Creative Meditation:
Inner Peace Is Practically Yours

Richard Peterson

A.R.E. Press • Virginia Beach • Virginia

Table of Contents

"Mindful Doings"
Mini-Meditations
Momentary Meditations

How Did We Do?
In the Service of Peace

List of Self-Inventories, Figures, and Closeups

Acknowledgments

Mark Thurston has been an ongoing source of both insight and inspiration in my study and practice of meditation since 1978 — through his courses, his conference lectures, his books, and now his editorial guidance. I deeply appreciate not only Mark's efforts on behalf of this book, but his significant contributions to the universal understanding and practice of meditation.

My wife, Anita Harkin Peterson, lovingly and patiently made it possible for me to write this book. Without her encouragement, sensitivity, and judgment — not just during the past year, but over the past 12 years — it would not have been written. I am thankful for her presence in my life.

Finally, I must acknowledge the significant influence which the Glad Helpers Prayer Healing Group has had on my life — especially my meditation life. I feel fortunate to be able to participate in the ongoing response this group makes to the needs for healing, peace, and at-oneness throughout the world.

TO THE GLAD HELPERS, I DEDICATE THIS BOOK
WITH LOVE AND THANKSGIVING.

INTRODUCTION

"You sure look relaxed, lying there with your book. What are you reading?"

"A new book on physical fitness called *Mind Over Matter*. Can you tell I'm doing 'mental pushups'?"

"A lot of good they'll do you, stretched out on the couch, not moving a muscle!"

"You don't understand. This book says fitness is all in the mind, so the exercises are done mentally. Then you just wait for the fitness to manifest physically! No more sweat and strain!"

"I can see why it's 'mind over matter.' If you think this'll work, you're out of your *mind*, and then it doesn't really *matter*!"

Everyone who can write or arrange to appear on a talk show seems to be an expert on how to improve the quality of our lives. And they assure us that what they teach, preach, or counsel may not even cost much in time or money. We wouldn't even be surprised to see titles like these: *Achieving Your Perfect Weight Without Changing Your Diet, How to Live Luxuriously on Five Dollars a Day ($3.50 If You Just Want Comfort)*, and *You Can Make Friends Even with Your Enemies*. The message often seems to be: If you just use perfect self-control and have nothing but love in your heart, you have it made!

I'm up against that kind of competition for your attention to this book — on the surface just another book on meditation. How can I persuade you that your life *will* be changed for the better if you put the ideas in this book into practice? Why should you believe that *creative meditation* can transform feelings of being out of control or stressed out into feelings of self-empowerment and inner peace?

Creative meditation is *not* for everyone, however. Consider it only if you are ready to accept greater calm in your life, more inner peace, and a feeling of being "at one" with the world and with the universe. You can be as immersed as you want to be in the *outer* world and still keep in touch with the source of creative energy at the *inner* center of your being. Be certain that's what you want before you attempt *creative meditation*.

Why Another Book on Meditation?

Creative Meditation is not the first book to present meditation as a practice helpful in coping with life and conducive to finding peace of mind in a crazy world. So why another book? Part of the answer lies in the fact that meditation is about to "go public" and can well stand a treatment especially suited to the wide range of individuals who will consider it.

Look at the stages through which the practice of meditation has moved in Western civilization, especially in recent years:

From antiquity through the 1940s. Off and on throughout the history of Western civilization, meditation was a serious spiritual practice for members of certain religious groups. We tend to assume that, across the centuries, meditation has been practiced in the West predominately by mystics, monks, and members of the clergy. Less well known is the fact that meditation was an accepted spiritual practice among many Jews and early Christians until their respective religious establishments discouraged or prohibited the practice.

Even after meditative practice was branded heretical for the Christian layperson — "Who do you think you are that you can commune directly with God?" — individuals periodically arrived on the scene not only to rediscover the value of the practice for themselves, but also to share it with others. For example, two significant spiritual movements in the 17th century included meditative practices: The followers of German cobbler-mystic Jacob Boehme formed Boehmenite societies throughout Germany and Holland early in the 17th century. Later in the century, the Englishman George Fox founded the Society of Friends — the Quakers. He extended the Society not only throughout England, but into Holland and America as well. He personally traveled from New England down to the Carolinas to spread his message and confirm his followers in their faith.

In the late 1800s and early 1900s, some form of meditative practice was fundamental to the ideas and writings of several individuals who became known for their spiritual philosophies. For example, Edgar Cayce and Rudolf Steiner both referred frequently to meditation. Charles and Myrtle Fillmore encouraged meditative "God talk" for guidance and healing. Georges Gurdjieff and P.D. Ouspensky taught the value of a meditative practice called "self-remembering." Groups that formed around these philosophies incorporated meditation into their personal disciplines.

x

The 1950s and 1960s. During this restless era of civil rights activism and questionable involvement in foreign conflicts, meditation found itself among companions of mixed reputation, such as psychedelic drugs, hippies, and new sexual freedom. "Consciousness raising" became a familiar, if equivocal, catch phrase of the time. A few people recognized that meditation was indeed a way to raise consciousness, but most leaders of popular causes had other agendas in mind. An influx of yoga-as-exercise from the East brought with it yoga-as-meditation. The work of the American mystic Joel Goldsmith attracted groups of dedicated seekers to "The Infinite Way," a spiritual philosophy in which meditation was an essential discipline. For the first time in modern Western history, meditation began to make a "crossover" from a largely exclusive religious or esoteric environment to segments of the general population.

The 1970s and 1980s. This period saw the blossoming of many "New Age" and "spiritual" philosophies and of groups associated with them. For example, *A Course in Miracles* appeared and attracted a large and devoted following, and many people became interested in the spiritual approaches of several Native American teachers and healers. The movements stimulated by the work of Cayce, Steiner, and the Fillmores flourished under their respective organizations: the Association for Research and Enlightenment (A.R.E.), the Anthroposophical Society, and the Unity School of Christianity. "New Age" movements got extra boosts through their association with charismatic individuals such as psychiatrist Gerald Jampolsky, Native American medicine man Rolling Thunder, and actress Shirley MacLaine.

This period also experienced the widespread dissemination of Transcendental Meditation (TM), an Eastern import modified for the West in a "non-sectarian, non-religious" form. A 1978 Gallup poll reported that about 2% of all Americans were using TM — a small percentage that nevertheless represented a large number of people. The same survey reported other indicators of increased spiritual activity: 6% of Americans were involved in inner or spiritual healing, 3% in yoga, 1% in other Eastern religions, 2% in the charismatic movement, and 19% in Bible study groups. Gallup's report on this survey says, "One of the most remarkable trends in the 1970s is the continuing interest in the inner or spiritual life." Meditation was becoming an integral part of many lives — another significant step in the crossover.

Meanwhile, the medical and psychological professions were working experimentally with meditation. They began to recognize and recommend its physiological and psychological benefits to patients and clients. The book *The Relaxation Response* by medical researcher Herbert Benson became a best-seller. Popular magazines and major newspapers began publishing articles with titles such as "The No-Sweat Diet: Meditate and Lose Weight" (*Harper's Bazaar*, 1980), "Meditation Merges with the Mainstream" (*Esquire*, 1983), and "What's Your Mantra?" (*The Wall Street Journal*, 1986). If we were waiting for meditation to be properly sanctioned, we need wait no longer. After all, if the medical establishment recommends it and it appears in *The Wall Street Journal* ...

The 1990s and beyond: A new era is beginning for meditation — one in which meditation is viewed as no more weird than prayer or jogging (neither of which is everyone's cup of tea) — a period which may see, for example, many organizations encouraging the regular use of meditation by employees. In this era, meditation will complete its crossover from the occult and the esoteric to the practical and the acceptable. Edgar Cayce frequently referred to a systematic progression of ideas related to "the work" of enlightenment: "... first to the individual, then to the groups, then to classes and masses" (254-91).[1] If you look back over meditation's history, it has clearly reached the stage of the masses.

This book and its principles of *creative meditation* are designed in preparation for this era of the 1990s and beyond. Furthermore, this book is the first which is designed with these features:

- to present meditation concepts in a framework of self-empowerment — the need we all have for taking control of our own circumstances;
- to integrate the information on meditation in the Edgar Cayce psychic readings with information from a rich variety of other Western sources, including Christian and Jewish traditions over many centuries;
- to provide you with opportunities for self-appraisal on aspects of your life relevant to meditation, as well as opportunities for experimentation in meditation;
- to help you create personal meditation practices that match your unique lifestyle and needs; and
- to present meditation information and guidance with a light touch, encouraging you to awaken your sense of humor and to associate a feeling of joy with your meditation practice. As Cayce puts it,

> "... above all, *keep* that ability to see the humor in any experience, whether it is the most sacred, the most cherished experience, or that which comes as a trial or as a temptation from outside influence" (2560-1).

---

[1] This is the reference number by which the Edgar Cayce readings are identified. The numbers were assigned to maintain confidentiality. The first number represents the code number for the person or group receiving the reading, or the code number for a special requested topic; the second number refers to the sequence of readings for this individual, group, or topic. This excerpt, for example, is from the 91st reading on the special topic 254 – the work of the Association.

The theme of this book is as follows:
- If you will meditate regularly with a clear spiritual focus,

and

- if you will creatively extend the resulting attunement throughout your life,

then

- you can experience...
  - inner peace regardless of outer circumstances,
  - the realization of being at one with the universe, and
  - the assurance of making choices that lead to greater control over the circumstances of your life.

If I am able to present principles and practices advancing this theme in a clear, helpful, and enjoyable manner, I may be justified in presenting yet "another book on meditation."

For Whom Is This Book Written?

In preparation for the 1990s and beyond, *creative meditation* is designed for those choosing to spend more time "at one with life" and willing to integrate meditation practice into their daily activities. If my readers include people who would not have considered the practice of meditation ten years ago, I have achieved one of my goals for writing this book.

If you are *new to meditation*, the book will serve as a practical introduction to the concepts as well as the steps of *creative meditation* with everything you need to fit its practice into your daily life, whatever your circumstances.

If you are an *experienced meditator*, you will discover numerous ways to enrich and extend your meditation practice so that, throughout your life, you can realize greater benefits than you ever realized before.

Dialoguing with the Reader

As an instructor of adults in university, business, and conference settings, I have found that understanding and learning is facilitated when I interact with the learners, the practitioners-to-be. In a book, I am confined to the printed page, so our give-and-take must be limited. As a partial substitute for that unavailable dialogue, I have designed two kinds of activities to help you interact with me — that is, with what I have written — so you can most effectively fit the information to your own background, experience with meditation, lifestyle, and living circumstances:

"Search Me!" Several self-inventories and other exercises will help you learn about yourself in ways that allow you to relate the ideas to your own life and tailor your meditation practice to your own interests and needs. As expressed in the lesson on meditation in the study books entitled *A Search for God*, "The first and last obstacle to overcome is understanding ourselves" (Book I, p. 19). Suggestions for scoring and interpreting the self-inventories are provided at the back of this book, based on a sample of people who completed the inventories as the book was being written.

"Try Me!" These are activities and experiments to put the ideas into action. The Edgar Cayce readings repeatedly remind us:

"For it is in the application, not the knowledge, that the truth becomes a part of thee" (826-11). Also "It is the 'try' that is the more often counted as righteousness, and *not* the success or failure" (931-1).

Please excuse my teacherly gesture of pointing my finger at you and stating what may be obvious: *The value you receive from this book will be proportional to the amount of effort you put into applying its principles through the suggested activities.*

Occasionally, I describe incidents, feelings, and other examples from my personal experience to illustrate or clarify a point, just as I would in a live, interactive setting. I present these not in pride or affectation, but in empathy and understanding of our common purpose. Accept the examples simply as the experiences of another individual learning to cope with life — with indispensable support from meditation.

Who Says What I Say Is So?

For every reader willing to take my word for what I write, there are others who might well ask, "Who says so? Why should I believe what he reports as his experiences and opinions?" To support many of my ideas as well as to enhance my presentation of them, I include a diverse selection of references to the writings of others. I acknowledge these sources in the text and give bibliographic references to them at the back of the book.

These sources include several fascinating people whose own lives have exemplified "becoming at one with life." I have chosen people and writings that represent our Western culture —predominantly American and European. Such information is more interesting, as well as more credible, if you know something about the individuals quoted. To share with you some of the splendid tradition of meditation, I have borrowed a technique from photography, occasionally *Zooming In for a Closeup* of some of these people. For example, one of my principal sources for ideas and information is the work of Edgar Cayce. Do I hear anyone asking, "Who's Edgar Cayce?" Here's the first of our closeups:

Zooming In for a Closeup. Whether you refer to him as a psychic, a seer, or a prophet — all those terms and more have been applied to him — surely Edgar Cayce would have preferred being remembered simply as a man who served God by helping others. He knew that was to be his life's work when, as a child, he experienced a vision through which that purpose for his life was affirmed. Later, as a young man without much education or apparent promise for carrying out his purpose, he discovered his ability to give a "reading" for an individual in which he not only diagnosed ailments, but recommended treatments and remedies generally composed of natural ingredients. These "physical" readings and several other types of readings became the means for fulfilling his life's purpose, always in quite modest living circumstances.

At the beginning of each twice-a-day reading session, everyone present (including Cayce himself) participated in a prayerful meditative process that focused on a desire for connection with the universal source of information. Only after this initial period of group concentration did Cayce lie down and begin the process of personal attunement and connection that allowed him to extend his consciousness to the person requesting the reading and to the information source. The words spoken by Edgar Cayce during these connections were recorded on the spot in longhand or shorthand by someone attending the reading.

The body of Cayce readings — over 14,000 of them are on file — represents a "philosophy of life" from which we can gain an understanding of ourselves and our purposes, and learn how to live more attuned to God's love. The consistency of the philosophy is especially remarkable when you realize how it evolved over a period of 40 years: from readings usually less than an hour in length —for many different individuals (and a few groups and special topics) — in response to questions about a wide range of physical ailments, mental concerns, or spiritual needs. The information in the readings continues to be relevant for today's world in spite of the fact that the readings were given in the first half of this century.

In addition to using a meditative approach to prepare for the readings, Cayce set aside a short period every afternoon for meditative prayer for himself, his family, and others working with him. He often asked visitors to pray and meditate with him, sometimes as part of the counseling they sought from him. He also spent as much time as he could outdoors — fishing, walking, caring for his garden — periods when he was effectively meditating through nature. Meditation in a variety of forms was clearly an integral part of Cayce's own life.

References in this book to "the Cayce readings" or "according to Cayce" represent my interpretation of information obtained from typed transcripts of the readings maintained by the Edgar Cayce Foundation and from several of the 24 volumes of the published Edgar Cayce Library Series. As you have already seen, brief quotations are occasionally cited to provide the reader with a direct sense of their richness in idea and expression. I have also included direct quotations from some of the other reference sources so you can share directly their expressions of ideas and feelings and, in some cases, draw your own conclusions.

The result of my planning and presentation lies before you in three parts:

Part One. BUILDING THE CASE FOR MEDITATION: In three chapters, you will examine what keeps you from your inner peace, try to define what that desirable state might be like, and consider why meditation may be the perfect tool for reaching that state.

Part Two. CREATING YOUR OWN MEDITATION STYLE: These six chapters present you with a wide range of both essential and optional building blocks from which you can experimentally develop a meditation process suited to your own needs, interests, and lifestyle.

Part Three. TAKING CHARGE OF YOUR LIFE: These five chapters guide you in the understanding and activities necessary for taking greater control of your circumstances, especially through self-guidance and self-healing and through the extension of attunement throughout your life. You will also be guided in the direction of serving the cause of peace in the world.

We begin by taking a look at the challenges of our lives — as Shakespeare's *Hamlet* identified them, "the slings and arrows of outrageous fortune"!

PART ONE

BUILDING THE CASE
FOR MEDITATION

Chapter 1

Slings and Arrows of
Epidemic Proportions

"Say, you haven't been looking so frantic or frazzled the last few days. Quite a change for you!"

"Now that you mention it, I do feel peculiar lately — kind of laid back, not worrying about anything, sort of peaceful inside. I wonder what's wrong with me."

The word "epidemiology" has long fascinated me. It rolls so rhythmically off the tongue: *ep'*-i-*de'*-mi-*ol'*-o-gy. I first heard the word in 1955 when my boss told me he was going to graduate school to major in epidemiology. I thought he was going to become some kind of skin doctor. But my *Random House Dictionary of the English Language* defines the word as

"... the branch of medicine dealing with the incidence and prevalence of disease in large populations and with detection of the source and cause of epidemics of infectious disease."

In the interest of epidemiology, I am alerting you to an epidemic in which an insidious dis-ease is being contracted by new and unsuspecting victims

1

every day! The symptoms may vary widely from one victim to another, but they frequently include anxiety, hair-trigger emotions, hyperactivity, and general inner turmoil. People differ in their susceptibility to the dis-ease, some having a higher threshold of tolerance than others.

It seems to occur most frequently in the presence of multiple responsibilities, competing commitments, countless opportunities, and shifting priorities. It hits adults in all walks of life throughout the so-called civilized world. More surprising, it strikes some victims very young, according to a news report by Michael Horak in *The Virginian-Pilot*: A recent study among Kansas schoolchildren found symptoms of "negative stress behavior" in 42 percent of 4,000 children from kindergarten through third grade, with similar results for a study of 18,000 children through grade 12.

The dis-ease is difficult to diagnose because its destructive symptoms are often masked by feelings of being useful, needed, competent, vital, and "in the swing of things." Even when the dis-ease subsides — often only when the victim's life circumstances change — the victim may be easily reinfected.

A generic label too often applied to this dis-ease is *stress*. I would call one form of it *crisiphilia* — an abnormal attraction to crises — and another, less severe form would be *busimania* — an excessive enthusiasm for being busy. In his book, *Reconciliations: Inner Peace in an Age of Anxiety*, psychiatrist Theodore Rubin tells about

> ... a man I know who asked me, "Without all this [competition, striving, pecking orders, heirarchies of esteem and power, prestige], what can we do? Where can we go? What purpose is there in life?" For him, life on a spontaneous basis, without the stimulation of imposed striving, had no meaning. Over a lifetime he had exchanged real vitality born of inner peace and self-realization for the synthetic aliveness of a pressured existence imposed by a competitive, malignant, hierarchical society. He had already had one heart attack and was justifiably afraid of another. He saw only two possibilities. One was stress, and the other was deadness. (p. 18)

This lifestyle is not only reinforced by its high level of stimulation and apparent purposefulness; it becomes addictive, according to Rubin:

> Relative inner peace is the antithesis of deadness. Many of

us have unwittingly become stimulation and crisis addicts. And many of us feel "dead" unless we feel very high or very low, so we engineer crises in order to feel alive. Of course people suffering in this way are terrified of inner peace, even relative inner peace. (p. 14)

Even if you are not a victim of crisiphilia or busimania, simply trying to get on with your life today is to be exposed to enough challenges to undermine your calm, cool inner self. Are any of these situations familiar?

- Just before the sales clerk finishes ringing up your purchase, another customer gets her attention for "just a moment," and five minutes later you are still waiting for your change.

- The "service representative" at your car dealership is not really listening to your description of the clackety-thump under the rear seat and the squooshy feel of the brake pedal, since he has already decided what the problem is — just as he did a month ago — and the month before that.

- Your boss just told you it's time the two of you had a serious talk.

- Right after the warranty expires, so does your television set. . .or your washing machine ... or your _____ (you fill in the blank).

"The Slings and Arrows of Outrageous Fortune"

Hamlet knew the dilemma all right:

> Whether 'tis nobler in the mind to suffer
> The slings and arrows of outrageous fortune,
> Or to take arms against a sea of troubles,
> And by opposing end them?

(From Shakespeare's *Hamlet*, Act III, Scene 1)

It's not always the *big* slings and arrows that wear us down, but the incessant barrage from the *little* ones, like those just illustrated. Often we are not even aware of what is disrupting our peace of mind, and we lay the blame on familiar but innocent sources. Consider the kinds of slings and arrows

3

from which you choose — and you *do* choose:

> **Slings and arrows from your physical responsibilities**: the home chores that always need doing; the yard and garden work to be done; the home projects you want to do, but can't find time for; the condition of your automobile, your kitchen appliances, your TV set; the deadlines and pressures of your work; the degree of satisfaction and fulfillment from your work; your finances; your health, your weight; your clothes; your appearance; even your pets and their care.
> **Slings and arrows from your encounters with other people**: your spouse, family, close friends, boss, coworkers, neighbors, salespeople, those who treat your ailments, the people who work on your car, those who preach to you in one way or another.
> **Slings and arrows from happenings near and far**: accidents, hurricanes, droughts, earthquakes, inflation, recession, taxes, acid rain, the greenhouse effect, terrorism, crime on the streets, alcoholism, drugs, child abuse. In *Edgar Cayce Answers Life's 10 Most Important Questions*, John Fuller speaks to the emotional impact on us when

> ...we are bombarded on a daily basis with the turmoil of our turbulent world. News stories of political upheavals, bloody uprisings, and strife can't help but create within us a feeling of personal distress, a feeling that we are being tossed about by events fully out of our control. Faced with epidemics, natural disasters, and widespread crime, we are bound to feel vulnerable, helpless, sometimes even hopeless. (pp. 89-90)

Challenges like these are new to our high-tech, overstimulated, civilized society, right? We've never had it so bad, right? Wrong! They may differ in the form they take or in the speed with which we know about them, but life has always been filled with challenge. That's the nature of living on this earth!

> I cry aloud to God...that he may hear me. In the day of my trouble I seek the Lord; in the night my hand is stretched out without wearying; my soul refuses to be comforted. (Psalm 77:1-2 RSV)

> My grief is beyond healing, my heart is sick within me. (Jeremiah 8:18 RSV)

4

In the world, you have tribulation ... (John 16:33 RSV)

Throughout history, writers have documented lives characterized by "calamitous living," yet seeking peace of mind and soul — in the Dark Ages, the Renaissance, the recent centuries of revolutions, civil wars, and world wars, and on up through recent years in Vietnam, Afghanistan, and Nicaragua.

Zooming In for a Closeup. To English mystic Evelyn Underhill, the life of a religious person, even a mystic, should not be one of solitude and monasteries, but one concerned with the problems of everyday life, including those created by wars and violence. In World War I, she herself served England's efforts as a translator in Naval Intelligence. Her longstanding personal concern was for the poor, to whom she devoted time every week in later years. Her choice of religion evolved from years of deliberation and study. Finally convinced she wanted to become a Roman Catholic, she instead joined the Anglican Church when the Pope denounced the "Modernist" scholars with whom she had great sympathy. In fact, through correspondence, the Modernist Baron Friedrich von Hugel was her mentor and spiritual teacher for many years.

A longtime meditator, she authored 37 books on the devotional life and religious experience and, although she was never formally educated in religion, her work was held in high esteem among religious leaders. She was the only woman ever chosen by an Oxford college as an outside lecturer on religion. During World War II, she devoted herself to her writing and to leading spiritual retreats with meditation at their core. Her writings on mysticism and meditation are still relevant, informative, articulate, and colorful.

In the Preface to her 1915 book *Practical Mysticism*, Evelyn Underhill acknowledges the seeming contradiction of being at war and considering a meditative approach to life:

> ... Many will feel that in such a time of conflict and horror, when only the most ignorant, disloyal, or apathetic can hope for quietness of mind, a book which deals with that which is called the "contemplative" attitude to existence is wholly out of place...The thoughts of the English race are now turned, and rightly, towards the most concrete forms of

action — struggle and endurance, practical sacrifices, difficult and long-continued effort ... (p. vii)

... your attention to life has been deliberately adjusted to
a world of frittered values and prismatic refracted lights: full
of incompatible interests, of people, principles, things.
Ambitions and affections, tastes and prejudices, are fighting
for your attention. Your poor, worried consciousness flies to
and fro amongst them; it has become a restless and a
complicated thing. At this very moment your thoughts are
buzzing like a swarm of bees. The reduction of this fevered
complex to a unity appears to be a task beyond all human
power. (pp. 37-38)

How universal such feelings can be! That last paragraph could apply to
many of us right now. Does any of it have a familar ring?

"Search Me!" Can you identify your personal slings and arrows, the
challenges — big and little — of your life? Self-Inventory 1 gives you
an opportunity to estimate your "challenge position." Where are you on
the road between Peaceville and Panicsville? This is not intended to be
a full-blown assessment of your circumstances, but to make you aware
of the range of opportunities you have chosen for yourself. When you
have completed Self-Inventory 1, you can find information for scoring
and interpreting the inventory in the back of this book.

Our Injuries, Ailments, and Scars

As a result of the epidemic of sling-and-arrow dis-ease, we sustain a wide
range of injuries and ailments, some of which leave us with scars. Of course,
if you are immune, then you do *not* experience many of the following
symptoms:

headaches	fatigue	digestive upsets
frustration	mood swings	feeling "no one cares"
cynicism	apathy	emptiness of life
forgetfulness	no new ideas	negative self-talk
clamming up	loneliness	loss of direction
muscle aches	irritability	finger-drumming

SELF-INVENTORY 1
What's My "Beef"?

On the next page are listed 14 areas of your life that may have given you some degree of challenge (worry, aggravation, frustration, or stress) during the past year. If one or two areas are not listed that were major challenges to you, add them at the end of the list.

A.   In Column A, rate each area according to its *FREQUENCY* of challenge for you. How often *during the past year* did this part of your life present you with a challenge? Use this rating scale:

0 = This was *never* a challenge in the past year.

1 = This was an *occasional* challenge in the past year.

2 = This was a *frequent* challenge in the past year.

3 = This was a *continual* challenge in the past year.

B.   For each area that challenged you (those you rated either 1, 2, or 3), rate them again in Column B according to the *INTENSITY* of challenge. *During this past year*, how strong were your attitudes and emotions about this part of your life when it challenged you (on the average)? Use this rating scale:

1 = This was usually a *mild* challenge — feelings not very strong, not much anxiety or aggravation, low impact on me at the time.

2 = This was usually a *moderate* challenge, or was mixed — had some severe challenges and some mild challenges in this area.

3 = This was usually a *severe* challenge— feelings very strong, a lot of anxiety or aggravation, high impact on me at the time.

7

A	B	AREAS OF POTENTIAL CHALLENGE IN YOUR LIFE
☐	☐	HOME/LIVING ARRANGEMENTS: convenience, maintenance, move, size, comfort, problems, yard work, furniture.
☐	☐	CAR/TRANSPORTATION: convenience, repairs, problems, purchase, accident.
☐	☐	FINANCES: bills, payments, taxes, loans, mortgages, losses, decrease in income, account keeping.
☐	☐	WORK/JOB/OCCUPATION: change, loss, ability requirements, retirement, type of work, satisfaction, security, compensation level, pressures, pace.
☐	☐	DAILY "NITTY-GRITTY": meal preparation, laundry, other housekeeping, errands, mail, phone.
☐	☐	CLOSEST RELATIONSHIPS (spouse, mate, best friend, pet): loss, communication, responsibilities, quality of relationship, demands.
☐	☐	FAMILY (children, parents, other relatives not spouse): responsibilities, communication, demands, loss, quality of relationship, child care, parent care.
☐	☐	WORK RELATIONSHIPS (boss, coworkers, customers, clients, contacts): changes, atmosphere, quality.
☐	☐	HEALTH: general state of health, weight, injuries, illnesses, ongoing ailments or discomforts, energy level.
☐	☐	LEARNING: new skills, new equipment, courses, classes, new knowledge, lack of opportunity.
☐	☐	RIGHTS AND ENTITLEMENTS: women's rights, worker rights, minority rights, rights under purchase or service contracts, guarantees, policies.
☐	☐	VIOLENCE AND CRIME: personal safety, crime, child and spouse abuse, drug and alcohol abuse.
☐	☐	ENVIRONMENT: storms, droughts, air and water pollution, acid rain, food additives, greenhouse effect, misuse or loss of resources.
☐	☐	NATIONAL AND GLOBAL CONCERNS: nuclear arms, wars and violent conflicts, political confrontation, hunger, poverty, homeless, terrorism.
☐	☐	_____
☐	☐	_____

If you are symptom-free, the epidemiologists will certainly want to interview and examine you. Maybe they can develop an antitoxin based on your approach to life. If, however, you do experience some of these symptoms, this book presents at least a preliminary "treatment" that is both an antidote and a preventative for such symptoms and the dis-ease they represent.

The slings and arrows take their toll on us both physically and mentally:

Physical effects. There is no short list of physical symptoms caused by the challenges and stresses in our lives. They range from mild headaches to elevated blood pressure, and from there to ulcers, heart attacks, and cancer. Even the children in the Kansas study experienced headaches, inability to sleep, stomachaches, and fingernail biting. How much of our illness is a response to the stresses of our lives — either as a passive surrender to the assault of circumstances, or as an active separation of ourselves from the circumstances? Is a week-long bout with the flu the *passive* response of the body to the stressful circumstances around us, or is it an *active* response to remove us from the stress for a while? The reason for the choice of response may make a difference in how we heal ourselves. (An extensive summary of current information about the physical correlates of stress from a holistic viewpoint is presented by Dr. John Harvey in "An Overview of Stress and Stress Management," the opening chapter of the book under Harvey's editorship, *The Quiet Mind: Techniques for Transforming Stress*.)

Mental effects. We often give more attention to physical ailments than to mental ailments. When physical illness or injury occurs, the symptoms are usually apparent both to ourselves and to others, and we can usually give them specific physical attention. But mental symptoms are often not as apparent, as treatable, nor as socially acceptable. Besides, we say, we can always take care of that inner problem ourselves. Actually, because our mental reactions to stress and overwhelming circumstances are less apparent, their consequences are more ambiguous, more suspect, and more insidious. Those consequences may include feelings of burnout, futility, uselessness, low energy, irritability, depression, and ultimately severe mental illness. Furthermore, when such consequences recur or continue unabated, they may become integrated with the stress-producing circumstances, greatly affecting our ablities to respond further. We may eventually become immobilized. The study of Kansas children reported mental symptoms even at their tender ages, manifesting not only in short tempers and worry about doing poorly in school, but in an alarming rate of suicide — one every nine days in the 1987–'88 school year in the state of Kansas. (Dr. John Harvey has also written a comprehensive summary on the subject of mental effects of stress, "The Mind and Stress," in *The Quiet Mind*.)

That's enough time cataloguing our challenges for now. We'll even admit we don't like some of our reactions to them. Yet we also realize that the slings and arrows of our continuing outrageous fortune are not likely to disappear spontaneously, especially when some of us seek even more and greater challenges, addicted as we are to them. So what can we do to be more constructive, more creative, more peaceful and loving to ourselves?

Strategies and Tactics of Coping

The approach we take in meeting and handling our life circumstances helps set the tone for our lives. To live a relatively satisfying life, we must select effective ways to *cope* with the ongoing stream of challenges. If we don't choose coping techniques consciously, the selection is made for us at a subconscious level, and our bodies and lives pay the consequences.

As we grow up, we observe how those around us cope with life. We learn a little about what seems to work and what doesn't. When circumstances require us to cope, we try out the strategies we have learned, or we discover new ways to respond. We keep the strategies that work for us and discard those that don't. In this way, each of us gradually builds a personal "style" of coping. This style has a repertoire of patterns of how to react to a challenge in our circumstances. Some patterns show little variety of response (for example, we get angry at everything that gets in our way), while others call for a complex variety of responses (we react differently to the same circumstance according to who else is involved, how serious it is, and what time of day we encounter it).

Following are descriptions of eight common strategies for coping. The first is the fundamental strategy you apply when you know what to do and want to do it. The other seven are common strategies for coping with stressful circumstances over which you have no apparent control or where you otherwise don't want to do what is needed. At the end of these descriptions is an exercise to help you profile your coping style. As you read the definitions, think about your own reactions under difficult circumstances.

Do it! This is simply taking appropriate action as you know it, doing what you can to "take care of business," trying to alleviate or eliminate the stressful circumstances and move ahead with life. We might paraphrase an ancient prayer this way: "Lord, give me the ability to handle the things I can do something about, the courage to accept as they are what I can do nothing

10

about, and the critical discernment to know the difference."
(The discernment will get you every time!)

Ignore it. This strategy reflects an attitude of non-importance ("What difference does it really make?"), non-acceptance ("I will not do anything about it"), or non-responsibility ("It's not up to me"). "It" may not actually go away, but once you have adopted one of these attitudes, you tend to forget about "it." Unfortunately, although you ignore it at the conscious level, you may try to deal with it at the subconscious level, perhaps by internalizing it (another strategy).

Escape it. This strategy is accomplished by indulging in usually pleasurable activities that tend to numb one's sensitivities to life outside. Our daily news brutally reminds us of the frequent abuse of unsafe, even criminal forms of escapism: alcohol, abusive sexual acts, drugs, and "wildin'" — a form of virtually uncontrolled group violence. How much of this kind of activity occurs as a temporary escape in lives where other more acceptable forms of relief seem unattainable?

At a less destructive level, do you have favorite kinds of "escapist entertainment"? Television, movies, popular magazines, mysteries, romance novels, spy stories, games, and puzzles — all generally safe forms of diversion and relaxation, some of which are essential for balance in our lives. However, an average of 17 hours a week in front of the TV (according to a recent study of 5,000 Americans) means a great many people are spending a great deal of time watching programs they often admit are "mindless" and yet helpful in "getting their minds off other things."

Exercise it. This popular and essentially healthy coping style is well represented by the joggers, runners, walkers, swimmers, bikers, and aerobic dancers among us — apparently an ever-growing crowd. Although such total-body exercise is usually initiated through an interest in physical fitness, the participant often discovers its effectiveness in releasing tension and stress, mentally as well as physically. In fact, one may become "hooked" (positively) on the activity *because* of its effectiveness as a coping mechanism.

It's only fair to extend this category to include golf, hunting, and fishing, and even physically taxing activities like gardening and yard care, ongoing home improvement activities, and even normal housework. Hard work around the house can help in two ways: First, you can get so absorbed in it and use so much energy that you forget about your other problems; and second, when you're done with that work, you're glad to get back to the other problems!

Displace it. In psychoanalysis, "displacement" is the transfer of an

11

emotion from the original focus to a new object, person, or situation. One way to cope is to get yourself actively involved in another situation that can absorb your pent-up emotions constructively. Our volunteer and service activities, as well as our relationships with friends and family, often serve this function. One of Edgar Cayce's prominent themes is service, "the *outlet* through which the inner self may find the greater satisfaction" (1046-1).

Displacement is a *healthy* approach to coping when the new focus converts the energy of anxiety and tension into productive, helpful actions on behalf of someone in need. Displacement is *unhealthy* when the stressful emotions are simply transferred directly to others without constructive transformation. When you've had a "bad day" away from home, have you ever let out your frustration on a member of your family or a close friend? "Misplaced displacement"?

Internalize it. This approach may be least apparent to others but probably has the most devastating impact on you (along with abuse of some of the temporary escape substances like drugs and alcohol). Instead of displacing the emotion and tension or converting it to constructive activity, the energy is absorbed within the body and allowed to trigger hormonal and other reactions, releasing substances which over time are detrimental to the body. Discussed earlier as "mental effects," the results range from mild discomfort (headache, stomachache, other aches and pains) to forms of severe physical impairment (ulcers, heart disease, cancer, and other disabling health problems).

Wing it. This pattern of coping is *no* pattern. Each situation is met as if it were brand-new or unique. This approach may make use of all the above styles and therefore be most versatile. At one moment, the response to stressful circumstances might be anger and a lashing out at someone; a short time later, the same circumstance may bring on a stomachache; and if the situation repeated itself an hour later, the response might be to write a long letter that defuses the emotional energy.

On the one hand, flexibility in adapting to immediate circumstances may be generally commendable. On the other hand, a coping strategy that requires moment-by-moment choices of how to react, even when facing the same challenge, may compound the circumstances by adding indecision and anxiety to the process.

Revitalize for it. Exercise and some forms of escape may result in a sense of renewal and revitalization — a feeling of regaining composure, finding new energy, "getting your head on straight." Vacations that truly allow for a separation from the sources of stress — and don't in themselves add to it — may be quite effective for people working in stressful situations.

On a shorter-term basis, creative activity can revitalize —performing music, drawing and painting, writing, sewing and needlecraft, building and woodworking, engaging in other crafts or household projects of choice, gardening, and computer hacking. All of these can bring revitalization if, in fact, they involve a significant opportunity for creativity. A form of energy conversion takes place — the energy bottled up as emotion and anxiety is transformed and redirected into constructive, often creative channels. Furthermore, new sources of energy may be tapped.

For some people, attending religious services, praying, and reading scripture and other inspirational material may contribute to the renewal process. For example, comfort may come from reading that "God...will not let you be tempted beyond your strength, but with the temptation will also provide the way of escape, that you may be able to endure it." (1 Corinthians 10:13 RSV).

Finally, for some people, renewal comes through walking in the woods, sitting by the ocean, or watching the sunset — almost any activity in natural settings.

"Search Me!" Now take a look at your usual strategies of coping by completing Self-Inventory 2. The scoring and interpretation instructions are in the back of this book.

How well you see yourself coping (Self-Inventory 2) with your challenges (Self-Inventory 1) is a primary contributor to your feelings of calmness and inner peace — in fact, to your whole self-image:

Negative impact: Apparent inability to keep up or cope well, tendencies to worry, to see problems everywhere, to be anxious — these prompt the feelings of being out of control and tarnish your self-image. At the extreme, ineffective or inappropriate reactions to stress coupled with low self-esteem will almost certainly take its toll in both physical and mental health.

Positive impact: The more effective you perceive your coping to be, the better self-esteem you have, the greater your feelings of inner peace and well-being, and the more you feel in control of your life. Also, you are more likely to think about yourself with words and phrases such as "in harmony," "all together," and "at one."

SELF-INVENTORY 2
My Coping Profile

Listed below are the eight strategies for coping with challenges in your life. Refer to the preceding pages if you need to review the description of any of the strategies.

A. In Column A, rate all the strategies according to *FREQUENCY* of use. How often did you use this strategy *during the past year*? Use this scale:

0 = I *never* used this strategy in the past year.

1 = I used this strategy a *few times* in the past year.

2 = I used this strategy a *moderate* number of times in the past year.

3 = I used this strategy *many times* in the past year.

B. In Column B, rate the strategies you used (those you rated either 1, 2, or 3) in terms of their *BENEFIT* to you, their *effectiveness* in helping you cope, their *contribution to your well-being* in times of challenge and stress. This rating may be difficult for some strategies. It may help to think of specific times you used each strategy, and make an estimate from the results at those times. Use this rating scale:

0 = This strategy was of *no benefit* in helping me cope.

1 = This strategy was of *limited* benefit in helping me cope.

2 = This strategy was of *moderate* benefit in helping me cope.

3 = This strategy was of *significant* benefit in helping me cope.

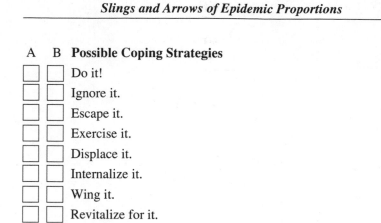

A	B	Possible Coping Strategies
☐	☐	Do it!
☐	☐	Ignore it.
☐	☐	Escape it.
☐	☐	Exercise it.
☐	☐	Displace it.
☐	☐	Internalize it.
☐	☐	Wing it.
☐	☐	Revitalize for it.

I have referred repeatedly to a sense of inner peace and well-being — of feeling calm, cool, and collected. But what is this apparently desirable state really like? Will you recognize it if you stumble into it? In the next chapter, you'll find out.

Chapter 2

Inner Peace and
"Being at One with Life"

"What do you think it would be like to have it all together — to feel
like you're really with it — to be cool about whatever comes
along?"

"Do you know anybody like that?"

"Oh, sure! And they're all very rich, unburdened by jobs, and
living on a beach in Tahiti!"

A variety of colorful words and phrases suggests a state of being that
combines inner peacefulness and self-control with outer awareness and
involvement. Do you sometimes feel like any of these?

mellow	at peace within	on top of the world
centered	tranquil	feeling all together
with it	self-possessed	in tune with the Universe
in control of my life	calm, cool, and collected	being *in* the world but not *of* the world

In this book, the phrase **"being at one with life"** is used to represent these qualities.

What Does "Being at One with Life" Feel Like?

The experience of "being at one with life" is probably different for each of us. Yet we should each have a conception of what it is like so we will know where we're headed and recognize it when we get there.

"Search Me!" Before reading anyone else's ideas about this desirable and elusive quality, take a few minutes on Part A of Self-Inventory 3 to express your own ideas about what "being at one with life" would be like for you. Then in Part B, estimate how far along its road you are now. Your responses here will serve as a baseline for later reference.

After you write your ideas, you may want to compare them with ideas expressed by others who responded to this self-inventory. Sample responses are presented at the back of this book in the scoring section.

Over the centuries, philosophers, spiritual leaders, and others writing about their lives and their work have referred to a state which sounds like "being at one with life." For example, a longtime missionary to the Philippines, Frank Laubach, wrote of a state where "worries have faded away like ugly clouds and my soul rests in the sunshine of perpetual peace" (from Laubach's book, *Letters by a Modern Mystic,* reprinted in *The Practice of His Presence,* p. 33).

Psychiatrist Theodore Rubin told us earlier about the man who saw his only options as stress or deadness. Here Rubin describes his own ideas of inner peace:

What is this inner peace, and where does it come from? For me, it means a state of *relative well-being*, "feeling good," or "feeling together."... Listening to music, looking at paintings, or reading a wonderful book may sometimes help for a little while. But a major reevaluation and struggle are usually necessary for any kind of sustained state of well-being or "feeling together." When I think of inner peace what comes to mind is a long, lazy, languid, Huckleberry Finn kind of summer afternoon, during which neither stimulation of any kind nor boredom plays any significant role. (From *Reconciliations*, pp. 13-14)

SELF-INVENTORY 3
To Be "At One with Life"

Part A: Consider the desirable state of "being at one with life." You may prefer to think of it as feeling "all together," "with it," "centered," "mellow," "at peace within," "on top of the world," "in tune with the universe," or "calm, cool, and collected."

Using details from your life and expressing the kinds of feelings you have or would like to have, describe on a separate sheet of paper what it would be like for you to "be at one with life." You need not write sentences. Jot down words and phrases, situations, attitudes, emotions, physical and mental states that might be a part of that state of well-being for you. (Examples: "only pleasant and loving thoughts about everyone in my life"; "no anxiety or pressure from my work once I set it aside"; "satisfied with what I have"; "happy just to be.")

Part B: Consider a rating scale from 0 to 10, where 0 is complete lack of "being at one" and 10 is perfect realization of it. Rate yourself as follows:

Thinking about your life *over the past six months or so*, what is the *highest* rating you would give yourself at any time during that period?

What is the *lowest* rating you would give yourself at any time during that period?

What rating would you give yourself on the *average* for that period?

A closeup will introduce a person who demonstrated at-oneness through his day-to-day actions:

Zooming In for a Closeup. A 17th-century Frenchman named Nicholas Herman would probably not be remembered today if he had not decided to change careers at age 55. Born into poverty, Herman served his country as a soldier, and then became a footman to a family of French nobility. In 1666 he became a "lay brother" in the community of Carmelites in Paris, taking the name Brother Lawrence. He served in the community for 25 years, mostly in the hospital kitchen. He is remembered primarily through his short, unpretentious writings that have been assembled under the title, *The Practice of the Presence of God*. It is reported about Brother Lawrence that

> His very countenance was edifying, with such a sweet and calm devotion appearing in it as could not but affect its beholders. It was observed that in the greatest hurry of business in the kitchen, he still preserved his recollection and heavenly-mindedness. He was neither hasty nor loitering, but did each thing in its season, with an even, uninterrupted composure and tranquillity of spirit. (From the Laubach and Lawrence book, *The Practice of His Presence*, pp. 104-105)

Inner peace in action!

Some of the most down-to-earth views of "inner peace" were given to us by the woman who called herself Peace Pilgrim and spent 28 years of her life walking more than 25,000 miles across America, teaching the way of peace. Her "signs and symbols of inner peace" are these:

> a tendency to think and act spontaneously rather than on fears based on past experiences

> an unmistakable ability to enjoy each moment

> a loss of interest in judging other people

> a loss of interest in interpreting the actions of others

a loss of interest in conflict

frequent, overwhelming episodes of appreciation
contented feelings of connectedness with others and nature

frequent attacks of smiling

an increased susceptibility to the love extended by others as
well as the uncontrollable urge to extend it.

Reflected here is the warmth as well as the wisdom of at-oneness.

In these days of rampant drug abuse, it's only natural to wonder if drugs
— psychedelics or hallucinogenics — produce something akin to feelings
of at-oneness with life. Here's a profile of a man who has explored both
paths:

Zooming In for a Closeup. In the early 1960s, Harvard University
became the site of controversial experimentation with psychedelic
drugs. Psychologist Richard Alpert joined with Timothy Leary and
other colleagues to create altered states of consciousness through drugs
such as LSD (lysergic acid diethylamide) and to study in themselves and
others the behavioral and psychological effects. Alpert himself took
over 300 doses of psychedelic drugs and found his experiences profound, but disturbing and limited compared with what he felt the change
in consciousness could be. In the late 1960s at the age of 36, Alpert
journeyed to India to explore spiritual traditions that he understood
taught self-induced ways of achieving altered states of consciousness.
He found his guru in Neem Karoli Baba, who named him Ram Dass and
directed him to study Raja Yoga. Later, as a spiritual teacher in his own
right, Ram Dass returned to the United States to lecture and write,
periodically journeying back to India and the Far East to continue his
studies.

Most recently, Ram Dass has been advocating service — one of the
predominant themes in Cayce's readings — as the greatest opportunity
each of us has for joy and self-realization. Ram Dass himself serves, for
example, through his activities with prisoners and in his work with the
dying.

In his "Meditator's Guidebook," *Journey of Awakening*, Ram Dass reminds us of the moments in our lives when we have been pure awareness — making no attempt to express it in words, having no thoughts about being aware — just openness and a spacious quality in our existence. He assures us we have all had such experiences — moments when we "lost ourselves," were "taken out of ourselves," or have "forgotten ourselves" — "moments in flow":

> It is in these moments of your life that there is no longer separation. There is peace, harmony, tranquillity, the joy of being part of the process. In these moments the universe appears fresh; it is seen through innocent eyes. It all begins anew. (p. 2)

Returning to the question of drugs and at-oneness, apparently psychedelic drugs can produce feelings of at-oneness for some individuals, along with heightened sensory experiences. Such drug-induced euphoric feelings are, however, quite temporary, often contaminated by destructive emotions and irrelevant sensations, and at the risk of experiencing serious and disturbing side effects. Drugs are not the means for reaching a healthy, safe state of at-oneness with life.

The Cayce readings frequently refer to a state of "at-onement," saying, in fact, that "attunement, atonement, and at-onement are *one*..." (2174-3). This reading goes on to say that each person "knows within when it is in an at-onement."

In one reading, Cayce compared our seeking at-onement with a musician's tuning of an instrument: "Attune yourself almost in the same manner as you tune the violin for harmony" (1861-18). The violin's A string is first tuned to a standard of pitch, such as an oboe in the orchestra, and then the musician tunes the four strings on the instrument to one another for internal harmony; similarly, we are attuned by aligning the equivalent of our A string to the Infinite, and then tuning the rest of our strings to one another for balance and harmony. To me, this parallel suggests that, when we are "at one with life," we will feel not only an *inner* sense of harmony and peace, but we will also have a sense of being in tune with *life around us* and, beyond that, with the universe.

What follows are the qualifications I propose for the state of being at one with life. See if your responses in Self-Inventory 3 relate to these criteria (the word "It" refers to the state of at-oneness):

It works for all kinds and degrees of challenges. The preceding

22

chapter illustrated the abundant sources for slings and arrows — our physical responsibilities, our encounters with others, and happenings near and far. Being at one should be as effective in helping us find inner peace when we are coping with a severe financial crisis as it is when we are coming to terms with physical pain or working through the challenges in a close personal relationship.

It reduces or eliminates the negative effects of our challenges. The preceding chapter also illustrated the physical and mental effects of our slings and arrows — everything from finger-drumming to heart disease and cancer, from worry to clinical depression. Being at one should help protect us from developing these symptoms and should reduce their severity when they do occur.

It is readily available and can be effective for long periods of time. When negative effects of inner stress and turmoil occur, we can't always take time off or get to the gym or even leave the meeting. Once we have attained a state of inner calm, we want to remain in it as long as possible without too much effort. Consider the analogy of ideal body weight: Once you've achieved it, you'd like to maintain it forever. To do so, however, you will need self-discipline on diet and exercise. Similarly, you just may have to adopt some regular disciplines if you are to maintain a state of being "at one."

It facilitates clear thought and "right action." We don't need a condition that wipes us out, makes us feel lethargic or indifferent — possible consequences of drugs, tranquilizers, alcohol, other medications, and even too much exercise. Rather we look for a state that lets us pull our thoughts together, reach into our deepest resources for information and ideas, and make wise decisions. It should also allow us to relax and find quick sources of renewal when needed.

It promotes creativity and productivity. Most of us would like to be more creative in our thoughts and actions — and more spontaneous in our creativity, not having to dredge it up as if from some deep pit. Also, given what time we have, we would like to get the "must do's" out of the way so we can spend time on the "want to do's."

It helps you feel more in control of yourself and your life. No one likes to feel as if "everything and everyone out there is running my life for me." Although our circumstances cannot be changed overnight, we may be able to change our perception of them, seeing them in a more constructive light until they do change. We want to feel empowered in our lives, not victimized.

It creates a state of calm extending far below the surface. A calm exterior can mask anxiety, inner churning, and disorientation. It can also signal apathy, passivity, disinterest, remoteness, and lack of enthusiasm. None of these inner states would be a desirable goal. We should be able to choose our outward demeanor — from unruffled calm to wild enthusiasm — while retaining the peaceful inner feeling of being at one.

It inspires personal traits favorable for sustaining the condition. Being at one should help us not only take care of current concerns, but also develop personal qualities consistent with at-oneness — in fact, traits that help us perpetuate being at one with life. One series of such qualities — frequently referred to by Edgar Cayce — appears in the apostle Paul's letter to the Galatians as the "fruits of the spirit": love, joy, peace, patience, kindness, goodness, faithfulness, gentleness, and self-control (Galatians 5:22-23 RSV).

It is consistent with our fundamental values. Any state we advocate and adopt must agree with our deep inner values — those ideals we hold within us for ourselves and for our lives. These inner motives go beyond physical needs such as food and water, money and shelter. They go beyond mental drives such as comfort and convenience, fame and power. We begin to perceive these deeper values when we identify our personal standards of integrity and morality, justice and responsibility. Many people are not in touch with what those deeper values and motivations are for them. These deep-seated values are part of our *spiritual* nature, a topic we will address in the next section.

These then are nine criteria for a model state of well-being:

At-oneness with life will eliminate the negative effects of our slings and arrows of all kinds and degrees, will be easily invoked and long-lasting, will help us think and act appropriately while feeling in control of our lives, will permeate our beings, will stimulate personal traits consistent with its tone, will foster creativity and productivity, and will be consistent with our inner values and ideals.

A rigorous set of qualifications!

24

What's All This About Our "Spiritual Nature"?

The last criterion above — relating to fundamental values and our "spiritual nature" — is at once the most vague, the most slighted, and the most essential criterion of the lot. Let's address those three qualities one at a time:

Reducing the vagueness of "spirituality." This is not the place for a long discourse on metaphysics, but several metaphysical concepts are fundamental to our understanding of spirituality:

Everything in the universe is a form of energy. The original and ongoing infinite source of that energy is variously referred to in the Cayce readings as the Creative Force or Forces, First Cause, the Universal Source, the Father, God, Lord, and Spirit. We are created from that energy, as are our homes, our food, our pets — even our mountains and oceans.

Although everything in creation is a form of the one universal energy, human beings differ from all non-human forms in two ways: First, we differ from one another as well as from other non-human matter because of our differing patterns of energy vibration. That's not a unique manner of differentiation — everything differs from everything else because of its vibratory pattern.

The second set of differences **is** unique to humans and goes back to the original creation of us in spirit. At creation, even before we were human beings, we each acquired two special gifts: a soul and free will. The soul became the repository for all the pure Spirit-like attributes we would develop in our experiences on a journey toward "oneness with God"; and free will became the capability through which we would, as humans, choose many of our experiences on earth. Having these special gifts puts us humans in a unique relationship to Universal Spirit. It is because of this unique relationship that we characterize ourselves as *spiritual* — that is, having a special relationship with Spirit, with God. Of all the products of creation — animal, vegetable, and mineral — only human beings have the choice of attuning themselves to God or not doing so; only human beings can choose to call upon the infinite resources of God for the purpose of moving toward oneness with God. Although everything in creation is of the same energy, the same spirit, only human beings can claim the quality of truly being *spiritual*.

The bodies we take on when we come into the earth give us our physical nature and provide a vehicle for our mental nature, but our most fundamental lineage remains spiritual. We are not just close to God; a portion of God is in us! An analogy by the American mystic Joel Goldsmith likens God's presence in us to the presence of gold in a ring:

> Gold is the ring; gold constitutes the ring. There is no possible way to remove the gold from the ring without destroying the ring, because there is not gold *and* a ring; there is only a gold ring. (From *The Art of Meditation*, p. 18)

Our spiritual nature never allows us to forget totally our spiritual origins. In fact, according to the Cayce readings, we each have a spiritual purpose, and each of us has adopted spiritual ideals and values which are often buried under the physical and mental details of our lives — the very slings and arrows about which we are concerned.

Did that discussion make "spiritual" less vague for you? In simplest terms, think of spiritual as meaning "having a special, direct relationship to God."

Recognizing our inclination to slight our spiritual nature. To many people, the words "spirit" and "spiritual" suggest traditional religion, and for some of those people, religion is represented by experiences and understandings from which they feel separated — perhaps without much regret. Or maybe the religious connection is an obligation, but not a high priority or a major influence on beliefs and actions. In a 1976 Gallup poll (the same question has not been asked in more recent years), 94% of the national sample of Americans said they believed in God or a universal spirit. Yet only 65% in 1979 considered "religion" very important in their lives; by 1988, that figure had dropped to 53%. In this book, "spiritual" does not depend on any religious connotation, but it is consistent with the theological idea of a relationship with God.

To some folks, "spirit" may be associated with spiritism, ghostly apparitions, and seances, all of which have low credibility for them. To still others, the concept of the spiritual is just too intangible to merit serious consideration. Most of us have beliefs and ideas we do not feel comfortable talking about, partly because of the haziness of the ideas and partly because such topics are just not matters of everyday conversation.

So we tend to ignore our spiritual nature; in fact, we tend to push it aside into personal oblivion. An understandable reaction, but one that prevents us from recognizing all the spiritual "good" waiting for us.

Realizing the central role of spirituality in our lives. To clarify the relationship among the physical, mental, and spiritual aspects of our lives, I introduce one of the most far-reaching — and mind-boggling — universal laws under which we operate: "...the spirit is life; the mind is the builder; the physical is the result" (349-4): To bring something into physical existence, we draw energy from pure spirit, where life originates; then we give shape to it with the mind, after which its physical form results.

The energy itself is God, and God is predisposed toward qualities such as love and wellness. Therefore, the spirit we draw upon in this law is predisposed toward "good" and "right" —if we don't get in the way. Unfortunately, our gift of free will *can* get in the way, challenging the naturally positive qualities of the spirit and building instead something selfish, unhealthy, even destructive. Because of the direct impact we — through our minds — have on everything we bring into our experience, understanding and acting "in sync" with this law of manifestation is probably the most important lesson we can learn in life.

The concept of "the spirit is life" was central to a philosophy espoused by a controversial theologian whose life bridged the 13th and 14th centuries and whose work gave rise to a popular mystical movement in 14th-century Germany:

> **Zooming In for a Closeup**. Born Johannes Eckhardt around 1260, the man now referred to as Meister Eckhart studied, took vows, and taught in the Dominican order of the Roman Catholic Church. The theme of his teaching and writing was a burning sense of God's nearness to humanity, in contrast to the then-current Church view of God's distance and the indispensable role of the clergy in interceding between God and His people. Meister Eckhart preached that life itself was the creative energy of God in action, sometimes referred to as a "creation-centered" tradition. He adopted as a principal audience for these ideas the poor, the humble, and the ignorant, urging them to seek the divine spark in humankind through direct communication with God. His activities and ideas were considered unsound and, near the end of his life, he was charged with heresy, although his Dominican order supported him. According to Matthew Fox in his introduction to *Meditations with Meister Eckhart*:
>
> > Meister Eckhart...was mystic and prophet, feminist and philosopher, preacher and theologian, administrator and poet, a spiritual genius and a declared heretic. While all reputable scholars today agree he was unjustly condemned — his condemnation bears all the earmarks of an attempt to silence his prophetic preaching on behalf of the poor in his

society — his way of spirituality remains too little known in the West ... [M]any, many Christians hardly know the name, much less the spiritual tradition he presents so beautifully. (p. 3)

Meister Eckhart's own writings clearly express the fact of "God in us":

We ought to understand God equally in all things, for God is equally in all things. (p. 26)

The seed of God is in us. Now the seed of a pear tree grows into a pear tree; and a hazel seed grows into a hazel tree; a seed of God grows into God. (p. 28)

Meister Eckhart and Joel Goldsmith (he gave us the gold ring metaphor) would probably agree with Edgar Cayce on this issue: Whether or not we choose to acknowledge our spirituality, we *are* spiritual beings and function well only when we acknowledge the spiritual in our lives — that is, our direct and special relationship with God.

As to achieving inner peace and being at one with life, there are dozens of ways we can get it all together and suppress that turmoil and anxiety that bubbles over from time to time — dozens of ways that will bring "temporary relief for the minor aches and pains" from our slings and arrows. But the Cayce information makes it clear that the only "long-lasting relief" against future disturbances can be brought about through the *spiritual connection*. The Cayce approach is distinctive in its potential for guiding each individual toward at-oneness in a manner unique to that individual, using the inner spiritual motivation of that person.

Therefore, when we ask "What's all this about our spiritual nature?" we answer that we must grow in our acceptance of our spirituality and in our understanding of spiritual laws, seeking ways to make them a focus of our lives.

Getting Comfortable with "God"

That intangible "something" that most people believe exists in the universe has a purpose for us: "... we were made for the purpose of becoming companions with Him, a little lower than the angels ..." (1567-2). (And all this time, you wanted to become an angel!) As part of the process of becoming "companions," we are given the opportunity to "... become aware of [our] relationships to the Creative Forces or God" (1567-2) — that is, to recognize our spirituality. For that relationship to work, we must find comfortable ways to address this Spiritual Force, to talk about It, and to express ourselves to It.

Let's set the stage with some ideas from others who have considered the question of what Spirit is and how we address It. First, let me introduce you to Charles Merrill Smith and his book, *How to Talk to God When You Aren't Feeling Religious*. In one of Smith's conversations with God, he says:

> ... how am I to think of pure spirit, which You are? I have to clothe it, in my imagination, with some kind of form I can visualize. So I play this game of picturing You as a perfect human. I know it is a game, but it doesn't have to be a bad game so long as I don't confuse it with reality.
>
> It becomes a bad game, though, when I move from picturing You in human terms to believing You are my sidekick, my best friend, a cosmic amigo who pals around with me in a special way. When I think of You in this way, which I'm always tempted to do, then I'm attempting to possess You and use You for my own benefit. If You and I had this relationship, You wouldn't be God any more. You'd be an object, an acquaintance with plenty of clout. I might like You, and enjoy Your company, and all that — but You wouldn't be the Ultimate Being any more, and sooner or later I'd be looking for an Ultimate beyond You.
>
> ... If I understand the Gospels, Jesus said that he came in order that we could have a glimpse, a clue as to what You are like.
>
> That's enough for me. (pp. 175-176)

Robert Fulghum astonished the publishing world with his best-selling *All I Really Need to Know I Learned in Kindergarten*. In an interview with Sydney Trent, Fulghum shared this analogy for God:

> The closest analogy I have for my idea of God is water. Water is every place on this earth. You and I are 95 percent water. Water comes in the form of steam and ice, drinkable and non-drinkable. There is not life without water. It seems strange to me that you and I would argue over the name of this liquid, or the fact that you drink it out of a glass and I

29

drink it out of a mug. What we have in common is our thirst.
(From "Accidental Author" in *The Virginian-Pilot*, June 2,
1989, p. B3)

Now what shall each of us do about referring to Spirit, God, the Creative
Force? In this book, I have chosen the word *God* as the term with which I
am most comfortable. Cayce captures my concept of God this way:

First we begin with the fact that God *is*; and that the heavens
and the earth, and all nature, declare this. Just as there is the
longing within *every* heart for the continuity of life.
What then is life? As it has been given, in Him we live
and move and have our being. Then He, God, *is*! Or Life in
all of its phases, its expressions, is a manifestation of that
force or power we call God ... (1567-2)

What about the gender of God? Why do we usually refer to God as "He"
and "Father"? Rabbi Aryeh Kaplan speaks of the male and female forces of
God's providence — the male force which acts upon the world, the female
force which allows the world to be receptive to God's power:

... although we usually refer to God as a male, in His true
essence He is without gender. We refer to Him as a male,
however, because we want Him to act upon the world
through the male force of providence. We then leave
ourselves open to God's providence, as a female is open to
her mate.
... The Torah presents man and woman together as com-
prising the image of the Divine. (From *Jewish Meditation*,
p. 154)

I personally like the androgynous image conveyed by the term *Father-
Mother God* — a form of address expressed at least once (849-76) in the
Cayce readings. To remind you of the androgyny, I will sometimes refer to
God as He or Him, and sometimes as She or Her — these latter pronouns
being appropriate when I am emphasizing the female/receptive aspects of
God the Mother.
As to my style of speaking with God, I choose to be informal, avoiding
Thee's and Thou's along with other traditional prayer words. I am more
inclined to talk with God when I don't have to adopt a new vocabulary for

the purpose. In her biography, *The Spiritual Journey of Joel Goldsmith*, Lorraine Sinkler gives us insight into Goldsmith's style of speaking to God while seeking guidance for a series of classes he was being asked to teach:

> A few days before that first Friday night [class,] Joel went to his office and spoke to God: "Look, Father, if You sent these people to me, it must be for a reason. Tell me what it is. If You didn't send them, that's all right. Within four weeks, they will know all about it, but if You sent them, let me in on the secret. What are they here for? What is it You want me to do?"

> [Joel said,] "I talked to the Father as if the Father were another man. That isn't very metaphysical, but that is my way, and that is the way I still talk to the Father..." (p. 47)

"Try Me!" For your own spiritual activity, think about the various ways of referring to and addressing the universal power that I call God. Several have been mentioned earlier: Spirit, Creative Force, Father, Infinite Source. The word Lord is often used in the Cayce prayers, as well as Lord God and Father God. A spiritually devout friend of mine uses the wonderful term Holy Companion. Select one or two forms of address or personal reference that you find most comfortable and expressive of your attitude toward God.

Consider your conversational style with God. If you feel the need for formality, Thee's and Thou's will help keep you in that frame of mind. Whatever style you select, practice speaking with God, expressing thanks and concerns in words you are comfortable with.

As you watch the news on television or read about it in newspapers and magazines, talk with God about how you feel. Find aspects of the news events on which you would invite God's blessings and protection — even "bad" news. For example, reading about death can lead to asking God to guide those who have passed over and to comfort those left behind. Develop a habit of using the news as a trigger to talk with God.

Get to feel comfortable with your selected forms of address and your expressions of thoughts and concerns. Expressing thankfulness and love are always good first steps to feeling comfortable with God.

31

Remember that the point of this chapter has been to define the desirable state of inner peace that I call "being at one with life" — and that got me to discussing the vital role of our spirituality. Now I'm ready to talk about the strategy that can, with conscientious practice, produce this state. The strategy is built around the process of *meditation*. "Meditation?" you echo, maybe with a little condescension in your voice. "The stock-in-trade of gurus, mystics, and flaky eccentrics?" Whatever you know about meditation, I'll bet that meditation — as *we* will discuss it — is both more and less!

Chapter 3

Meditation Is Both More and Less

"What's that you're working on?"

"Slogans for bumper stickers. I want to let everyone in on the world's best kept secret."

"What is it? The cure for whatever ails you? A new way to make love? A recipe for happiness?"

"All of those."

"I don't believe you! Let's see those signs."

DON'T MEDICATE — MEDITATE!

ANSWER TO FRUSTRATION — MEDITATION

WANT TO BE CREATIVE? — BE MEDITATIVE!

Most people who have heard of meditation have some conception of what it is, how it is done, what its effects are, what kinds of people meditate, and even how acceptable it is to mention meditation in polite society. Whether you are new to meditation, are already a meditator, or meditated at some time in the past, in this book you're likely to discover that meditation is both less and more than you expected: less mystical and mysterious, less Oriental and guru-centered, less restrictive and "formularized," and generally less off-putting; and more Western in tradition, more practical in both manner and results, more adaptable to your own lifestyle and personality, and ultimately more beneficial than you ever imagined.

This chapter highlights meditation's Western traditions, illustrates benefits that may be realized through meditation, clarifies some terms associated with meditation, considers several definitions of meditation, and presents the basic principles of *"creative meditation."* Set aside your preconceptions and think of meditation *not* as a technique, but as a *state of being, attained by a disciplined, individualized process.*

The Traditions of Meditation: East vs. West

A personal note. Growing up in a conservative, Midwestern, Protestant home, what I learned as a young person about meditation was next to nothing. I knew about monks and religious scholars who apparently spent all day in meditation, which I imagined as somewhere between praying and dreaming. This kind of experience was as foreign to me as the life of Australian aborigines — and I doubt that my early impressions about meditation were unique among those who grew up in the 1930s and 1940s.

My first experiences with meditation as an adult were not very promising — and also probably not unique. In the early 1970s, I was exposed to Transcendental Meditation (TM) and to meditation associated with yoga. At first, I was intrigued by mysterious elements that I now label as Eastern: sitting in a lotus or half-lotus position, fixating on an object such as a piece of fruit or a candle, repeating a secret Sanskrit mantra. I did not make much effort to understand the philosophy that undergirded meditation, especially the spiritual aspects. Although I felt relaxed following the yoga-related meditation, after several months I gave up my halfhearted efforts to meditate, never experiencing the "inner peace ... profound self-knowledge ... physical grace ... and spiritual serenity" promised on the cover of a popular meditation guide I was using. Do you suppose the quality of my experience was affected at all by my uninspired level of motivation, sincerity, and persistence?

I justified my relapse by wondering why I should adopt something that originated in India and the Orient and was practiced mostly there (I thought). The very qualities of the meditation technique that first attracted me — the mysterious Eastern elements — now helped to turn me away from it. Since I didn't separate the *technique* of meditation from the *state* of meditation, I threw the baby out with the bath water, as the saying goes.

Years later, as a student of the ideas and information expressed through the readings of Edgar Cayce, I rediscovered meditation and I learned processes for meditating that are sensible, comfortable, and flexible for me. More significant, I find benefits to my physical and mental health and values to my spiritual well-being that I never anticipated. As I continue to study meditation information both Eastern and Western, I find my appreciation for the gifts of meditation continually growing.

A universal note. The practice of meditation is far more universal and timeless than I had realized. In a book of essays entitled *Meditation in Christianity* is the following statement by Arpita, who serves on the staff of the Himalayan International Institute of Yoga Science and Philosophy in Honesdale, Pennsylvania:

> Meditation is a practical and simple method of spiritual practice that transcends era, culture, and religion. All the great religions of the world have utilized some method of meditation, each with its own identifying but nonessential embellishments unique to the background of those who developed it. The meditative tradition itself is universal, because the practice of meditation is an intrinsic aspect of human nature. (pp. 73-74)

In another essay in the same book (for which he served as editor), Swami Rama of the Himalayan Institute speaks particularly to the Christian tradition:

> Western Christians are not aware of an overlooked tradition, one in which meditation was taught widely. The meditative tradition at one time dominated early Christianity in the Middle East. After studying the history of the early Christians and the Desert Fathers, we know that they meditated day and night, and that meditation was not a new concept for them. (p. 6)

Rabbi Aryeh Kaplan not only relates a Jewish parallel in meditation history, but also suggests a significant link between Eastern and Western traditions through Jewish meditation:

> People are often surprised to hear the term "Jewish meditation." Otherwise knowledgeable Jews, including many rabbis and scholars, are not aware that such a thing exists ...

It is therefore not surprising that many current books on meditation give scant attention to Judaism... For students of meditation, this is a serious oversight. Judaism produced one of the more important systems of meditation...Furthermore, since Judaism is an Eastern religion that migrated to the West, its meditative practices may well be those most relevant to Western man. Without knowledge of Jewish meditative practices, an important link between East and West is lost. (From *Jewish Meditation*, p. v)

... during the period when the [Jewish] Bible was written (until approximately 400 B.C.E.), meditation was practiced by a large proportion of the Israelite people. The Talmud and Midrash state explicitly that over a million people were involved in such disciplines. (p. 42)

With such a fertile tradition in the West, we need not draw upon the meditation sources of the East, prolific as they are. Therefore, in the remainder of this book, most of the references cited will be Western sources, including both Jewish and Christian — both Roman Catholic and Protestant.

The Western Meditation Tradition

In her book, *Beyond TM: A Practical Guide to the Lost Traditions of Christian Meditation*, Marilyn Morgan Helleberg traces the thread of Christian meditation through the centuries, beginning with Jesus and His disciples, most notably John; the apostle Paul, possibly the first great mystic after Jesus; Augustine of the 4th and 5th centuries; Francis of Assisi, 12th and 13th centuries; Teresa of Avila, 16th century; the German cobbler-mystic Jacob Boehme of the late 16th, early 17th centuries; George Fox, 17th-century English founder of the Quakers, who taught his followers to listen for the "still small voice within"; and William Blake, the English poet-mystic of the late 17th, early 18th centuries, whose prophetic writings resulted from his avowed communion with God.

One of the classic instructional guides to meditation was a product of the same medieval period that saw the efforts of Meister Eckhart condemned. In fact, the English writer of this guide remains unknown apparently because he was concerned about being accused of heresy.

36

Zooming In for a Closeup. In the 14th century, the acceptable way for an ordinary person to approach and commune with God was through the formal channels of the Church — the priests and the saints. It was presumptuous to think one could speak directly to God, and Church authorities did not deal kindly with those who so proclaimed. In this lively medieval controversy appeared an Englishman, probably a monk in the northeast Midlands area of England. His writings which have endured for 500 years reveal that he was remarkably well read, familiar with the theological work of such figures as Dionysius of the 1st century, Augustine of the 4th and 5th centuries, and Thomas Aquinas of the 13th century.

The Cloud of Unknowing is addressed to an unidentified young man as a set of instructions on a form of meditation sometimes referred to as contemplation. His approach rejected the typical meditative practice of that time which allowed thoughts and images to flow freely during the meditation. Such conscious thought and imagery were replaced by direct communion with God. This concept of moving close to God is so central to the approach that it gives the book its title: The meditator is to bury all thoughts and images beneath a "cloud of forgetting" while pure love rises to God hidden in a "cloud of unknowing." His strong feelings against trying to work with meditation as a mental process are expressed early in the document:

> Some will probably hear about this work and suppose that by their own ingenious efforts they can achieve it. They are likely to strain their mind and imagination unnaturally only to produce a false work which is neither human nor divine. Truly, such a person is dangerously deceived. (From William Johnston's edition of *The Cloud of Unknowing,* Chapter 4, p. 52)

The guide to meditation is practical and down-to-earth, as well as insightful and inspirational. The personality of the unknown author is reflected throughout the 75 short chapters of the work.

In *Beyond TM*, Marilyn Helleberg reminds us that Martin Luther's revolt in the early 16th century was aimed at breaking up the Roman Catholic Church's rigid emphasis on external forms of worship and devotion, so that the spiritual possibilities of the inner person might be freed and expanded.

37

She also points out that John Wesley's great 18th-century appeal concerned the need for intimate personal experience between God and the individual.

Helleberg cites several people who have contributed to the 20th-century views of meditation: Joel Goldsmith, William Johnston, Paul Tillich, George Mahoney, M. Basil Pennington, Thomas R. Kelly, and Morton T. Kelsey. I would add to this distinguished group Rabbi Aryeh Kaplan, as well as Edgar Cayce and his readings, his son Hugh Lynn Cayce, and the spiritual teacher and writer Mark Thurston.

As I read about Western meditative practices, I am impressed with both the "sameness" and the "differentness": they often reflect many of the same motives, the same steps of preparation and practice, the same difficulties to be overcome, and the same experiences of spiritual communion with God; while differing in principles of philosophy or theology; in the nature of mental focus; in the regularity, frequency, and length of practice; and in the benefits realized through the meditative state. These similarities and differences have led me to formulate the process of *creative meditation* so that it builds on the similarities and encourages experimentation on some of the differences.

Research on Meditation and Its Effects

Finally, someone has done it! Michael Murphy and Steven Donovan have completed a monumental survey of the research on *The Physical and Physiological Effects of Meditation: A Review and Comprehensive Bibliography, 1931-1988.* The title could have included the word "psychological," since the book refers to effects on behavioral and psychological factors such as creativity, perception, self-esteem, and flexibility. Although I have read only a few of the over 1200 studies reported on in that book, I suspect: (a) that most of the research is based on meditation without an intentional spiritual focus and (b) that none of the studies attempted to assess effects either accruing *to* spiritual outcomes or stemming *from* spiritual elements in the process. The physical, physiological, and psychological results would probably not be lessened by the addition of a spiritual component, and a whole new range of spiritual outcomes might be realized.

The compilers, Murphy and Donovan, point out that the reports are largely from experiments with beginning meditators. Some results would probably be enhanced in comparable studies with experienced meditators. Many long-term meditators regularly reach an altered state of consciousness typical of deep meditation. I would speculate that, even without an intentional spiritual focus, such experienced meditators have "spiritual experiences" that include a feeling of oneness with God or with the universe.

In *The Meditative Mind: The Varieties of Meditation Experience*, Daniel Goleman, psychologist and frequent writer for *The New York Times*, summarizes a number of remarkable physical and physiological effects of meditation (and relaxation):

- Probably the single most reported physiological benefit of meditation — indeed, of systematic relaxation techniques generally — is the drop in blood pressure. Even the National Institutes of Health (NIH) have recommended meditation (along with salt and dietary restrictions) above prescription drugs as the first treatment for mild hypertension.
- Relaxation through meditation relieves suffering from angina and arrhythmia, lowers blood cholesterol levels, and can enhance blood flow to the heart.
- Although changes taking place through the endocrine system are still not well understood, some research results are startling. For example, the deep relaxation of meditation may enhance the immune function of the body, with research showing increased defense against tumors, viruses, colds, flu, and other infectious diseases.
- From meditative relaxation, diabetics can experience a lessening of the emotional reactions that often precede attacks.
- Asthmatics can experience improved flow in constricted air passages.
- Chronic pain patients can reduce their reliance on pain-killers and lessen the level of pain. Backaches, migraine headaches, and tension headaches may all be relieved with long-term carryover through proper training.

Other meditation research has demonstrated this wide range of psychological benefits:

- Improvement in measurements of personality
- Decrease in neurotic tendencies
- Increase in psychic sensitivity
- Improvement in study efficiency and exam performance
- Increase in efficiency of problem solving
- Improvement in creativity in the visual arts
- Decrease in drug and alcohol abuse

Of special interest is Daniel Goleman's own research demonstrating the greater tolerance for stress by those who meditate. He gives us some insight into how meditation accomplishes this:

> People who are chronically anxious or who have a psycho-somatic disorder share a specific pattern of reaction to stress; their bodies mobilize to meet the challenge, then fail to stop reacting when the problem is over... their bodies stay aroused for danger when they should be relaxed, recouping spent energies and gathering resources for the next brush with stress.
>
> The anxious person meets life's normal events as though they were crises. Each minor happening increases his tension, and his tension in turn magnifies the next ordinary event — a deadline, an interview, a doctor's appointment — into a threat. Because the anxious person's body stays mobilized after one event has passed, he has a lower threat threshold for the next. Had he been in a relaxed state, he would have taken the second event in stride.
>
> A meditator handles stress in a way that breaks up the threat-arousal-threat spiral. The meditator relaxes after a challenge passes, more often than the non-meditator. This makes him unlikely to see innocent occurrences as harmful. He perceives threat more accurately, and reacts with arousal only when necessary. Once aroused, his rapid recovery makes him less likely than the anxious person to see the next deadline as a threat. (From *The Meditative Mind*, pp. 164-165)

Subjective Experience with Meditation

To many of us, as impressive as the "hard" research are the reports of individual experiences with meditation and the evidence of personal trans-formation and well-being reported by meditators. For example, Marilyn Helleberg reports what happened when she brought meditation into her own busy life:

> When I first started meditating, all six members of our family were living at home, I was a part-time, college teacher, a correspondent for a national newspaper, a Sunday

40

school teacher, and a free-lance writer. How in the world could I ever find time to meditate twice a day? Well, I discovered an astonishing thing. The more regularly I meditated, the more I got done! Instead of *crowding* my day, it seemed to *ease* the congestion! It's because meditation drains off stress and helps us to *order* our lives. (From *Beyond TM*, p. 14)

In his book *You'll See It When You Believe It*, psychologist and psycho-therapist Wayne Dyer describes not only his personal approach to meditation, but also his remarkable and moving "personal transformation." At the deepest level of his meditation, Dyer says:

"Exquisite peace" is the best term I can think of for this place... When I leave this level I feel totally connected to all of mankind. In fact, I call this meditation my connection to all of eternity, because someplace deep inside of me I am freed from my form completely. After meditating I know that I can accomplish anything! Some of my most profound ideas, my very best speeches, and my most personally satisfying writing emerge after meditating. And my appreciation for my loved ones can only be described as a peak experience. (p. 45)

A young German pastor found that meditation was essential to his survival under appalling circumstances:

Zooming In for a Closeup. Dietrich Bonhoeffer, born in 1906, grew up in a distinguished and highly educated German family. His theological studies were undertaken at Berlin University where he was much influenced by the writings of Karl Barth. After a short pastorate in Spain and a year studying at Union Theological Seminary in New York, he returned to Berlin to teach, until he was forbidden to do so by the Nazis in 1936.

Then, while preparing for a visit to Gandhi in India, Bonhoeffer was asked to conduct an emergency seminary program for young ministers. During this period of 1937-'38, he wrote some of his most controversial works on the compromises being made in the German church under National Socialism. Although he was trying to remain a pacifist, he learned through friends about the attempts to overthrow the

41

Nazi government and realized pacifism was not a legitimate position for a conscientious German citizen.

After a lecture tour to the United States in 1939, he took one of the last ships back to Germany before the war began, being of two minds about returning. He then worked for the Resistance Movement in Germany, coping with the obstacles the Gestapo had placed before him — prohibiting him from lecturing, writing, making speeches of any kind, even staying in Berlin. He was able to travel in and out of Germany, however, meeting with sympathizers and supporters in other countries.

Finally, in April 1943, Bonhoeffer was arrested and spent the first 18 months of his confinement in Berlin's Tegel Prison. His correspondence during that period is not only a remarkable testament to his faith in God and in ultimate justice in Germany, but a demonstration of the inner strength and peace sustained by the practice of meditation. Even during his internments in the death camps at Buchenwald, Schoenberg, and finally Flossenburg, he seemed to "diffuse an atmosphere of happiness, of joy in every smallest event in his life, and of deep gratitude for the mere fact that he was alive," according to another prisoner. "He was one of the very few men that I have ever met to whom his God was real and close to him" (from *Letters and Papers from Prison*, pp. 13-14). In April 1945, the day after holding a service for other prisoners at Flossenburg, he was hanged by the Nazis.

In 1942, before his imprisonment, Dietrich Bonhoeffer writes:

Our previous ordered life has been broken up and dissolved in these present days, and we are in danger of losing our inner sense of order, too, because of the rush of events, the demands of work, doubts, temptations, conflicts, and unrest of all kinds. Meditation can give to our lives a measure of steadiness... Meditation is a source of peace, of patience and of joy; it is like a magnet which draws together all the forces in our life which make for order; it is like deep water which reflects the clouds and the sun on its clear surface. It also serves the Most High by presenting him with a place of discipline, stillness, healing, and contentment in our lives. Have we not all a deep, perhaps unconfessed, longing for such a gift? Could it not become for us once more a source of health and strength? (From *Meditating on the Word*, pp. 51-52)

Over and over again, we read of meditation experiences that echo words and phrases like those cited in our discussion of "being at one with life" in the preceding chapter — "tranquillity of spirit," "connectedness with others and with nature," "enjoyment of each moment," "peace and love." Also, repeatedly in the Cayce readings we find references to the extraordinary benefits of meditation:

> Of course, meditation.. helps self more than self can be aided in any other way. (3226-2)

> But if there is set a definite period or manner of meditation ... there may be had a balancing. And... there may come an activity that will enable the body-physical ... to "snap out" of these expressions, those depressions, those feelings of floating, those feelings of losing control, those feelings of the inability of concentration. (1089-2)

> ... the quicker way [to overcome conditions of being over-tired mentally and physically], the greater response, physically and mentally, may be found by the perfect relaxation in meditation... (257-92)

> As the [person] may experience in some of its moments of meditation, the finding of peace in self enables the [person] to give more assurance, more help to others... (3098-2)

One of our principal goals of this life is to know ourselves and to understand our relationship to God. "... to know *yourself* to *be* yourself and yet one with God" (281-37, A-12) is how Cayce expresses it repeatedly in the readings. Second only to this goal is that of understanding our relationships to one another, often mentioned by Cayce through reference to Jesus' second great commandment — "You shall love your neighbor as yourself" (Matthew 22:39 RSV). The means to gain this understanding? "Meditation is the safest and surest way to understand ourselves" (from *A Search for God*, Book I, p. 19).

Definitions, Distinctions, and Non-Distinctions

Do all reports of research and experience use the word "meditation" to mean the same thing? They clearly do not. So how do we deal with that ambiguity? Also how does meditation differ from prayer, and how does it relate to mysticism, for example? As we move toward a series of principles of *creative meditation*, we need to clear up several overlapping and ambiguous words and concepts.

Mystics and mysticism. In reading about meditation, we occasionally encounter the words "mystic" and "mysticism." In a nutshell, *mysticism* is the practice of putting oneself into a state of consciousness in direct contact with God and remaining there, and a *mystic* is a person who does that. The *Random House Dictionary* qualifies that somewhat: A mystic is

> "... a person who claims to attain, or believes in the possibility of attaining, insight into mysteries transcending ordinary human knowledge, as by direct communication with the divine or immediate intuition in a state of spiritual ecstasy."

Other uses of the word "mystic" are in general use — some of them not very flattering. Cayce's own use of the words "mystic" and "mysticism" appears to be based on a 13th-century use of mystic to mean specifically a person initiated into religious mysteries; thus he uses "mystic" or "mystical" to suggest mysterious (282-3, 1265-3), and "mysticism" to mean spiritualism and the influence of mysterious forces, in contrast to spirituality (1101-2). In this book, "mystic" is used in the sense defined in the paragraph above.

Is our aim to become mystics? Our jolly friend, Charles Merrill Smith, expressed concern to God about this:

> After many years of waiting for that transforming, edifying, ecstatic experience the mystics say I should receive, I have concluded, Sir, that I am just not the mystical type. Perhaps I do not believe strongly enough. Or maybe I have a spiritual gland missing. I have decided that I'll just have to muddle along as best I can without mystical experience.
>
> Sir, there must be millions of nonmystical Christians like me. And I'll bet if You questioned them You would discover that they all feel a bit guilty for not having had a mystical experience. All of us suspect we are missing out on something tremendous, because our more mystically inclined Christian friends tell us that we are.
>
> ... At any rate, I hope You don't downgrade us nonmys-

tics. I'm sure we all would be mystics if we could be, but some of us can't. Perhaps the mystical spirit is a gift You give to some and deny to others. (From *How to Talk to God When You Aren't Feeling Religious*, pp. 151-152)

Mysticism is not a requirement for at-oneness!

Meditation. The writings of mystics and spiritual teachers allow us to reflect on what meditation may be. You have met the English mystic Evelyn Underhill, who will be quoted; it's time to meet the American mystic, Joel Goldsmith.

Zooming In for a Closeup. Although Joel Goldsmith was born a Jew in 1892, his parents did not practice Jewish customs or attend religious services. When he was age 12, however, they did see that he received instruction in a Reform Jewish temple for his confirmation at age 13. According to Joel, he went to temple only once again in his life.

His formal education ended at eighth grade at which time his father began teaching him the family business — importing lace and similar goods. When his father was taken seriously ill on a European buying trip, a friend's father, who was a Christian Science practitioner, prayed for him. His father's miraculous recovery led Joel to study Christian Science. Later, while he was traveling as a very successful salesman, he sought out a practitioner for healing a cold. Talking and praying with this man, he had his first spiritual experience, not only healing his cold, but causing him immediately to discontinue smoking, drinking alcoholic beverages, playing cards, and going to the races! Soon after that, much to his surprise, his customers spontaneously began asking for his prayers and healing, often resulting in their healing. He began to realize a transformation had taken place and that his thoughts were continually on God and healing.

As his healing activity increased, however, his sales business decreased until, at age 36, it died. He then opened an office as a Christian Science practitioner, also serving in various functions within the Christian Science Church. Goldsmith's former assistant and biographer, Lorraine Sinkler, reports that the day she first met him in his office, he had seen nearly 50 people!

Sixteen years later, he left the Christian Science movement to follow his own guidance and revelation. His healing, teaching, and writing came together in what he called "The Infinite Way." The essential process of this approach is meditation, and his books *The Art of Meditation* and *Practicing the Presence* are filled with his guidance and experience on the process as he practiced it.

An unpretentious man, both in actions and in appearance, Joel Goldsmith dedicated his life to healing, to writing— about 30 books — and to teaching all over the world. He was truly a mystic — a man continuously in touch with the Divine — a man whose life was always ready for immediate response to the direction of God. His work — simple in concept and rich in his expression of it — has been the focal point of groups of spiritual seekers all over the world. He died in 1964 at the age of 72.

From Joel Goldsmith on what meditation is:

> As we begin to recognize our good as the gift of God, we let the reasoning, thinking, planning mind relax. We listen for the still small voice, ever watchful for ... the Father within. It will never leave us nor forsake us. It is our permanent dispensation.
>
> This listening is the art of meditation, in the learning of which we come to a place of transition where truth leaves the mind and enters the heart. (From *The Art of Meditation*, p. 6)

From Evelyn Underhill:

> Meditation is a word which covers a considerable range of devotional states. It is perhaps most simply defined as thinking in the Presence of God. [It requires] recollection — a deliberate gathering of ourselves together, a retreat into our own souls. (From Kepler's *The Evelyn Underhill Reader*, p. 167)

From Swami Rama, founder of the Himalayan Institute in the United States, headquartered in what was once a Roman Catholic monastery in Honesdale, Pennsylvania (an exception to my rule about only Western sources, since this Eastern spiritual leader wrote this articulate passage for a Western audience):

> The word *meditation* is used in various ways, but however it is used, it always refers to techniques that deal with one's

46

inner nature. Through these techniques one finally trans-
cends all levels of the mind and goes on to Christ consciousness and realization of the absolute One. Meditation does
not require a belief in dogma or in any authority. It is an
inward journey in which one studies one's own self on all
levels, and ultimately reaches the source of consciousness.
The aim of meditation is Self-realization — a direct vision
of Truth. It is not an intellectual pursuit, nor is it emotional
rapture. One's whole being is involved. It is neither
suppression, which makes one passive, nor is it the acquisi-
tion of any experience that is not already within us. Meditation leads one from want to wantlessness. It is a way of
going from the known to the unknown. The process can
hardly be explained by words, but it leads one from the
personal, through the transpersonal, and finally unites one
with the highest One. It transforms the whole personality.
(From *Meditation in Christianity*, pp. 11-12)

Notice that all three of these quotations express a spiritual purpose for
meditation. Many people writing about and teaching meditation — perhaps
most of them — do *not* include a spiritual focus or any spiritual component
in the processes they recommend. The spiritual focus is, however, *essential*
to the process of *creative meditation*.

As I have studied the Cayce readings, I admit to being perplexed about
the relationship between meditation and prayer. In my earlier book, *Miles to
Go: The Spiritual Quest of Aging,* I separated the two spiritual activities,
because the readings often recommend "meditation and prayer" as if they
were independent actions; for example, "set definite periods for prayer; set
definite periods for meditation" (5368-1). This dichotomy is strengthened
by Cayce readings like these:

Prayer is supplication to God and meditation is listening to
His answer. (2946-6)

Prayer ... is appealing to the Divine within self, the Divine
without self, and meditation is keeping still in body, in mind,
in heart, listening, listening to the voice of thy Maker.
(5368-1)

This distinction does make it easy to talk about what we normally refer to as prayer and then to address separately a process called meditation.

In the present book, however, I define *prayer* broadly as any communication with God, and define *meditation* as a special form of prayer. This conception is also reinforced by many Cayce readings, one of which is an instructional reading on meditation for the prayer healing group called the Glad Helpers:

> Meditation ... is prayer, but is prayer from *within* the *inner* self... (281-13)

Cayce characterized meditation with words that differed in their attention on one or another aspect of meditation. He apparently chose to emphasize the ideas that would be most helpful to the person or group for whom the reading was given:

> Meditation is prayer from within the inner self (281-13).

> Meditation is attuning the mental and physical forces of the body to the spiritual source (281-41).

> Meditation is participating in the spiritual vitalization of the energies of the bodily system (270-33).

> Meditation is emptying self of anything that hinders the inner creative forces from rising (281-13).

> Meditation is meeting and talking with God, as if God were physically present (281-28, 1152-9).

> Meditation is listening to the Divine within (1861-19).

My own experience with meditation leads me to conceptualize it in this way:

> I am urged by my inner self to maintain ongoing, direct contact with God through frequent *prayer*. I am also urged to refresh my relationship with God daily in an extended prayer experience of *meditation* — a sort of daily appointment to meet God in a quiet place for an uninterrupted period.

During that meditation period, I try to put aside everything physical and mental and, with the help of a spiritual focus, I try to tune myself in to Her unending love and mercy and to His infinite wisdom and power. I must empty myself of anything that might block either the inflowing of creative energy or its flow within me. The attunement not only allows me to receive ideas and experiences directly from God, but it also quickens and revitalizes the creative forces already within me.

Throughout this experience, I remain aware in human consciousness, yet am unaffected by my mental and physical states. Both the process of becoming attuned and the state of attunement itself contribute to a condition of inner calm and well-being that may be called "being at one with life."

The essence of this idea is caught in a word borrowed from the English mystic of the late 14th and early 15th centuries, Juliana of Norwich: "Prayer oneth the soul to God" (the second word being read as "one-eth," meaning "makes as one"). A simplified expression of meditation then becomes *"Meditation ones me to God."*

Principles of "Creative Meditation"

First, why *"creative meditation"*? The term keeps visible four essential features of meditation as presented in this book:

- Meditation leads to attunement with the *Creative* Forces that we call God, giving us total access to that Source of infinite energy.
- Meditation also quickens the *creative* energy already within our own bodies.
- Meditation is in itself a *creative* process, in that it can bring about *physical* changes within the body through the action of this law: The spirit is life, the mind is the builder, the physical is the result.
- The process of meditation is to be adapted *creatively* to your own needs, your own experience, and your own lifestyle, and it may be varied *creatively* as your interests and circumstances change, allowing you to grow with and through your meditative experiences.

Seven principles underlie *creative meditation*:

49

1. **Creative meditation is a state of being.** As noted earlier, meditation is not a technique; rather, it's the state achieved by the process through which an individual attunes himself or herself to God. A universal "best" technique or process does not exist. The Cayce readings suggest that each of us must find the approach that serves our needs, since "The activities of meditation are personal" (1158-25). No one can tell what will work for you in meditation any more than "one may tell another how to fall in love ..." (2441-2). A major goal of this book is to guide you in your discovery of the meditation approach for you.

2. **No special talent or innate ability is required for creative meditation, although it does require learning and practice.** In one of the principal readings on meditation, Cayce says you "must learn to meditate — just as [you] have learned to walk, to talk ..." (281-41). In *The Art of Meditation*, Joel Goldsmith reminds us that things worthwhile deserve the time they require: "Meditation is a difficult art to master" (p. 52); therefore, "even though we seem to feel no response, let us not become discouraged ... To expect immediate results from the practice of meditation would be the same as expecting to play Bach or Beethoven after the first music lesson" (p. 27).

3. **The goal of creative meditation is spiritual, and a spiritual focus is essential to the attunement process.** Our three-part nature — spiritual, mental, and physical — and the law "the spirit is life, the mind is the builder, the physical is the result" make it essential that the spiritual element be included in *creative meditation*. Admittedly, individuals may have a spiritual meditation experience without consciously addressing the spiritual element. However, the spiritual focus, coupled with prayer for protection, helps to insure that the meditative state is reached safely and that the meditator remains under God's protection in that state.

4. **Creative meditation is a state in which the meditator has direct access to and communication with God and God's infinite resources.** The goal is at-onement, which is attunement to the Creative Forces which are God. Once attunement is made, communication may take many forms, and results beyond at-oneness may be realized. Everything is available through this channel, as suggested in this reading:

For, thy body is indeed the temple of the living God. There He — as all knowledge, all undertakings, all wisdom, all understanding — may commune with thee, if ye but give that opportunity... He stands continually at the door of thy consciousness, of thy heart. If ye will open, He will enter. (2533-4)

5. **The creative meditator develops and regularly practices a variety of meditative forms and actions, ranging from the momentary to the extended.** Meditation will be effective only when it is done mindfully, rather than mindlessly or by rote. Variety in form and action helps to prevent mindlessness and boredom in meditation. Also, conditions of daily life vary in how accessible meditation can be, so methods must permit accommodation to the circumstances.

6. **Creative meditation is integrated into all phases of life experience.** Its foundation is a regular extended prayer experience during a scheduled period once a day. In addition, meditative actions are recommended for use throughout the day for reconnection to God even momentarily. The variety of meditative forms associated with the preceding principle facilitate this integration.

7. **Creative meditation is first directed to at-onement with God without expectations of benefits; the resources of God are then accessible for self-knowledge, self-guidance, and self-healing.** The primary goal of meditation is always at-onement, rather than to obtain something from God or through God's help. Once at-onement is attained without conditions imposed by the meditator, then God's resources are truly available.

A Meditation Experience

This section completes Part One, *Building the Case for Meditation*. If I have built my case well, you are now eager to begin learning the *creative meditation* process. And there's no time like the present for us to begin practicing meditation together. (If you are already an experienced meditator, I suggest your trying *creative meditation* at first as if you were new to meditation.)

First, read over these six general steps of an extended meditation process without carrying them out:

1. Prepare yourself physically and mentally for meditation, seeking physical relaxation and a quiet mind, using special activities or aids as you find them helpful.

2. Direct your whole attention to your spiritual focus. Concentrate on it for a short period.

3. Release the words of the spiritual focus and feel only the emotional essence of the spiritual concept. Enter a period of inner silence with both mind and body stilled. Remain aware and alert.

4. In the period of stillness, feelings of at-onement may be perceived. Be receptive to inner experiences that may represent a connection with God, whether the experiences are mental, emotional, physical, or spiritual.

5. Make use of the creative energy for prayer, healing, insight, and guidance.

6. Emerge from meditation slowly and deliberately, and rejoin the world!

Now you are ready to begin meditating.

"Try Me!" Select a comfortable, straight-backed chair where your spine will be vertical, and choose an uninterruptible period of 10 to 15 minutes for your experience.

Follow these steps for your first several meditation experiences:

• Use music or uplifting reading material for a few minutes to divert your mind from ongoing concerns.

• Sit comfortably and straight in the chair, feet flat on the floor, hands touching and resting in your lap, eyes closed. Relax your entire body from head to toe so you feel you are sinking into the chair and the floor. Observing but not controlling your breath may help you relax and avoid distractions.

- As you relax your body, focus your mind on the word LOVE and the emotional feelings that go with the idea of love of family, love of others dear to you, love of God.

- When you are relaxed, breathing easily, set aside the word LOVE and sense only the feeling of LOVE. As thoughts try to distract you, let them gently slide away, without getting caught up in them. Return to the word LOVE if you need to refocus. Try to hold the feeling of LOVE in the stillness for a minute or two. You may have to refocus several times.

- After that stillness period, before you move or start thinking again, send that feeling of LOVE to someone you name. Hold that person in your mind for a few moments.

- As you start moving your body, stretching a little, consider for a moment how you feel. Bring yourself back to your full senses and capabilities, ready to rejoin the world again.

Repeat this simple meditation at least once a day for a week or so without change or amplification. In the meantime, you may begin reading Part Two, especially Chapters 4, 5, and 6.

Stick around! The adventure is just beginning!

PART TWO

CREATING YOUR OWN MEDITATION STYLE

Chapter 4

What Counts in Your Life?

Just below the shimmering blue surface of the Caribbean swam a beautiful chameleon rainbow fish. As he darted among the reds and browns of the coral, he took on those hues. When he swam among the sea anemones, he became blue and green, almost invisible among the waving tentacles of the sea creatures.

As he drifted with the water's movement, a graceful silver angelfish appeared, seemingly from nowhere. "How are you doing, Rainbow?" she asked.

Startled at being so addressed by a stranger, he coolly replied, "Fine, thank you, Miss Angel." (Somehow he knew that was her name.) "Just drifting around ..."

"... letting the currents carry you along, taking on the color of your surroundings, with no special direction. Don't you ever dream about something higher in life than drifting?"

"Now, look, Miss Angel," he said, turning orange with annoyance, "I'm just fine without any high-falutin' dreams. What counts is keeping my stomach filled and keeping out of another fish's stomach! Who has time to worry about something better? Leave me alone!" A note of melancholy crept into his whisper, "Do you suppose I'm really missing out on something?"

Moral: If you have no dream to guide your life, then it makes no difference where you go or what you find when you get there.

With the presumption of a guardian angelfish, dare I ask if you're clear about what counts in your life? When serious choices have to be made, do you have any kind of vision or dream against which to compare your alternatives? Do you have any idea what is truly "best" for you? Maybe you find yourself drifting from the sunny surface to the shadowy coral below, just trying to keep away from predators (rhymes with creditors).

What on earth, you are wondering, do my personal standards have to do with meditation? As emphasized earlier, *creative meditation uses a spiritual connection* to facilitate attunement. That's why we begin our preparations for meditation by examining what it is that counts in your life — from a spiritual viewpoint.

How We "Measure" Our Lives

Our finances and other physical assets — homes, cars, clothes, furnishings — weigh heavily in how we perceive our state of well-being. They seem to be what count in life; consequently, many of us measure our status in life — and the status of others — by yardsticks of income and assets. Other popular yardsticks are those that gauge prestige and power through what kinds of jobs people hold, who their friends and acquaintances are, and what their social standing is. We may also measure our lives in terms of our health and fitness, our talents and abilities, our knowledge, and our material accomplishments.

As most people realize, market research and advertising both influence our perception of what counts in life, from the games and toys advertised on the popular children's television programs, to the automobiles associated with opulently successful, attractive, and sophisticated men and women in ads during adult programs. In a recent article in Hampton Roads' *Port Folio Magazine*, for example, John Sherwood described six audience categories into which the population of the 12-city/county area of Greater Hampton Roads is distributed. The categories are used for planning marketing strategies; for example, these six are used in planning advertising and possibly programming for a local television station. According to a market research firm under contract to the station, the categories are: Upscale Sophisticates, Upscale Traditional Families, Blue Collar Traditionalists, Struggling Starter Families, Content Survivalists, and Free Spirits. The people who presumably fit into each category are identified by words and phrases such as socially active, smart shoppers, traditional sex roles, religious, or alienated from politics. (Contractual agreements between the television station and the market research firm prevent me from illustrating further.) Even though most people don't fit precisely into one of the categories, Sherwood says that "the research suggests that each person, no matter what age, will discover an 80 percent identification with just one group" (p. 10).

Once the advertisements or programs appear, a sort of self-fulfilling prophecy sets in. We "near-types" see the ads and programs that appeal more strongly to our category, and we may become even more aligned with the type, because we see images and we hear ideas that represent others "like ourselves." Thus do we tend to fulfill our own stereotypes.

My point is that many of the physical and mental standards for our lives are presented to us full-blown by our life circumstances without our conscious seeking of them, and without our expressed willingness to adopt them. *We may be accepting them by default because we haven't identified our own.*

If we give weight to such imposed standards, we are empowering others "out there" to have control over a very important key to our lives — our values and our standards. Perhaps even more significant, we may be giving first priority to the physical and mental values, while ignoring the third dimension of our three-part nature — our spiritual selves.

Taking the point a step further, part of our inner turmoil may result from our inability or unwillingness to meet all the standards and expectations imposed by others. Another contributor to our lack of inner peace is our realization — often subconscious — that we have deeper, personal values we are not expressing and living. Do we ever measure our lives by the quality of our interpersonal relationships? Or by our progress in creating conditions for peace? By our success in helping others overcome obstacles in their lives? Remembering the law that begins "the spirit is life ..." (349-4), we are putting the proverbial cart before the horse when we allow ourselves to be pulled along primarily by material and mental norms.

We begin to take control of our lives when we set standards grounded in our own well-considered values and priorities, our own sense of purpose in life, our own *ideals*. Furthermore, our inner sense of well-being — the feeling of being at one with life — will be more readily achieved when we put those ideals in their spiritual form at the center of our meditative work. Only then will all else follow. A 34-year-old man who had changed his occupation and relocated still appeared unsettled as he asked in one of his readings by Cayce, "In just what environ will I find the greatest opportunity for service, success, and happiness?" Cayce's response included the following:

Depends upon what is the measure of success set in the ideal
for the body. . .What is thine ideal? Then there may be set
as to what may be the measure of success and happiness and
pleasure and joy in that field of activity. (520-3)

What is success in one's life without a standard, a vision, an ideal with which
to measure success? The statement of the ideal carries within it the yardstick
for success — and for joy, happiness, and peace.

Ideals as the Measures of Our Lives

To me, no concept from the Cayce readings is more important or useful
than that of the *ideal and its spiritual, mental, and physical counterparts.*
Ideals make it easy to answer the question: What counts in life? That which
measures up to our ideals. Cayce himself says:

... the most important experience of this or any [individual]
is to first know what *is* the ideal — spiritually. (357-13)

In 1988, a research project conducted among members of the A.R.E.
examined the effect of ideals on how participants viewed the outside world
as controlling their lives. The hypothesis was that "by consciously working
with ideals for personal change, one would increase the sense of having
internal control over life situations." The 85 people who participated fully
in the study — probably highly motivated to experiment and change — demonstrated a significant shift in the expected direction. The report to A.R.E.
members on the Home Research Project states:

Evidence suggests that systematic focus on ideals, purposes, and motives leads to a measurable shift in how one
views the world. Problems may not go away immediately, but there is a greater sense that the power to shape
one's life comes largely from within.

As he does in defining meditation, Cayce selects words and phrases
suited to the individual he is addressing in his definition of "ideals." This
gives an elastic, elusive quality to the concept of ideal, one that leaves room
for each of us to adjust the idea to our personal needs and circumstances.
Catch the essence of the ideal from these segments of Cayce readings:

...what is an ideal? That not made with hands; that that is eternal — *that* is an ideal. (24-4)

An ideal means that to which the entity may, itself, ever look up [to], knowing itself to be gradually becoming a portion [of it], but n*ever* may it be the whole. Something to look up to, or to attempt to *attain* to; not an idea, that I may do this or I may do that, that I may accomplish such and such through such modes of operation! for then one reaches the goal! (256-2)

First, know what is thy own ideal. Not as to what others may do for thee, but what is the ideal way of individuals to live among themselves? (1755-3)

Q-2. What is [my] ideal?
A-2. *That* the body must set itself... The body *knows* within self that which it holds as the criterion for *every* developing life, from that *it* holds as its ideal. Then, *whatever* is set in self the body should work toward, and the results will be in keeping with that activity...[if] the body set the ideal wholly in making the material success, it may *not* expect to be content, nor will it bring happiness. If the body's ideal is set in that which is *right* in the sight of its ideal, or by the measurement of that it holds as its criterion, as its ideal, *that* it will develop to. That must be set by self. (4866-2)

Seeking the Spiritual Ideal

The spiritual ideal is a personal standard for our lives that can be expressed at several levels of abstraction — from the lofty to the lowly — from the inspirational to the "perspirational" — from the universal ideal to the lifetime ideal and the working level ideal.

The universal spiritual ideal. Every human being, according to Cayce, has the ultimate spiritual ideal of "oneness with God" — attaining perfection in soul development that allows the soul to return to God from whence it originally came and to remain in/with God as God's companion and even "co-creator." (Now isn't that better than being just an angel?) So at the most exalted level, the soul level, each of us has *the universal ideal of oneness with God.*

The lifetime spiritual ideal. While oneness with God is your ultimate spiritual ideal, your soul-self has chosen a single element of oneness as a kind of theme for your present life. It is the focus of the lessons you have decided to learn in this experience. Consider "oneness with God" as a fantastic diamond cut with hundreds of sparkling spiritual facets, such as "love," "peace," "service," "cooperation," and "justice." Your soul-self has chosen one of those facets as your "lifetime spiritual ideal."

This lifetime ideal — which is always operating in your life — can often be identified by looking for the deep inner motivation that impels you toward your most inspired efforts. What spiritual quality or condition (several are mentioned in the preceding paragraph) would give you the greatest experience of joy if you saw it coming to fruition all around you and within you? An exercise (described later) will help you identify your lifetime ideal.

Such a spiritual quality becomes an underlying theme for your life, even if you don't recognize or acknowledge it. How much more you can be at peace with yourself and at one with the universe when you bring this lifetime ideal to the surface and work with it consciously in your life!

The "working level" spiritual ideal. The spiritual ideal —along with its counterparts in mental and physical ideals — is to be used not only as a spiritual focus for your meditation, but also as a yardstick for your life. Therefore, actively working with your ideal requires you to relate it to the activities and choices of your daily life. Even though your lifetime spiritual ideal is more specific than "oneness with God," it may still be hard to relate to every part of your life. For example, if your ideal is "justice," can you relate that to decisions about a relationship?

To enhance the meaningfulness of your ideal, you may choose to express your lifetime spiritual ideal at a more specific level — what we'll call a "working level" spiritual ideal. For example, the lifetime ideal of "love" may be focused on the quality of non-expectation — "unconditional love"; the lifetime ideal of "justice" might become a working level ideal of "fairness and honesty."

The working level ideal can be helpful in another critical way: You may not be able to identify your lifetime spiritual ideal — regardless of the ingenious exercises I have provided! Instead, you can choose a working level spiritual ideal that seems to ring true for you. Use it as if it were a reflection of your lifetime ideal. Circumstances may lead you to adjust it or even change it to another facet that seems more applicable to your life. When you modify your ideal, keep a record of your changes. Eventually, you may perceive a pattern among the working level ideals that identifies your lifetime ideal. In a sense, you follow this same principle even when you think you have identified your lifetime ideal. You use your experience with the working level ideals to verify and confirm it or to make adjustments accordingly.

As the circumstances in your life change, you may find it desirable to focus on another aspect of your lifetime spiritual ideal or simply to restate your working level ideal. For example, a lifetime ideal of "the Christ pattern" may have led you to a working level ideal of "loving patience" — especially appropriate when family members were all living at home, you were working in a business setting, and you were involved in many outside activities. When these circumstances change, you may want to choose another aspect of the Christ pattern as your working level ideal — gentleness or kindness, for example.

How do you make the spiritual ideal even more tangible and relevant in your life? How do you focus it on a specific issue or activity where you experience frequent challenges? How does it guide your attitudes and actions? The answer to all three of these questions is: By means of *mental ideals* and *physical ideals*, which are derived from the spiritual ideal. After you have identified your spiritual ideal — at least a tentative version of it — we will discuss and illustrate the usefulness of mental and physical ideals.

Identifying your spiritual ideal. Discovering your lifetime spiritual ideal is made easier by the fact that it is already demonstrating its influence in your life, whether you are consciously aware of it or not. The exercise which follows is designed to help you examine experiences in your life when the influence of your ideal is likely to be felt and, from those experiences, to find a word or phrase representing your spiritual ideal.

> **"Search Me!"** Now is the time for all good readers to come to the aid of your lifetime spiritual ideal. Its faint cries of "Find me! Get to know me! Work with me!" can be heard whenever it gets quiet enough in your life to give you time to make wise choices. In this exercise, you will first try to identify your lifetime ideal. If it eludes your attempts at discovery for the time being, then you will choose a working level ideal that is meaningful for you.
>
> 1. You will use the meditation steps recommended at the end of Chapter 3 for spiritual preparation. Before you begin, have your journal or notebook within reach for making a few notes later. Also have this book beside you and open to the questions in Step 2 below.

Carry out the meditation through the attunement process, including the use of LOVE as your focus, until you have experienced (or tried to experience) the stillness and the feeling of LOVE for two or three minutes.

2. At the point when you would ordinarily send out light and prayer to another, consider instead these questions one at a time and make notes of any words or ideas that come to you:

   a. Who are your personal heroes or models — living or dead, personal acquaintances or historical figures? What do you admire about them? (For example, Eleanor Roosevelt for her continual struggle for human rights and for her restraint regarding her own personal desires and ambitions; and Edgar Cayce for his dedication to service for others without regard for personal reward and recognition.)
   b. If someone wrote a news story about you, what personal qualities would you be most pleased to have mentioned? What accomplishments would you like to see listed? On what occasions are these qualities most likely to be exhibited? Why are these qualities or accomplishments so satisfying to you?
   c. Think of moments in your life when you have felt deeply inspired or emotionally uplifted by something you experienced — times when you have felt "one with the flow" or have experienced pure joy or a feeling of being engulfed in love beyond words (without the assistance of drugs or alcohol, of course). Can you recall what was happening at the time that may have triggered such experiences?

3. Now review whatever information you have written from questions 2a through 2c above. Do you see any *pattern* of motivation and guidance that plays a significant role in your life, a *thread* that appears in several of your responses, a *theme* that may be trying to guide you toward your own personal best? From this kind of introspective activity, look for indicators of your lifetime spiritual ideal.

   When you select words or phrases to represent your ideal, choose those that will help you relate it to many areas of your life, rather than those with narrow relevance. Now write down a word or phrase for your ideal. Add today's

date. You will have opportunities to review and refine it
later.

If you have had prior experience with ideals or if you had an intuitive
flash as you were reading earlier, you may have had an idea of your
spiritual ideal before you began to meditate. Did your meditation
confirm it? Did it give you something else to consider? Use additional
meditations to clarify your ideal. If two different ideas emerged, one
may be a working level ideal and the other a lifetime ideal.

If you do not hook up with your lifetime spiritual ideal in this exercise,
either continue with love as your focus or choose from other examples
(such as service, peace, patience, justice, the Christ pattern), or select a
working level ideal (such as unconditional love, fairness and honesty,
loving service to others, peaceful relationships, etc.). You may prefer
to create one that feels especially meaningful to you, and use it as your
temporary spiritual ideal. When you start to work with it in the
meditations and exercises that follow, you will come to realize whether
it is yours or not. Repeat this exercise whenever you feel it might be
helpful. Also watch for signs in your life suggesting your ideal — for
example, repeated opportunities to serve may suggest service as the
ideal; frequent periods of frustration and impatience may suggest
patience as the ideal; encounters with injustice and dishonesty may
suggest justice as the ideal. You may be drawn to experiences that give
you an opportunity to apply your lifetime ideal, even if you have not yet
identified it.

Mental and Physical Ideals

As you would expect from our threefold nature, our spiritual ideals have
counterparts in the mental and physical dimensions of our lives. Mental and
physical ideals help guide you in day-to-day experiences to act in accordance with your spiritual ideal. In essence, they are the stepping stones in
your mental and physical actions that allow you to reach toward your
spiritual ideal.

Mental ideals are expressions of your spiritual ideal in your mental
activities — your thoughts, attitudes, emotions, ideas, and plans. For
example, if your spiritual ideal is "peace," your mental ideals will also relate

to peace, but they will be guidelines for specific mental activities (e.g., catching your attitudes of anger and impatience before they erupt into non-peaceful words or actions; looking for peaceful qualities in others you meet).

Physical ideals are expressions of your spiritual ideal in your words and actions. Continuing with the above example, your physical ideals will also relate to peace, and they will be guidelines for your spoken words and physical actions (e.g., not participating in arguments; expressing appreciation to others for their peaceful activities, such as resolving an argument amicably).

We will consider a detailed illustration of the relationships among these three types of ideals and how they are used as guidelines and yardsticks in our lives. To make the example easier to follow, let's look at a method for recording and displaying our ideals.

One way of expressing all three dimensions of our ideals is in a three-column format suggested by Edgar Cayce himself: the spiritual ideal in the left column, the mental ideals in the center column, and the physical ideals at the right. Another approach that helps you keep the spiritual ideal at the center (literally) uses three concentric circles, like a target with a bull's-eye. The spiritual ideal is written in the bull's-eye; the mental ideals are written in the ring immediately outside the bull's-eye; and the physical ideals are written in the outer ring, as illustrated in Figure 1.

A useful way of keying this approach to your daily life and areas of current challenge is also illustrated in Figure 1. The target is divided into two or more segments, like slices of a pie. Each slice is labeled with an area of challenge, such as "home," "job," "customers," "my husband," "Margaret," "the church project," or "myself." Then mental and physical ideals relating to that challenge are written in the slice labeled for it. If necessary, two or more bull's-eye targets can be set up to accommodate more than about four segments per target.

Let's use Figure 1 as an illustration of the three types of ideals and how they may be derived:

> In setting up my (imaginary) ideals chart, I decided to give special focus to four areas of my life: my relationship to my wife Kathryn, my relationship to Cameron at the office, my household responsibilities (that are a matter of concern by my family), and my new responsibilities as a member of the board of directors for a community agency having both financial and personnel problems. My lifetime spiritual ideal is justice, and I have been working with it as fairness

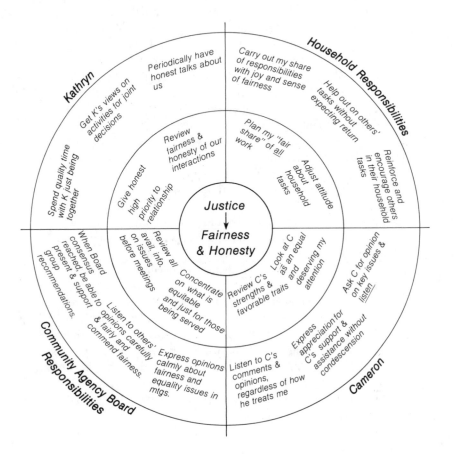

Figure 1. Example of Ideals Chart

CREATIVE MEDITATION: Inner Peace Is Practically Yours

and honesty. I have labeled the four quadrants of the bull's-eye according to my four special concerns, and I have entered my spiritual ideal — both lifetime ideal and working level ideal — in the center.

Regarding Kathryn: My spiritual ideal triggers two ideals to guide my mental actions. One set of thoughts goes like this: Am I being fair and honest in my communications and interactions with Kathryn? Do I tell her how I really feel? Am I giving her a fair chance to express herself to me and do I appreciate honesty when she does? Do our physical contacts — like touching, hugs, and kisses — arise from genuine feelings or are they for show? The mental ideal from that thinking is expressed: "Review fairness and honesty of our interactions." Another series of thoughts: Having made a lifetime commitment to this relationship, am I giving it high enough priority in my life? Is it fair to give it low priority in time and consideration? Am I being honest about its priority? The mental ideal from this: "Give honest high priority to relationship." I could go on to other considerations, but I'll concentrate for now on these two mental ideals regarding Kathryn.

It's fine to have mental ideals to guide my thinking about Kathryn, but how will they affect my actions toward her? I must take another step — to physical ideals. How will the ideal on our interactions be carried over into physical actions (which includes words)? One thing I should do is spend more time talking with Kathryn honestly about my feelings, and I should ask her to do the same ("Periodically have honest talks about us"). Another thing I should do is ask for her honest opinions and suggestions concerning family and household matters, vacations, our social activities, and I should appreciate her honesty and learn to negotiate and compromise, not override or ignore her desires ("Get K's views on activities for joint decisions"). From the mental ideal about priority, I have derived the physical ideal of "Spend quality time with K just being together."

Then I have gone on to the other three areas highlighted on the chart — the house, the board, and Cameron — setting mental and physical ideals for each.

This kind of chart should be reviewed frequently to bring the ideals to mind, as well as to realize when the chart needs to be revised because of changes in circumstances or priorities.

From time to time, you will encounter specific situations outside of your current ideals list or chart — situations in which you find it difficult to "measure" alternatives or guide your actions with your stated spiritual ideal. Do you cop out with the excuse that "It just doesn't fit this situation"? No, you can do better than that. You operate as if you were setting up a quadrant of a bull's-eye for the situation, and you can develop some "special purpose" mental and physical ideals that *will* relate to the situation. For example, suppose "unconditional love" is your working level spiritual ideal. You come to realize that you are more loving to everyone outside your family than to your own family. To address that area of your life, you might develop some mental ideals for "looking for opportunities to express unconditional love," with physical ideals that suggest what some of those expressions might be: "express your love to daughter Pat even when you don't like some of her clothes or her friends" and "tell and show son Jack you respect his views even when you don't agree with him." You can always find ways to make your spiritual ideals more tangible and meaningful relative to a specific problem. When you can't see this relationship in your head, try to work it out on paper. Your whole life will seem more joyful and fulfilling when you follow the guidance of your spiritual ideal.

"Try Me!" Try out the bull's-eye target approach for your own ideals:

1. Draw a set of three circles as in Figure 1.
2. Write your spiritual ideal in the center circle, expressing both lifetime and working level ideals if you have identified them. Use whatever words will help relate the ideal to most areas of your life.
3. Select four areas of your life for which you will write mental and physical ideals; for example, a family relationship, a work or social relationship, your work as a whole or a specific activity at work, and a nonwork activity in which you are involved. Divide the "pie" into four slices. Label the slices at the outside edge of each.
4. Working a slice at a time, first write two or three mental ideals, then two or three physical ideals, all in support of the spiritual ideal. Make them as specific and as action-oriented as possible,

67

as in Figure 1. Consider the kind of thought process illustrated earlier on the "Kathryn" quadrant.

Even though the spiritual ideal usually remains the same (once you feel you have identified it), the mental and physical ideals vary with the progress you make and according to changes in your circumstances. Be prepared to refer to your ideals chart frequently to help you remember them, and consider refinements or revisions every few months as you are learning to work with them — at least once a year thereafter.

An analogy may illustrate how these different layers of ideals relate to one another: You are a photographer trying to record on film the beauty and wonder of a view from the top of a mountain in summer. That panorama surrounding you is like your ultimate spiritual ideal, awesome for you to appreciate but difficult to capture on film. As you peer into your viewfinder with a wide-angle lens and gradually turn around full circle, you see many possible views to photograph, each like a lifetime ideal — one aspect of the ultimate view. With any one of these partial views, you can set your focus, select a pleasing and balanced picture, and produce a stunning photograph that partly represents the whole panorama. You are drawn to concentrate on one of these views — a lifetime ideal — that includes a grove of trees beside a stream with flowery meadows beyond. Removing the wide-angle lens, you frame a view with your normal lens, including all its main features — trees, river, meadow — analogous to a working level ideal. In addition to the working level view of this area, you single out elements within it for special emphasis, using your telephoto lens. Now you can see a hawk at the top of a tree, a rock jutting from the river, the shape of individual flowers in the meadow. These are a little like mental and physical ideals at the working level — singling out specific aspects of the view in order to better relate to them, yet still retaining the quality of their context in the larger view. This analogy is not perfect, but it illustrates how each level is either a more detailed or a more selective view of the whole.

Relish the process of defining and working with your ideals. Their use can remind you that you are a spiritual being — a child of God with a spiritual standard for your life.

Affirming Ideals

Virtually all meditation approaches use *some* point of focus for the mind in the early part of the stillness period. In fact, the retraining of attention through such a focus is one of the most fundamental requirements for any meditative technique. *Creative meditation* requires the use of a *spiritual* focus in the process of becoming attuned. Furthermore, attunement may be facilitated if the spiritual focus is *personalized* — for example, if it represents one's *own* spiritual ideal. Although the ideal is not the only spiritual focus you will experiment with later, it should remain your "home base" focus.

One of the most useful ways of working with your spiritual ideal is through the *affirmation* of your ideal. An affirmation is the first step in applying the law which begins "the spirit is life ..."

> In some traditions, an affirmation is a phrase or statement declaring that the stated principle or idea exists, is already accomplished, or is taking place *right now.* For example, if my spiritual ideal is peace, I might affirm simply: "As I live peace, it fills the world." Or for an ideal of loving patience, "I have the loving patience I need for today."
>
> Throughout the Cayce readings are many affirmations on a wide range of ideals and other qualities. Some take the form of requests, petitions, or supplications: "Not my will, but Thine, O Lord, be done in and through me." And "Let virtue and understanding be in me." And "Make me more aware of 'God is love.' "

Either or both kinds of affirmations — accomplished facts and petitions — are appropriate in meditation and can be used according to your preference and to the situation being affirmed.

One of Cayce's instructional readings on the meditation process for the prayer healing group says that, if the affirmation takes the form of the meditator's own ideal, then the meditator may "enter *through it* into the very presence of that which is the creative force from within itself..." (281-13). The ideal-as-affirmation becomes an open door — a channel — through which the meditator may more readily reach attunement with the Creative Forces which are God. I encourage you to use the ideal-as-affirmation frequently in your meditations.

The ideal-as-affirmation may be contained in the single word or short phrase by which you identify your ideal, unelaborated by other words. When we go a step further, the ideal-as-affirmation need not even use words, especially if we are trying to quiet the verbal, logical, left-brained part of our consciousness. We may use a picture or image, or we may simply work with an emotional feeling representing the essence of the ideal. (In the simple meditation you have been practicing, for example, after concentrating on the word "love," you dropped the word and went with the feeling the word generated.) Consider an ideal of patience, for example. Can you find within yourself a feeling "image" or a picture that would represent the ultimate feeling of loving patience?

The ideal-as-affirmation is by no means the only — or even the primary — use of the ideal, but it is our principal application of the ideal in this book. As you may have already experienced, there is sometimes a tendency to focus on other matters in the early stages of meditation — thoughts we cannot lay aside, desires for certain meditation experiences, body signals. Focusing on the ideal — as an affirmative statement, as a meaningful word or phrase, as a feeling — not only seems to "grease the skids" for attunement, but also helps the meditator stay focused and screen out distractions, further facilitating attunement. Reiterating the theme of this chapter: The ideal keeps you directed in meditation toward what *really* counts in your life.

The Cayce readings include many special purpose affirmations, some given for individuals with specific needs, others given for groups for general use in spiritual attunement. Many of those affirmations — often several sentences long — include phrases useful for individual ideal-as-affirmations. For example, the readings given on the small group approach to spiritual development — the study group readings (the series numbered 262) — include a lesson on patience with the following inspirational affirmation, adapted from the first two verses of the letter to the Hebrews:

How gracious is Thy presence in the earth, O Lord. Be
Thou the guide, that we with patience may run the race
which is set before us, looking to Thee, the Author, the
Giver of Light. (262-24)

An individual with the ideal of patience might *adapt* part of this affirmation for personal use; e.g., "I have the patience to run the race set before me. Lord, be my guide." To give renewed meaning to our ideals from time to time, we can review some of the affirmations from the Cayce readings to adapt ideas from them for our own affirmations. Examples of such adaptations for several possible ideals are presented in the back of this book.

"Try Me!" You will use an affirmation for many meditations. Write at least one affirmative statement representing your spiritual ideal. Choose words that have these qualities: (1) they are comfortable to you

70

(you may want to skip the Thee's and Thou's, for example); (2) they are easy to say aloud or silently and may even be rhythmic in their arrangement ("I live my life with patience" has a simple beat, for example); and (3) you are likely to remember the words.

You may find it helpful to develop several affirmations and write them on cards for ease of reference during meditation or for carrying in your purse or wallet.

As the second part of this exercise, begin to use your spiritual ideal or your ideal-as-affirmation in your meditation practice, in place of the word "love." In those meditations, you may get feelings of confirmation about your ideal, or words may come to you that suggest a rewording of your ideal or even a different ideal. Keep yourself open to possible guidance on adjusting your ideal, but don't be hasty about switching to a different ideal. Remember the earlier exercise of finding signs of your ideal working in your life? If you feel moved to change your ideal, check it against the kind of questioning and exploration you did earlier.

The first and most essential key to *creative meditation* is now within your reach in the forms of your spiritual ideal and your ideal-as-affirmation — your opportunities to recognize and affirm what counts in your life. It's time now to explore the stillness — the most challenging and yet the most "simple" experience of meditation.

Chapter 5

Exploring Stillness

"Do you realize how much a good meditator has in common with
a bad stand-up comedian?"
   "No, but I'm sure you're going to tell me."
   "They both spend a lot of time experiencing the silence."

The heart of the meditative process is simple to describe: Being com-
pletely still in body and mind, while attuning our consciousness to God.
Reaching and holding the stillness, however, is *not* simple to experience.
Our bodies and especially our minds object to stillness.

You've had some experience with meditation by now, focusing on a
spiritual thought and then releasing it while you held only to the feeling the
thought aroused. Were you able to still your mind of wandering thoughts and
images? Could you keep your attention focused on the word "love" or on
your ideal-as-affirmation? When you released the words, did you experience a stillness, a deep inner quiet with no distractions? If your honest
answer was "No" to any of those questions, your experience is not unusual
among beginning meditators. Even experienced meditators do not find it
easy to achieve and hold stillness.

We will first explore the phenomenon of stillness in meditation so you
have an idea of what you may experience. Then we'll examine ways of preparing for stillness and staying in the stillness.

The "Stillness"

Throughout this book, references to "the stillness" always mean the state of consciousness you experience from the time you begin your spiritual focus, until the time you begin to emerge from meditation. Actually, you may experience more than one state of consciousness during this period.

Your body is relaxed and your mind is relatively free of thoughts and other distractions. You concentrate on your spiritual focus and the feelings that correspond to it. This is the first stage of stillness, often referred to as *concentration* — one-pointedness of thought. During this stage, the mind itself "relaxes" and is emptied of thoughts, concerns, and ideas about everything other than the spiritual focus. The spiritual nature of the focus helps direct the mind and spirit of the meditator toward God, especially if the focus is the spiritual ideal.

When the spiritual focus has served its purpose as a path to God, it is set aside and the second stage of stillness begins — *mindfulness*. As the meditator's awareness becomes more internal, a shift in consciousness may be perceived. The mind remains alert, undistracted by body, thought, or surroundings, not focused on any idea, word, or image, although the *feeling* of the affirmation may continue. This state is often referred to as a "deeper" stage of meditation, suggesting that the meditator is more deeply turned inward, more removed from the "surface" of immediate surroundings. In this stage of mindfulness, we commune with God without words or images, but through feelings and pure spirit. The message of our communication may be that of joy, wonder, thankfulness, trust, and love. This is the state of attunement.

Concentration and Mindfulness

In brief, stillness in *creative meditation* has two stages, the second a deeper meditative state than the first:

Stage 1: Concentration
The mind focuses on the spiritual ideal or concept to the exclusion of everything else. The focus acts as a path to the presence of God.

Stage 2: Mindfulness
After release of the focus, the mind remains alert, undistracted by body, mind, or surroundings, but not focused on any object, word, or idea.

74

Strong spiritual feelings may be experienced, such as joy and love. In this stage we experience attunement with God.

From his study of meditational techniques, Daniel Goleman differentiates between these two states in the following way:

> In concentration, the meditator's attentional strategy is to fix the focus on a single precept, constantly bringing the wandering mind back to this object. . . (From *The Meditative Mind*, p. 105)

> The essence of concentration is nondistractedness; purification is the systematic pruning away of sources of distraction. Now the meditator's work is to attain unification of mind, one-pointedness. (p. 7)

> In mindfulness, control of the senses comes through cultivating the habit of simply noticing sensory perceptions, not allowing them to stimulate the mind into thought chains of reaction. Mindfulness is the attitude of paying sensory stimuli only the barest attention. (p. 4)

In my own meditation experience, moving from concentration to mindfulness has prompted an analogy: Have you been in a large recreational swimming pool that has a deep diving area at one end and a shallow area at the other end? To me, walking from the shallow end toward the deep end of such a pool is analogous to the two stages of meditation, concentration and mindfulness. As you begin to walk away from the shallow end, you feel the bottom securely beneath your feet (like the spiritual focus in concentration). As you continue to walk, the water gets slightly deeper, but your feet still touch the bottom. Then you pass a point where the bottom begins to slope more steeply downward, and soon your feet can no longer touch the bottom (releasing the focus). You must now float or swim in the deep water (being in mindfulness).

To me, crossing through that area where the slope becomes greater is like moving myself from concentration to mindfulness. It's not a sudden change, but there comes a point — subtle as it may be — where there is a choice between proceeding into the deeper water or remaining in the shallow end. Of course, if you feel you can't or don't want to float or swim, you must stay where your feet still touch the bottom.

Meister Eckhart defines the boundary to deep meditation and the presence of God in terms of our ability to empty ourselves:

> There, where clinging to things ends, is where God begins to be. If a cask is to contain wine, you must first pour out the water. The cask must be bare and empty. Therefore, if you wish to receive divine joy and God, first pour out your clinging to things. Everything that is to receive must and ought to be empty. (From Fox's *Meditations with Meister Eckhart*, p. 54)

Evelyn Underhill eloquently describes how to negotiate the shift between the two states, while we hold off any discouragement we might feel:

> [After holding your focus idea before you] Deliberately, and by an act of will, shut yourself off from your senses. Don't attend to touch or hearing: till the external world seems unreal and far away. Still holding on to your idea, turn your attention *inwards* ... and allow yourself to sink, as it were, downwards and downwards, into the profound silence and peace which is the essence of the meditative state. More you cannot do for yourself: if you get further, you will do so automatically as a consequence of the above practice ... and do not be disheartened if it seems at first a barren and profitless performance. It is quite possible to obtain spiritual nourishment without being consciously aware of it! (From a 1908 letter in Kepler's *The Evelyn Underhill Reader*, pp. 155-156)

Psychologist Wayne Dyer visualizes light as his focus:

> I visualize a pastel kind of light. Any thought is pushed away by the power of the light. As I become more and more peaceful I see a white light in the center of the field of pastel and feel I am moving closer and closer to the white. When I finally go through that light ... I feel energized and totally in control of myself and my surroundings. "Exquisite peace" is the best term I can think of for this place. (From *You'll See It When You Believe It*, pp. 44-45)

One of Cayce's readings addresses the hesitation some people experience as they approach mindfulness, the reluctance to let go of the comfortable, mentally directed state of concentration. In answering a question about the individual's feelings during meditation, Cayce says:

> More oft it is the fear of "letting go," or at others the interference from without — *from* fear. Yet ... by the surrounding of self with the Christ, the loving Son's consciousness, this will be taken away; and the *joy* of knowing ye are a channel of blessing will enter in. (412-7)

Perhaps no two meditators have exactly the same kinds of experience in the stillness, and yet some similarities are reported by many:
- the gradual movement in consciousness that leads to descriptive words like "sinking," "moving away," "going deeper inward," "detaching from surroundings," and "freeing my mind."
- the pleasant, sometimes ecstatic, often spiritual feelings that suffuse your whole being and get labeled as "profound silence," "exquisite peace," "the experience of God," and "a world filled with love."

"What If I Don't Feel Anything Special?"

Remember that these reports and descriptions of what happens in stillness are by experienced meditators. I cannot speak for others, but exhilarating and profound experiences in meditation are very rare for me. I am quite satisfied with a whole lot less than ecstasy. Goldsmith refers to a "click" that, for him, signals the presence of God within, and he reports that he spent eight months meditating five to ten times a day before he experienced the first one.

As Underhill implies above, more may be happening at the spiritual level than we are consciously aware of, so we should not be discouraged if we have no "peak experiences." In fact, this reference to feeling discouraged suggests that the quality of meditation can be measured on some scale of success or achievement. But I urge you *not* to evaluate your meditations. Instead, recognize that even the attempt to meditate, to quiet the mind and body, to carry out some of the preparatory activities is worthwhile. Even when you do not reach the deepest meditative state, you will reap some of the benefits of the quiet time and the efforts at concentration — some of the physiological and mental benefits highlighted in Chapter 3. Also remember that you are on your way to a visit with God. *She* knows you are serious about it and you are getting yourself ready. She is very patient!

Remember Cayce's encouragement, "It is the 'try' that is the more often counted as righteousness, and *not* the success or failure" (931-1). So much for discouragement and self-disparagement!

Retraining the Attention

Goleman's study of many meditative approaches leads him to conclude that the need to train attention is "the single invariant ingredient in the recipe for altering consciousness of every meditation system" (from *The Meditative Mind*, p. 107). Wouldn't you know that the skill we most need to develop — focusing the attention, one-pointedness — goes counter to much of our upbringing and cultural reinforcement? We have been brought up in a society that often requires us to attend to several things at once, to reward us for keeping several balls in the air at the same time. As a result, we seldom do one thing at a time: We listen to music while we shop or eat, we wear headsets when we run or do housework, we read the newspaper while we watch TV. Can we train ourselves to be one-pointed — to concentrate on one thing at a time? Yes, and we can do it outside of meditation periods.

Remember the earlier Goldsmith quote that compared learning to meditate with learning to play music? We wouldn't expect to play Bach or Beethoven after the first music lesson, he said. Just as we can practice scales and other useful instrumental exercises in preparing to play musical compositions, we can practice exercises for meditation at times when we are not trying to meditate. Some of them can be practiced in normal daily activities and environments.

You can approach ultimate one-pointedness through two intermediate steps: Through practicing the "nowness" of an activity and through practicing "sensory focus" in an activity. Let me illustrate both of them:

The "nowness" of present activity. Today was a beautiful early October day in Virginia Beach. Although I was eager to work on this chapter, I decided to spend time outdoors — pulling weeds in the flower beds, moving a woodpile, trimming the lawn edges, raking some early leaves — jobs that had to be done, and this was a good day to do them. You must understand that yard work is *not* my favorite way to spend a day *any* time of the year. Not long ago, I would have spent much of the time outdoors resenting the effort, losing patience, wishing I were inside at my computer, and generally feeling stressed. But I have been practicing "nowness": When I am engaged in one activity — whether chosen by me, by someone else, or by accident — I try to keep my attention on that activity, finding things to enjoy (even about restacking a woodpile), refraining from thoughts about other activities and other places. In other words, I focus my full attention mentally and emotionally on the present activity. I have committed myself to this activity, so I give it my best effort, knowing it is just the right activity for me at that moment. I invest my feeling self as well as my mental self in the activity, instead of just going through the motions. (I realize with surprise that I really enjoyed the yard work today. Such enjoyment often happens with activities performed with "nowness.")

This practice is not only helpful for meditation, but it also has the benefits of keeping you in the now, helping you to enjoy the present moment, and avoiding some sources of frustration, resentment, and stress. These practices are presented here, however, to help retrain your attention.

"Try Me!" While you are reading this book, have you had any thoughts about other activities you "should" be doing, other places you "should" be, things waiting to be done? Make a contract with yourself to this effect: "When I choose to take time to read this book, that reading is the most important activity for me at the time. I will be in the now, investing myself emotionally, relishing the nowness of this reading activity. I will have no place for thoughts and feelings about any other activity."

As another "nowness" exercise, pick one of your less-preferred activities around your home. When the time comes to perform that activity, consciously decide to use the nowness approach. Ignore any intrusive, distracting thoughts about other activities by keeping your attention joyfully — not begrudgingly — on the activity underway.

The sensory focus. Another kind of practice is a further step in training the attention. I will illustrate it from an activity earlier in my day: My wife, daughter, and I are regular lap swimmers at a YMCA several times a week. Sometimes while swimming, I get ideas related to a current writing project, or I mentally list chores that need doing, or I let my mind drift from one thought to another. This morning while swimming, I focused my attention not only on the swimming activity — the nowness approach — but more specifically on the sensations I felt while swimming: the stretch of the muscles in my arm and shoulder and along my sides when reaching forward for the water; the pressure of the water under me and against my pushing hand; the water rushing past my mouth as I open it at one side for air; the tightness of the goggles around my eye sockets; and so on. For attention training, I focus on just one of these sensory "clusters" at a time — maybe for a couple lengths of the pool feeling the water rushing past my face. Then I refocus on another cluster, like the stretches of my body. Lap swimming is a wonderful activity for this kind of sensory focus, because the sensations are plentiful and distractions are few. The water puts you into another world.

A sensory focus experience can be readily created for any restricted physical activity — working on a weight machine, stationary bicycle, or other exerciser, as examples. It also works for activities like jogging, running, and walking, but for safety's sake, you need to keep part of your attention on traffic, the ground under foot, and other unpredictables in your physical environment. You might even try it while scrubbing the floor on your hands and knees, washing windows, or folding laundry.

"Try Me!" Select a repetitive activity (indoors, as a starter) as a candidate for sensory focus. I hesitate mentioning this, but washing and drying dishes by hand lends itself quite well to such a focus. For example, notice the sensations on your hands of the warm sudsy water, the feel of "squeaky clean" on the dishes, the scent of the detergent, the shapes of cups, glasses, plates, and silverware. Keep your attention focused on a small set of sensations — sights, sounds, touch, smells, tastes (where appropriate). Relish them as if you were experiencing them for the first time. Then choose another set of sensations and repeat the process.

Exercises like leg lifts, situps, and running in place are good candidates for sensory focus experiences. In meditation itself, observing your breathing is a limited form of sensory focus.

Practicing nowness and sensory focus on a variety of activities outside of a meditation period can make a noticeable contribution to your attention focus during meditation. You may even find yourself practicing these attention skills for their own sake — for the contribution they make to your enjoyment of the focus activities themselves.

Here are four additional exercises to help train your attention. They are designed to be practiced as separate exercises. Some of them may be used as meditations in themselves.

80

Exercise 1. *Visual sensing in nature:* Find a quiet, unobserved spot to rest — in your yard or garden, in the woods, on the beach, beside a lake, in a field. When you are comfortably seated or lying down, focus your attention totally on an object or small area not far away and in front of you. Concentrate on that object or spot — draw it toward you with your eyes, absorb it, see every detail of it without labeling it or intellectualizing about it. Concentrate as if you were trying to capture the object or spot with your mind. Hold your concentration for several minutes. Then close your eyes, relax, and observe your breath for a minute or two. Repeat the exercise several times, focusing on a different object or place each time.

Exercise 2. *Body sensations in nature:* Choose a place in nature where your body will be subjected to the feel of rain, wind, or water at a beach or lake or in a stream. Sit comfortably where you can feel the movement of the wind or water on your face, your hands, or your feet. With your eyes closed, concentrate on one of those body areas feeling the water or wind on your skin. Simply feel the sensations without any other thought, without trying to describe the feeling. As in Exercise 1, concentrate for a minute or two. Relax and observe your breathing for a few minutes. Then concentrate on the feeling in another part of your body. A variation of this exercise is to choose a spot in nature where you can hear sounds of birds, insects, rustling leaves or cornstalks, or other natural sounds. Focus your attention on one type of sound at a time.

Exercise 3. *Object study:* In this exercise, select an object with a pleasant and varied surface — one good for holding and feeling with your hands. Possibilities include sturdy glass or wooden figures, cut glass dishes, small metal sculptures, wooden bowls or toys. (Once you try this exercise, you'll know what kinds of objects to use the next time.) Find a quiet place, perhaps your meditation location, where you can sit with your eyes open and focus all your visual and touch attention on the object as you hold it, turn it, caress it. Feel and visually study every part of its surface. As before, concentrate on it for several minutes and then relax and observe your breath. You may then want to repeat the exercise with a second object — one very different from the first.

Exercise 4. *Inner object study:* After doing Exercise 3 with your eyes open, set the object aside and close your eyes. Concentrate on going through the same kinds of activities with the same object, but only in your mind. Visualize holding it, turning it, feeling it. This is the most difficult exercise, since it is entirely an inner exercise. For that same reason, it is probably the most helpful for training the attention. A step

81

beyond this exercise is concentration on a spiritual concept or thought or the feeling it engenders in you, just as in meditation.

Dealing with Distractions

What has been your experience so far with distractions during the stillness in meditation? For most people, distractions will gradually diminish if you don't give them any attention. Because they are such a common phenomenon, many meditator-writers report how they deal with distractions.

One of the earliest descriptions of mental distractedness comes from the Greek philosopher Plato, who

> ... likened the mind of man to a ship on which the sailors had mutinied and locked the Captain and the Navigator below in the cabin. The sailors believe themselves to be perfectly free and steer the ship as they feel like at each moment... The task of a human being, wrote Plato, is to quell the mutiny, to release the Captain and the Navigator ... to choose a goal and to steer ... consistently and coherently toward its attainment. (From LeShan's *How to Meditate*, p. 15)

Brother Lawrence cautions us:

> If your mind sometimes wanders or withdraws from the Lord, do not be upset or disquieted. Trouble and disquiet serve more to distract the mind further from God than to recollect it. The will must bring the mind back in tranquillity. If you persevere in this manner, the Lord will have pity on you. (From *The Practice of the Presence of God*, pp. 85-86)

Dietrich Bonhoeffer seems to have been especially patient with distractions (the "text" he refers to here is any Biblical passage being used as the spiritual focus):

> Do not become confused and upset because of your distractedness ... If your thoughts keep wandering, there is no need for you to hold on to them compulsively. There is nothing wrong with letting them roam where they will; but then

82

incorporate in your prayers the place or person to which they have gone. So you will find your way back to your text, and the minutes spent in such diversions will not be lost and will no longer be any cause for worry. (From *Meditating on the Word*, pp. 34-35)

Evelyn Underhill addresses another frequent kind of distraction — the feeling of getting nowhere and even of boredom:

> A restless boredom, a dreary conviction of your own inca-pacity, will presently attack you. This, too, must be resisted at swordpoint. The first quarter of an hour thus spent in attempted meditation will be, indeed, a time of warfare; which should at least convince you how unruly, how ill-educated is your attention, how miserably ineffective your will, how far away you are from the captaincy of your own soul... Never before has ... fifteen minutes taken so long to pass. Consciousness has been lifted to a longer, slower rhythm, and is not yet adjusted to its solemn march.
>
> ... as your meditation becomes deeper it will defend you from the perpetual assaults of the outer world. You will hear the busy hum of that world as a distant exterior melody, and know yourself to be in some sort withdrawn from it. You have set a ring of silence between you and it; and behold! within the silence you are free. (From *Practical Mysticism*, pp. 51-53)

Finally, Joel Goldsmith recommends an almost passive approach to distracting thoughts:

> When we close our eyes in an attempt to meditate, we are amazed to discover a boiler factory inside of us. All sorts of thoughts flash through our minds...
>
> As often as our thought wanders in meditation, we gently come back, with no impatience, to the subject of the meditation. There will come a time, as we continue in this practice, when these extraneous thoughts will not impinge on our consciousness. We will have starved them by neglect... But if we fight them, they will be with us forever. (From *The Art of Meditation*, p. 56)

The Cayce readings on meditation frequently remind us that the physical and especially the mental conditions we take with us into meditation will seriously influence what happens during that period. For example, in one of the basic readings on meditation, he says that some individuals "have so overshadowed themselves by abuses of [their] mental attributes ... as to make scars, rather than the mark, so that only an imperfect image [of the spiritual ideal held as a focus] may be raised within themselves that may rise no higher than the arousing of the carnal desires within the individual body" (281-13). To me this says that negative or destructive thinking and attitudes outside of meditation ("abuse of mental attributes") create mental obstacles ("scars") which prevent such individuals from being able to focus on the spiritual ideal ("the mark"), and instead material world thoughts and feelings ("carnal desires") will interfere with meditation. Thus many readings stress the importance of "cleansing" the mind and body before attempting to meditate, as well as performing other preparatory steps to get the physical and mental conditions into a state favorable for meditation and less prone to distraction.

Do you feel reassured that you are not alone in dealing with distractions? Can you adapt some of their suggestions to your own practice? In your next meditation period, consider a gentle approach that includes at least these two steps:

- When a distracting thought or image draws your attention, acknowledge its presence with the idea, "Not now, thank you. Come back after meditation." Give it no more attention. Watch it drift away as you ...
- Refocus on the words or feeling of your spiritual ideal. Recapture its essence, letting it fill your whole mind. When you feel centered on it, release the words again, concentrating on the feeling.

The "Itches and Twitches" Syndrome

For many beginning meditators, sitting motionless for several minutes is a colossal challenge. You may begin to experience physical distractions: Your nose itches, the front edge of your chair is digging into your legs, your eyelid suddenly has a tic, your stomach is working on your pizza, your neck aches, your foot is going to sleep, and you have to go to the bathroom.

Physical distractions such as these may occur for any of these preventable reasons:
- Your body is not sufficiently relaxed in your present position. More

84

extended and systematic relaxation exercises may need to be done. For example, try tensing the offending muscles, momentarily holding them, and then releasing them completely.

• Your chair is not suitable for meditation. Try other chairs — straighter or less straight, softer or less soft, and so on.

• Your body is overly tired or stressed due to prior activity. Vigorous activity before meditation creates body stresses or rhythms that you may never notice except when you try to sit motionless in meditation. Plan a period of relaxation after such activity and before meditation.

• Your bodily eliminations were not attended to before meditation.

• Before meditation, you ate a meal or snacked on foods that have set digestive processes going.

These are genuine causes of physical distractions. If your body is objecting to immobility and none of these are at fault, then you probably have to react to your symptoms either by ignoring them through willpower or by giving in to them — scratching, shifting your position, rubbing the ache briefly, and so on. Experiment with willpower on some (like ignoring an itch or ache) and giving in to others (like shifting position to get circulation going in your legs).

Some of the preparatory steps described in later chapters are designed to minimize these bodily distractions.

Falling Asleep During Meditation

Meditators often feel embarrassment or dismay when they realize they fell asleep during meditation. Edgar Cayce gave a comforting response on this concern in one reading:

> **Question:** Why have I never been able to meditate? I go to sleep.
> **Answer through Mr. Cayce:** This...is the surer, safer, saner way of meditation. For, when the mind is absent from the body it is present with thy Lord, thy purposes, thy hopes. (1152-13)

I don't believe Cayce is recommending sleep instead of meditation, but he implies that, if you fall asleep when you meditate, don't get upset over it. You are, in fact, meeting with God in another mode.

Two conditions will probably reduce the likelihood of falling asleep in meditation: Getting sufficient regular sleep and sitting up rather than lying down for meditation. However, I will be the first to admit to catching a few winks while sitting in meditation fully rested.

Other Meditation Experiences in the Stillness

Through meditation, we are seeking the feelings and emotions of being at one with life and with God. Most such experiences, illustrated in Chapter 2, are at the emotional level — serenity, awe, wonder, faith, trust, and love, for example.

Along with that sense of oneness, some meditators have other physical, mental, and spiritual experiences during the stillness, *none* of which is a goal of *creative meditation*. Since experiences do occur, usually unbidden, the meditator needs to know what can occur and how to react to such experiences. As we alter our state of consciousness through meditation, we undergo several normal physiological changes. For example, we are lowering our brainwave rate from the normal waking beta frequency range to the lower frequencies of alpha or theta waves.

Another desired effect of meditation is the increased flow of energy through a series of spiritual centers associated with the endocrine glands (discussed at length in later chapters). We might well expect that some of these physiological changes would be accompanied by bodily sensations or experiences perceived by the meditator. (We will explore those later as well.) However, most of them are undetectable to meditators much of the time.

Acceptable inner experiences in the form of visualizations may result from our mental set as we go into meditation — a kind of special image we associate with the stillness. Done often enough, this visualization becomes an habitual experience in meditation. Wayne Dyer's visualization of pastel light and then a white light through which he passes is probably an example of this. Another example comes from a meditator friend of mine who frequently sees the figure or face of Jesus, to whom he often feels very close.

Some meditators have occasional disturbing, negative experiences in meditation. In 11 years of meditation, I have never had any, and I know other meditators who have never had such experiences. However, you need to know a little about them, especially how to prevent them. As you are attuning yourself to God, your vibrations may attract patterns of thought and energy which are not useful to you and which may, in fact, be distracting and even unsettling to you. These thought and energy patterns have been created by others — living and dead — through their misuse or abuse of God's energy which is normally biased toward good. To reduce the likelihood of your having such encounters, you can protect yourself with prayer that shields you from negative influences. For example, this prayer is adapted from the Cayce material:

> As I approach the throne of grace, beauty, and might, I throw around myself the protection found in the thought of the Christ.

In summary, consider three cautions about meditation experiences:

1. The meditator should not anticipate or try to achieve any specific experience in meditation other than being in the presence of God or being at one with life. Helpful visualizations may be exceptions to this.

2. If unusual experiences occur, even if they are pleasant or awe-inspiring, the meditator should not hold on to them nor give them special value or attention. They may distract from the spiritual goal of meditation — attunement with God.

3. The meditator should regularly pray for protection early in the meditation process. A Cayce-based prayer was suggested earlier; an alternative is a prayer to be surrounded with a protective golden light.

Several new ideas about the meditation process were mentioned in this chapter. Begin trying them out in your own meditation practice:

- Review the precautions listed as ways of avoiding the "itches and twitches." Observe them as you prepare for meditation.
- Before focusing on your ideal-as-affirmation, offer a prayer for protection, as worded earlier or in your own words.
- Try the gentle technique for discouraging distracting thoughts: acknowledge the thought, dismiss it, and refocus on the ideal, if necessary.
- Also observe your experience in the stillness. Do you sense any shift in your consciousness as you move from concentration to mindfulness? Don't force anything — just observe or reflect on it later.

As suggestions for your meditation practice are presented, you may feel undecided or even overwhelmed with all the possible ways of preparing for and carrying out meditation. The next short chapter sets the stage for how to handle the many suggestions. It outlines an approach to help you select options for your own meditation style. Ready to be experimental?

Chapter 6

Experimenting with Style

"It looks like you're baking up a storm. Look at all those different flours and spices, nuts and dried fruits. What're you making?"

"I'm going to create the most delicious, most nutritious bread you ever tasted. I'm experimenting with different combinations and amounts of ingredients and baking times. I've already planned 261 different recipes."

"That will take you months to try all those!"

"But think of all the good eating I'll do in the meantime."

If I were to promise to teach you the *one* most satisfying, comfortable, and effective approach to meditation, you should be suspicious. Those qualities can be determined only by you. Remember that the activities of meditation are very personal, according to Cayce; no one can tell another individual what will work for that person.

The experimental approach to *creative meditation* applies to both of these situations:

- If you are a beginning meditator or someone who is "rediscovering" meditation, then you're looking for the approach that will best meet your initial needs — the one you find most helpful in learning to become attuned, to experience being at one with life.

• If you are an experienced meditator, you may be looking for ways to enhance your present meditation process, or you may want to develop an alternative style for special situations or for variety.

Creative meditation encourages you to experiment with a variety of meditation-related activities, discovering combinations that best suit your needs, interests, and lifestyle. This experimental approach is not complex or burdensome. It simply helps you plan and try out meditation activities in a systematic way, so you won't get overwhelmed by choices and you will have time for those choices to be evaluated.

When you experiment with your meditation process, your conclusions will be based on what "works" or "feels best" for you. While meditation is likely to have effects noticeable to others around you, it's *you* who must be satisfied and comfortable with your meditation.

In the next two chapters, many different activities and variations will be presented for your consideration in preparing for and carrying out a meditation period. Some activities are necessary — like selecting a place for regular meditation. Others are optional — like playing music before meditation. Most of them, required and optional, have several alternatives — like how you hold your hands or what kind of music to use. How do you decide which activities and variations to try — and when? How do you know if they "work" for you? This chapter provides a few simple guidelines on experimentation. Apply whatever is helpful for you.

Define your baseline process. Begin by outlining the steps you are now following in your meditation process. Whether you have just begun to meditate or are experienced, list the steps you would take in your next meditation if you learned nothing new before then. We'll call that your "baseline process."

Continue with this baseline form of meditation until you feel you are ready to experiment. One overriding principle of our experimentation is *You have all the time in the world to experiment—don't try too many new things at once.* Meditation is a gentle art, not a product for market research.

Make note of interesting additions or changes. As you read about activities and variations in the upcoming chapters, consider each one a possible addition or substitution in your baseline meditation. Make a note — inside the back cover of this book, for example — of those you find most appealing, those you would like to try sometime. Write down the page number where it is discussed, so you can return to it quickly later. (A list of alternatives introduced appears near the end of each of the next two chapters.)

Create an experimental meditation process. When you feel ready to start experimenting, select one or two activities to add to or change in your baseline process, and outline the new sequence for your next meditation. You can use more than two changes, but remember the principle of not trying everything at once. You may want to put your outline of the experimental process on a card to refer to at your meditation location.

Use your experimental meditation process. Follow your experimental sequence for several meditations unless something you have changed or added seems immediately and strongly unsatisfactory for you. Many activities need to be practiced several times before they start fitting in or having a desirable effect. A breathing exercise, for example, may first seem awkward but can become a very smooth and helpful part of the process with regular practice.

Review and evaluate your experience. While you are experimenting, mentally review after meditation how you felt about the meditation as a whole and about any activities that seemed either very helpful or very distracting or difficult.

Questions you might ask yourself: Did the activities flow smoothly from one to another? Did any step or activity seem especially helpful or comfortable? Any that seemed distracting or awkward? Were my mind and body more relaxed at the start of concentration? Was my spiritual focus more consistent? Was I less distracted? Did I sense a shift to a mindfulness stage? Did I experience mindfulness? Was the meditation any "deeper" than usual?

The next time you use the same sequence of activities, try to overcome any distractions or difficulties you experienced. Continue to notice your feelings and experiences.

Earlier I expressed cautions about evaluating the quality of your meditation experiences against some expectations. Those cautions still apply. However, when you are experimenting, look for differences in your feelings of satisfaction or comfort from one meditation to the next. Compare your recent experience with your own previous experiences and with your intuitive feelings about what's "right" for you — not with someone else's experience or your preconceptions.

Create your personal style. From the alternatives which you try and will evaluate, you will eventually create a meditation process that becomes your personal style — a new baseline for you, a kind of *"personally relevant ritual."* The value of a familiar personal style is that it lets you get into meditation without stopping to recall what comes next. Yet, to realize attunement, your meditation process must remain mindful and purposeful, and not become routine in the sense of boring and mindless.

There's a parallel in the liturgy of a religious congregation: The activities of the liturgy (a "denominationally relevant ritual"?) are intended to "attune" the congregation to God. Even attending the liturgical service signifies some degree of interest in that attunement. However, if elements of the liturgy — for example, the Christian's recitation of the Lord's Prayer or the receiving of communion — are experienced mindlessly, attunement is less likely to result.

"Try Me!" If you have not yet taken the first step above — outlining your baseline process — do so at this time.

You may want to check your outline during your next regular meditation.

Experimentation is one facet of *creativity* in *creative meditation. You* decide what steps are helpful and meaningful to you as you create or enhance your own approach. And *you* always remain in control of the process you create. Don't let it control you by causing you resentment over the time it takes or making you feel guilty about skipping an activity. If you start having negative feelings about your meditation, uncover the cause and make changes accordingly. On to experimentation!

Chapter 7

Preparing for a Visit with God

"The phone rang. When I answered, this voice says, 'This is God. I've been meaning to stop by for a chat. If it's OK with you, I'll be there in an hour.' I sputtered and stuttered and finally said, 'Sure, God. I'll be here. I look forward to ... uh ... seeing You.' Then the voice was gone."

"Someone playing a trick?"

"Oh no, it was God, all right. And me without a single bush for burning!"

No Mount Sinai or burning bushes for us! As the Cayce readings frequently point out, "For thy body ... is indeed the temple of the living God. There He has promised to meet thee" (3488-1). If God is always with us — in fact within us — why should we set aside a separate time and make special preparations for communicating with God? Doesn't She know our minds and hearts before we speak them? Yes, but...

- We don't make it easy for ourselves to communicate with God — that is, to put ourselves in touch with the infinite Creative Forces available to us. We simply do not put it high in our priorities. Also, we are so used to an environment overflowing with both physical and mental distractions — inner and outer — that we are not skilled at single-pointed concentration and stillness. "Sure, I want to talk with God, but ... just a minute, there's the phone."

• Through Jesus, God has said, "Seek and you shall find; knock and it shall be opened to you," which I understand to mean the ball is in our court. We need to take the initiative. God does not hesitate to "speak" to us spontaneously from time to time, but for ongoing communication, we must take the first step — through meditation and prayer. "By the way, Father-Mother God, I've been meaning to tell you ..."

The purpose of *creative meditation* is to stay in touch with God — and thus with the Creative Forces — to check in daily as a step toward keeping your life on track and under control. Yet even before you begin the meditation process, you are already influencing what will happen in meditation.

Always Preparing

Most of your life is *not* spent meditating. What goes on in your "non-meditation" time, however, has impact on your ability to attune yourself to God at meditation time. In a very real sense, when you are not meditating, you are always preparing for your next meditation.

The topics addressed below include suggestions for ensuring that your "non-meditation" time contributes only positively to your meditation time. Consider some of these ideas in your experimentation.

Attitude adjustment. No, I'm not talking about the late afternoon "attitude adjustment hour" offered by some drinking establishments. The Cayce readings emphasize the need to enter meditation without a grudge or any feeling of ill will against another person. Here's part of a Cayce affirmation in a lesson on fellowship:

> Though I come in humbleness and have [anything] against
> my brother, my prayer, my meditation, does not rise to Thee.
> Help Thou my efforts in my approach to Thee. (262-21)

Negative attitudes and emotions get in the way of attunement. It's too late to resolve those feelings when you sit down to meditate. When you decide to become a meditator, you should also decide to put your attitudes and emotions under scrutiny and control, working to resolve issues of resentment, anger, fear, and guilt, for example.

In addition to working on existing attitudes, you can facilitate attunement and meditation by developing or accentuating certain positive qualities and attitudes. In several readings, Cayce suggested that the way to improve meditation or to interpret what is received in meditation is by demonstrating in daily life some of the "fruits of the spirit," expressed by the apostle Paul as love, joy, peace, patience, kindness, goodness, faithfulness, gentleness, and self-control (Galatians 5:22-23 RSV).

Spiritual study group. One of the most effective resources for working constructively on attitudes and emotions and for developing the fruits of the spirit is the spiritual study group. Many find this approach to self-study and personal change without equal because of its opportunities to join in spiritual studies, discussion, application, and meditation with a small group of individuals of similar interests.

One type of spiritual study group is the A.R.E.-affiliated *Search for God* Study Group. The first such group was formed by Edgar Cayce in 1931 and, over a period of 11 years, received a series of 130 readings that helped to produce two group study manuals titled *A Search for God*. From that landmark effort with one group has evolved a network of about 1500 groups around the world. My own spiritual development took giant steps forward as I participated in one of them. Other spiritual study groups use as their resource *A Course in Miracles*, for example, the writings of Joel Goldsmith, or the Bible. A regular part of many study group meetings is a period of group meditation.

Spinal adjustment. Because of the importance of the flow of energy along the spine in meditation, it is well for a meditator to keep the spine properly aligned through the combination of correct posture and bearing, appropriate body weight, exercise, and spinal adjustment. Consider adding to your regular health reviews a spinal checkup and alignment by a qualified professional practitioner of osteopathy or chiropractic.

Physical exercise. The Cayce readings point out that the energies of the body are affected by the balance between mental and physical activity. Cayce frequently recommended getting enough physical exercise, outdoors when possible, to keep unexpended physical energies from becoming "detrimental" (341-31). On the other hand, any physical activity that drains a lot of your energy is best not carried out just before meditation. If, however, a sequence of vigorous activity followed by meditation fits best with your schedule — such as having your morning run before meditation — then you will want to experiment with that sequence for yourself.

Eating. This popular non-meditation activity is mentioned here in two regards. First, in the matter of health, Cayce emphasized in his physical readings that nothing was more important than proper "assimilations" and "eliminations." We *are* what we eat — *and* what we consume mentally. And this must be followed in normal cycles by what we eliminate from our minds and bodies. Meditation is most effective in a healthy body and mind, and the Cayce readings have much information to share about the dietary contributions to health.

The second reason for mentioning eating here is a caution: Eating just before meditating may result in distracting sensations as you try to sit quietly while your food is digesting. Also, digestion uses body energy, which may decrease the energy flow during meditation, thus tending to be sleep-inducing (haven't you ever been drowsy after a meal?). On the other hand, if your stomach is craving food and telling you so, you may want to drink water or eat something light to keep it from raising objections during meditation. If your most convenient meditation period is after a meal, experiment to check out for yourself the effects of eating.

Getting Ready to Meditate

The first stage of the meditation process is *preparation for attunement*. When you feel that God is "family," you will meet and talk with God as informally as you please — and that's one of the long-range objectives of your work with *creative meditation*. Meanwhile, if you are just beginning to communicate regularly with God, the occasions are special and they call for special preparations. One Cayce reading says, "The preparations for [meditation], to some individuals, are just as necessary as the meditation itself" (1158-25).

Daniel Goleman points out in *The Meditative Mind* that approaches to meditation throughout the world vary most widely in the preparatory steps and in the setting for meditation. The range of different approaches gives us plenty to experiment with in developing our own style of meditation practice.

Length, time of day, and regularity of meditation. Your current baseline meditation process probably takes between 15 and 30 minutes. As you begin to experiment with additional activities, you may add to your total time. You may also choose to spend more time on certain activities without adding new ones, also increasing total time.

Cayce's general recommendation on "the best time period" for meditation was "Early in the mornings and as the day goes to rest" (256-4). He occasionally suggested meditating at 2 a.m. because the physical body (if it has slept) is in a vibratory pattern "where it is between the physical, the mental, and spiritual..." (1861-19).

Cayce emphasized the need for regularity of meditation — at the same time and in the same place every day — yet urged an openness to meditate "Whenever there is the call, as it were, to prayer, to service, to aid another" (275-39).

Consistent with Cayce's basic suggestion, many new meditators find it most convenient to their daily schedule to meditate either every morning, soon after waking up, or every night, just before going to sleep. Early morning seems best for me because my mind has not yet shifted into high gear and, once I wash the sleep out of my eyes, I am less likely to fall asleep than at bedtime. For some unfathomable reason, I have not found it convenient to adopt Cayce's recommended 2 a.m. time, although I have occasionally wakened around that time and meditated (on my way back to sleep). Consider experimenting with 2 a.m. — or some other middle-of-the-night time.

Location and position. As you realize, for meditating you need a quiet location with minimum distractions for a period of minutes. Meditating in the same place every day has benefits you may not have considered. Aryeh Kaplan says:

> You will come to associate that place with the serene mood developed during meditation, and after a few days, the calmness comes automatically as soon as you sit down in your meditation place. This tends to reinforce the process and make it easier to advance. (From *Jewish Meditation*, p. 60)

After repeated meditations in the same location, I believe the vibrations of the area and of the furnishings in it begin to increase, resulting in what is often referred to as "good vibes." Habit, associations with past states of calmness, and the vibrations of the area combine to make it progressively easier to become attuned in that spot.

Because you will usually remain in one body position for meditation, you will want to select a comfortable position that keeps your spine straight and your head aligned with it, while also allowing you to relax, probably with eyes closed, yet fully awake and alert. The Cayce readings do not emphasize physical position, except for suggestions such as, "Sit or lie in an easy position, without binding garments about the body" (281-13). Answering questions about position, Cayce said that individuals must find the position best for them and, in fact, "at times the pose or posture would be different" and "Do not let it become as a rote only, nor as form only ..." (903-24).

Joel Goldsmith describes probably the most generally used meditation position for the Westerner, contrasting it with the traditional Eastern position:

> Meditation is most easily practiced when we are not conscious of the body. If we sit in a straight chair, with feet placed squarely on the floor, the back straight as it normally should be, the chin in, and both hands resting in the lap, the body should not intrude itself into our thoughts.
>
> ... In the Orient, few people sit on chairs; therefore, it is natural for them to meditate sitting on the floor with their legs crossed. In that position, they are comfortable; but we, of the Occident, would find such posture not only difficult to achieve, but, for most of us, very uncomfortable to maintain. (From *The Art of Meditation*, pp. 50-51)

As to meditating while lying down, my body seems to associate the prone position with sleep rather than with meditation. However, many people find the prone position, even on the floor, quite satisfactory. Experiment with body positions in your own meditation practice — even with different chairs, if you choose to sit up.

New meditators often wonder about the position of their hands during meditation. In her book, *Healing Through Meditation and Prayer*, written from a Cayce perspective, Meredith Ann Puryear says:

> If a sitting position is adopted, the feet are to be flat on the floor, as a general rule; however, on occasion the ankles may be crossed as a way of shutting out negative outside influences. The suggestion for crossing the ankles and closing one's hands is recommended in a great deal of the literature on meditation. To "close the hands," join the thumb and index finger, put the hands palms-down on the thighs, or fold them across the abdomen with the thumbs touching. This closes the channels through which energy may flow out of the body; and since we desire to be *filled* with the spirit while meditating, containing the energy is highly desirable ... If the meditator is lying down, the hands should *always* be crossed over the solar plexus. (p. 7)

98

The latter suggestion is from a Cayce reading explaining to one person how to prevent "the terrifying sensation [that] results from lying on back and placing hands under head" in meditation (440-8).

Perhaps the most critical requirement in body position is the straight spine. Before presenting the physiological reasons for this, let me introduce you to a man with abilities similar to those of Edgar Cayce:

> **Zooming In for a Closeup**: Even at an early age, Ray Stanford exhibited unusual psychic abilities. Then in 1960 at age 22, he discovered he was able to use meditation as a method for reaching a state of consciousness in which he could provide helpful information on a variety of topics, including information unknown to him in the conscious state. Individuals and groups called upon Stanford for readings; some Stanford readings were initiated as requests for clarification of information in the Cayce readings. Stanford's readings on the seven "spiritual centers" of the body are among the most informative and practical of his readings.
>
> The Stanford readings began with a period of prayer and meditation in which everyone present participated. After meditation, Stanford reclined on his back and, within a few minutes, experienced an unconscious, meditation-induced state he called "the state of the readings." A voice identified itself as "the source of the readings" and asked what information was being sought. Occasionally, a "Brother" spoke before or after the source, or in place of the source. The Brothers, each with distinctive personalities and voices, identified themselves as brothers and servants of the Most High.
>
> Stanford no longer gives readings, but the edited transcripts of many of them have been made available to the public by the Association for the Understanding of Man with which he is affiliated.

In one of his readings collected in a book titled, *Speak, Shining Stranger*, Ray Stanford discusses the spine position in meditation along with the seven spiritual centers in the body. He emphasizes:

> ... good posture, sitting proper and erect, and having the spine in alignment. The spine should be positioned in such a way that it follows the more natural curve as found when standing or sitting properly; in that way, there becomes an alignment in the proper relationship of all seven centers so that the forces may flow properly, both physically through

the spine and also through those that are of a subtle nature.
(p. 21)

Cleansing. The Cayce readings are emphatic about preparing yourself physically and mentally for meditation through "purifying" and "cleansing" activities of your own choice:

Find that which is to *yourself* the more certain way to your consciousness of *purifying* body and mind, before ye attempt to enter into the meditation ... (281-13)

Cayce includes as alternatives for "cleansing": washing the body with pure water, using special breathing exercises, chanting, sounding bells or certain other instruments, avoiding food just before meditation, and preventing the mind from dwelling on

... those thoughts and activities that would hinder that which is to be raised from *finding* its full measure of expression ...

First, *cleanse* the room; cleanse the body; cleanse the surroundings, in thought, in act! Approach not ... the inner self, with a grudge or an unkind thought held against *any* man [or woman]! ... (281-13)

Notice the continual emphasis on "attitude adjustment." Listening to quiet music or reading inspirational material may be helpful for "cleansing" or at least redirecting the mind just before beginning other preparations for meditation.

My first-thing-in-the-morning meditation is enhanced if I first rinse my face and eyes with water, which has the practical value of waking me up and clearing my eyes for any reading I may do in my preparations or follow-up. And I feel even more self-respecting and sociable when I have brushed my teeth!

Relaxing the body. During meditation, you want no signals from your body that it is uncomfortable or tense. You may mentally survey your body as you prepare to meditate to see if a preliminary relaxation routine is desirable. If it's early in the morning, you may be so relaxed that your concern is more about keeping yourself alert and awake.

An effective way to relax the body and at the same time quiet the mind is through progressive relaxation. For example, starting with your left foot, concentrate on relaxing the toes one by one; then concentrate on the whole foot, then the ankle, and on up the left leg, one section at a time. Then do the same with the right foot and leg, the torso, the hands and arms, the neck, and the head, taking as much time as you like to feel relaxation in every part of your body. As you work through the entire body, visualize each body part relaxing.

You can vary your approach by briefly tensing muscles first and then releasing them, feeling the contrast between tension and relaxation. You can also be selective in your relaxation, concentrating only on those body areas where a mental survey of your body found tension.

Many people discover that muscles of the shoulders, the upper back, and the neck are often tight and even painful — places where we collect and shelter our tensions as if we didn't want to lose them. Since those same areas are closely associated with the spine, the circulatory system, and the energy flow among the spiritual centers, you may want to regularly spend a few minutes relaxing the neck, shoulders, and upper back.

One of the most effective ways of relieving tension in this area is by using the head-and-neck exercise that Cayce recommended in many of his readings — not specifically for meditation, but for many physical ailments and for increasing the circulation between the body and the head:

> Sitting erect bend the head forward three times at least, then back as far as it may be bent three times; to the right three times; then to the left side three times. Then circle the head and neck to the right three times, then to the left three times. (5404-1)

This exercise is a helpful way to relieve neck and shoulder tension at any time — for example, after sitting in one position for a long time. According to Cayce, if you drink water just before doing the head-and-neck exercise, you may experience a recharging of the battery force of the body (1554-4).

Prayers. We have defined meditation as a form of extended prayer. In general parlance, however, prayers are statements to God with words of praise, thanksgiving, concern, and desires. Prayers are as brief as "Thanks, God!" and as long as Psalm 119 with 176 verses.

Prayers may best be expressed at two times during the meditation process: During the preparatory steps to aid in attunement, and after attunement for guidance and healing, for example. Expressions of faith, praise, and thanksgiving are appropriate at both times.

Cayce frequently recommended a prayer statement of trust relating to the will, such as "Thy will be done" in the Lord's Prayer or in this statement from an affirmation:

> Not my will but Thine, O Lord, be done in and through me.
> (262-3)

I find just the phrase "Not my will but Thine" a helpful "mini-prayer" on many occasions.

I'm a firm believer in informal, conversational prayer, so Charles Merrill Smith is a good model for me. In a chapter called "I Don't Know How to Pray," Smith expresses his confusions to God — "Great Listener, Sir" — on the style and subject of prayers, concluding with:

> So, until I hear from You on the subject, I'll just go on sending up prayers of thanksgiving for the privilege of being alive in Your good creation, paeans of joy for the gifts of sight and hearing and feeling, appreciation for sunshine and food and friendship and sex, and praise for Jesus Christ who helps me make sense out of life.
>
> I hope You will consider this adequate. (From *How to Talk to God When You Aren't Feeling Religious*, pp. 39-40)

To aid in attunement, here are three suggestions for prayer with which to experiment:

- Expressions of praise, thanksgiving, and faith. For example, "Father-Mother God, I am thankful for the many blessings and opportunities I have received from You. I know You are always available for me with Your love."
- The Lord's Prayer, which has specific value as an aid in attuning the spiritual centers.
- Prayer for protection in meditation, such as the one suggested earlier.

The spiritual focus. As emphasized earlier, an essential skill for *creative meditation* is the ability to focus your attention on a spiritual idea, concept, or image during the stage of concentration. That focus is often a form of the meditator's spiritual ideal.

In *The Cloud of Unknowing,* the anonymous monk expresses the notion of "locking on" to such a spiritual focus:

If you want to gather all your desire [for God] into one simple word that the mind can easily retain, choose a short word rather than a long one. A one-syllable word such as "God" or "love" is best. But choose one that is meaningful to you. Then fix it in your mind so that it will remain there come what may. This word will be your defense in conflict and in peace. Use it to beat upon the cloud of darkness above you and to subdue all distractions, consigning them to the *cloud of forgetting* beneath you ... If your mind begins to intellectualize over the meaning and connotations of this little word, remind yourself that its value lies in its simplicity. (p. 56)

Evelyn Underhill dramatizes the need to hold to the meditation focus:

But, the choice [of meditation focus having been] made, it must be held and defended during the time of meditation against all invasions from without, however insidious their encroachments, however "spiritual" their disguise. It must be brooded upon, gazed at, seized again and again, as distractions seem to snatch it from your grasp. (From *Practical Mysticism*, p. 51)

You have a choice among the forms your spiritual ideal can take as your spiritual focus: the word or words expressing your ideal, an affirmation created from your ideal, or the feelings or images that represent the essence of your ideal. Experiment with all of these.

Choices, Choices, Choices!

As you were reading, you may have marked or otherwise noted several preparatory activities that appealed to you for experimentation. To give you another chance to add to your list, here is an inventory of choices to consider, grouped according to whether the whole activity is an option or it is necessary but has variations from which to choose:

Necessary activities with multiple alternatives
• Choosing a quiet location with a comfortable place to sit or lie.
• Setting the time of day and length of a regular meditation period.
• Releasing non-meditation thoughts and emotions, especially about

specific people, events, activities.
• Preventing negative attitudes from carrying over into meditation.
• "Closing your hands" comfortably; over abdomen, if reclining.
• Choosing the form your ideal will take as a spiritual focus.
• Holding your ideal as a focus.

Optional activities
• Participating in regular moderate physical exercise, preferably outdoors.
• Having a spinal adjustment by a skilled practitioner.
• Developing qualities represented by the "fruits of the spirit."
• Participating in a spiritual study group.
• Refraining from eating and vigorous physical activity just before meditating.
• Washing or rinsing hands and face, other physical cleansing.
• Reading inspirational material.
• Listening to quiet, uplifting music.
• Using the head-and-neck exercise and/or relaxation techniques that will relax your body from toe to head.
• Offering prayers as aids to attunement, especially a prayer for protection and the Lord's Prayer.

"Try Me!" Start experimenting with your meditation style, selecting from the alternatives presented. Hold off the temptation to try many new activities or variations at once, and also avoid the other temptation to cast aside options that don't satisfy you the first time you try them.

Whenever you wish, proceed to the next chapter and another array of activities and options, continuing to make notes of choices that appeal to you for future experimentation. Writing them on the inside back cover or highlighting them in your book will help prevent you from forgetting what you would like to try.

Your may instead decide to set the book aside until you have experimented with activities and variations presented in this chapter. This postponement is desirable if you are getting confused about the many options available to you.

When you feel ready to explore the "vibrations and rhythms" in your body and around you, please come along with me!

Chapter 8

Sensing the Rhythms and Vibrations of Life

"When I walked into that room, I felt such good vibes, I knew I was going to make some new friends."

"The last time *I* had good vibes was in a motel where I dropped a quarter in a slot and the mattress began to jiggle."

Have you ever been in a situation where you felt "good vibes" from the people in a room or from your surroundings — excluding mattress vibrators? Have you ever read a story or heard an idea expressed that "resonated" with you? Granted, some individuals use terms like these because they are fashionable, an "in" way to express positive feelings among "like-minded" people. Are these just figures of speech, or do they have some basis in fact?

George Leonard, for many years a senior editor of *Look* magazine, wrote a book with the intriguing title *The Silent Pulse: A Search for the Perfect Rhythm That Exists in Each of Us*. In it, he discusses an extraordinary phenomenon discovered by the Dutch scientist Christian Huygens in 1665 — "entrainment." As Leonard reports:

> This phenomenon, as it turns out, is universal. Whenever two or more oscillators in the same field are pulsing at *nearly*

the same time, they tend to "lock in" so that they are pulsing at *exactly* the same time. The reason, simply stated, is that nature seeks the most efficient energy state, and it takes less energy to pulse in cooperation than in opposition. (From *The Silent Pulse*, pp. 13-14)

Is there a parallel among us human "oscillators"? The first step toward such a parallel is to accept the fact that everything in the world is composed of the same God/Energy as everything else — each thing vibrating in its own complex energy pattern. One Cayce reading says:

... each home, each hall, each edifice, has [its vibratory pattern] — and there is felt the vibration of such a place. Some are in harmony, some are at disharmony. (2881-3)

It's not difficult to take another step and accept the idea that we can become sensitized to similarities and differences in the vibrational patterns in ourselves and others. One more step and we can hypothesize that, when we encounter vibrational patterns *nearly* synchronized or harmonious with our own, we may feel "good vibes." Then, through nature's principle of entrainment, we may lock in and resonate at *exactly* the same rate. A significant principle is: *It takes less energy to pulse in cooperation than in opposition.*

Meditation is a means for us to become more sensitive to our inner vibrations and rhythms. It may also be a means to facilitate entrainment, to tune our vibrations so that we are more "in sync" with our world and with the people around us. A Cayce reading states that "Every dis-ease or disease" creates in us an "opposite or non-coordinant vibration" (1861-12), so that we are no longer even in sync within ourselves. Then we must reestablish the body's correct vibration in our consciousness, and meditation can help us do that. Cayce cautions us, however, about meditating when debilitated by illness — when "A weakened condition of the body may be so overstimulated by concentration in meditation as to *overtax* the general physical system and become detrimental" (307-10).

George Leonard states the flip side of the disease principle:

Just as our internal rhythms are locked on "hold" with one another, they are also entrained with the outside world. Our physical and mental states change in rhythm with the seasonal swing of the earth and the sun, with the tides, with the day-night cycle, and perhaps even with cosmic rhythms that present-day science hasn't yet isolated and defined. When these rhythms are forced out of phase, disease is likely and dis-ease is inevitable. (From *The Silent Pulse*, p. 15)

We can promote control of our own bodies if we enhance our understanding of the vibrations and rhythms of our bodies and of how meditation both affects them and is affected by them.

"I Got Rhythm" — and Vibrations, Too

In *The Silent Pulse*, George Leonard refers to our pattern of vibrations by saying that each of us has at our center "a silent pulse of perfect rhythm, a complex of wave forms and resonances, which is absolutely individual and unique" (p. xii). In *The Healing Forces of Music*, musician and teacher Randall McClellan describes how our vibratory patterns originate at the cell level and combine to produce related patterns in each of the organs and body parts, reminding us that "We are a resonating system in process rather than a stable solid mass" (p. 44).

We seldom think about our bodily rhythms unless we experience a change in one of them:
• the breathing rate;
• the heart and pulse rate;
• the daily cycle of sleeping and being awake;
• the daily rhythms for food, water, and eliminations;
• the weekly cycles of habitual activities such as work and play;
• the monthly cycle of menstruation;
• the personal rhythms we experience for exercise, for sexual release, and for time alone/time with others;
• the "seven-year itch" cycles of change; the seven-year period in which Cayce says all the atoms of the body are renewed (3684-1); and other long cycles associated with human development, such as those identified by psychoanalyst Erik Erikson in his longitudinal studies.

Generally unperceived are the rhythms and resonances of internal systems we may not even know about:
• ordinary brain waves, which vary according to the level of consciousness and mental activity; for example, the stage of concentration in

meditation is probably in the "alpha" range of 8 to 14 cycles per second as measured by an electroencephalogram, and mindfulness is probably in the "theta" range of 4 to 8 cycles per second;

- the "superficial" vibratory patterns in the body initiated by the body's own functions; the ejection of blood from the heart to the aorta causes a skeletal oscillation of 7 cycles per second; this, in turn, sets up a series of wave patterns in the ventricles and the cerebral cortex, and pulsating magnetic fields in each hemisphere of the brain (from Randall McClellan's *The Healing Forces of Music*, p. 41);

- the complex vibrational pattern in the energy field at each of the seven "spiritual centers" (as referred to by Cayce and Stanford) or "chakras" (as referred to in Eastern traditions); each center has one or two large funnel-shaped whirlpools (vortices) of energy and from 4 to 972 small vortices of energy; each vortex produces an energy vibration that resonates at its own frequency (from Barbara Ann Brennan's *Hands of Light: A Guide to Healing Through the Human Energy Field*, pp. 41-49); the unhampered flow of energy among these spiritual centers is of great consequence in the meditative process.

As you are able to better direct your attention inwardly during meditation, you will become more aware of inner vibrations and rhythms. The obvious ones are the heartbeat and the rate of breathing; more subtle are the slight involuntary body sways that many experience and the pulsing of energy upwards through the spiritual centers.

The Cayce readings on meditation and healing suggest that, through the process of attunement to God in meditation, physical changes in the body may be brought about at the atomic level. This includes not only changes that alter the vibrational pattern in the cells, but also changes that may result in the creation of new cells (281-13, -24, -27). During an extended meditation process, might a person bring the vibrational patterns of diseased or damaged cells close to the patterns of healthy cells so that the natural principle of entrainment may take place?

You may accept the idea that each of us is a complex energy form that we call the physical body, but can you also accept the idea of a less visible, more controversial energy field around the body? McClellan describes the critical functions of this "etheric field," often called the "aura":

> The etheric field is an electro-magnetic vibrational field that shields and energizes the dense physical body and integrates it with the Earth's energy fields. It fluctuates continually in

response to vibrational waves with which it comes into contact. The etheric field is found around all living organisms, of both the plant and animal worlds, and gradually fades upon death of that organism. The etheric field can be easily perceived as a whitish hue if you gaze at or around a person. (From *The Healing Forces of Music*, p. 43)

According to physicist and healer Barbara Ann Brennan, large vortices of energy at each spiritual center/chakra extend out through this etheric field where they are accessible for diagnosis by means of a simple pendulum (see Brennan's *Hands of Light*, Chapter 10). This technique dramatically demonstrates the presence of the energy outside the physical body at the spiritual center and indicates the direction and strength of energy movement at the center.

This background information on vibration and rhythm of the body gives us a basis for considering several vibration/rhythm-related preparatory activities for use in meditation.

Breath Is Life

Lama Anagarika Govinda — a Westerner who journeyed to the East for his spiritual enlightenment — says:

... the process of breathing, if fully understood and experienced in its profound significance, could teach us more than all the philosophies of the world. By raising this process into the light of consciousness, we not only become aware of the basic functions of life, but we have a chance to get access to the formative forces of the subconscious, so that the integration of all qualities of body and mind is made possible. (From *Creative Meditation and Multi-Dimensional Consciousness*, p. 120)

Because of the remarkable, vital functions breath performs for us from moment to moment without our attention, we should reserve a place in our meditative practice not only to take advantage of the breath's perpetual rhythm, but also to experience its capability to draw energy and strength into our meditation.

Breath as exercise. In most Eastern forms of meditation, breathing exercises of several types are regularly practiced. One Cayce reading acknowledged the vital importance of the breath and the potential value of yogic breathing exercises. He stated, however, three conditions for their use: properly preparing for them, understanding what was happening during such exercises, and using wisely the outcomes resulting from their use, as in an attunement process:

> These [Yoga] exercises are excellent, yet it is necessary that special preparations be made — or that a perfect understanding be had ... as to what takes place when such exercises are used.
> For, *breath* is the basis of the living organism's activity. Thus such exercises may be beneficial or detrimental in their effect upon a body...
>
> Question: ... is further practice of the Yoga exercises of breathing and meditation recommended?
> Answer through Mr. Cayce: By all means! if and when, and *only* when, preparation has been made; and when there is the knowledge, the understanding and the wisdom as to what to do *with* that gained! Without such, do not undertake [them]! (2475-1)

In several other readings, Cayce recommended this yoga-like breathing exercise as preparation for meditation:

> Breathe in through the right nostril three times, and exhale through the mouth. Breathe in three times through the left nostril and exhale through the right [nostril]. (281-13)

This is usually interpreted to mean a series of *six* breaths: in through the right nostril and out through the mouth, repeated two more times; then in through the left nostril and out through the right, repeated two more times. One reading reminds us that the inhalation is taking in "strength," continually drawing a new supply of God/Energy into our bodies. The Cayce-recommended breathing exercise is frequently performed just after the head-and-neck exercise recommended in the preceding chapter.

Yogic breathing exercises sometimes require several quick intakes before exhaling. If the reading quoted above is interpreted literally, Cayce might have been referring to this technique — for example, in-in-in through the right nostril, then out through the mouth; in-in-in through the left nostril, then out through the right. Draw your own conclusions about the form of this breathing exercise, and then experiment to find your own pattern, usually to be repeated three times or more.

Breath as focus. A paradox: Because you do not normally pay attention to your breathing, the process of paying attention to your breathing can be very helpful in the meditation process. In learning to retrain attention for meditation, many people find it helpful to observe their breathing after completing other preparatory activities and before concentrating on the spiritual focus.

As you observe your breath, its rate or depth is not to be altered. Simply become aware of the rhythmic breath cycle. Observe the air going through the nose and throat and down into your lungs on inhalation, and also observe the air as it comes from the lungs through the throat and nose on exhalation. Notice that the breath feels warmer when it leaves your nose on exhalation than it does going in on inhalation.

I urge you to experiment with your breath in meditation, both as an exercise and as a focus. Breath *is* life, and by recognizing it as we seek at-onement with life, we honor its transformative power throughout our being:

> The breath of which the ancient texts speak is more than merely air or oxygen; it is the expresssion of a dynamic experience of vital force, generated with every inhalation. It does not end in reaching our lungs, but continues in our bloodstream, transforming itself into ever more subtle forms of energy conducted through the intricate system of our nerves, and thus it courses through our whole body, down to the further extremities until we can feel it reaching even our toes and the tips of our fingers, creating a new kind of body-consciousness. (From Lama Govinda's *Creative Meditation and Multi-Dimensional Consciousness*, p. 121)

From breath to ideal. If you begin the concentration stage using your breath as a focus, at some point you will shift your focus to your spiritual ideal. You may find it best to put all your attention on your spiritual focus. As an alternative, you may integrate the value of breath observation with the value of the spiritual focus by synchronizing your spiritual word, phrase, or affirmation to the rhythm of the breath. For example, silently speak your

111

ideal on each inhalation and again on each exhalation. If you are using a longer affirmation, divide it so you can comfortably express part of it during inhalation and the rest during exhalation. Suppose your ideal is patience and you are using part of the Cayce affirmation on patience. While inhaling, you might say: "Be Thou the guide that we with patience ..."; while exhaling: "... may run the race which is set before us."

Later in your meditation process, after you have set the words of the spiritual focus aside to move into mindfulness, you may find it helpful to use breath observation as a way to keep you mindful.

Sounds and Other Vibrations

Of music, music, music. Uplifting music as a prelude to meditation may help release thoughts and negative emotions in preparation for concentrating on the spiritual focus. That is the most frequent use of music in the meditation process, but there are others. You may be surprised how many bodily systems and functions are stimulated by music. Once you learn about the physical effects of music, you may want to experiment with music extending into the concentration stage and even into the mindfulness stage.

Randall McClellan reports in *The Healing Forces of Music* that music — in fact, sound generally — has a *physical* impact on the body, operating through a portion of the brain called the thalamus, "the relay station of emotions, sensations, and feelings." From the thalamus, the auditory impulses stimulate the cerebral cortex which sends response signals back to the thalamus, creating a reverberating circuit that may intensify as the music continues and may result in "thalamic reflexes" such as foot tapping, swaying, and other rhythmic movements. Located around the thalamus is the limbic system that interacts with the endocrine gland system with which the spiritual centers are associated. The endocrine glands themselves influence functions such as breathing, pulse, blood circulation, and secretions (such as epinephrine from the adrenals under strong emotional circumstances). The hypothalamus, which also gets stimulated, is associated with bodily functions such as metabolism and sleep patterns.

These physiological details may seem a bit confusing. The important fact is that marvelous, complex connections exist in the body. And the important consequence is that, with the help of music, you can take advantage of these connections to enhance your meditation, either in the preparation activities or during the stillness period.

McClellan and others have experimented with different types and

112

intensities of music to determine their effects. McClellan suggests that some kinds of slow music may be used during meditation — not just as a prelude — to deepen the breath and decrease its rate and thus still the body and mind. The slower the rate at which notes and phrases of music pass through our consciousness and the greater the silence between them, the slower our sense of time becomes. Our consciousness may "drop through" the silent spaces and begin to experience timelessness. To me, this suggests that slow, unobtrusive music — perhaps getting progressively slower, with more silences — might be played during the concentration phase while I focus on the ideal. When I move from the words to the feelings of the spiritual focus, the music may help me slow down and deepen my internal rhythms and thus facilitate mindfulness.

One other advantage music may give you during the stillness: It may mask other background sounds. But a disadvantage during the stillness is that you can get caught up in the music itself — melodies, harmonies, rhythms — and lose your spiritual focus.

Helleberg suggests a form of "music-induced" meditation in which you allow yourself to become completely absorbed in a piece of inspiring music, listening with your heart, she says, rather than your ears. Allow yourself emotionally to be carried along by the music, rising and falling, surging and gliding, swelling and floating. As it fades at the end, you find yourself in a profound silence in which you offer your spirit to God.

Of inner music. Many individuals can hear or "play" a variety of music silently in their heads, from simple melodies to symphonies. This is the audio equivalent to visualization. In both kinds of experience, the individual uses imaginative forces to reproduce an inner replica of an outer form. Just as the ability to visualize varies from one person to the next, so does the ability to hear inner music. Furthermore, an individual readily able to visualize may not be able to "audio-ize," and vice versa. Some people may be able to bring to mind only a short segment of a tune or musical theme without really "hearing" it, while others hear entire compositions. Some may sense a simple sound like a single instrument or a voice, while others hear complete orchestrations. Some people even create new inner sounds and music.

Listening to inner music is a good discipline for concentration. And how convenient to prepare for meditation without having to fuss with a disk or tape player! Simply turn on your inner music and find a selection suitable for meditation.

You may think offhand that you have never "heard" inner music. Have you ever had a dream with music? Give yourself the opportunity to look for music in your head — not just at meditation time, but any time you are in a quiet moment and place. Can you hear the tune for "God Bless America" or "Home on the Range"? What about your pop or country favorite, or maybe a familiar hymn like "Rock of Ages"? When you discover your inner music, consider experimenting with it as part of your preparation for meditation.

Of bells and drones and such. In an extended reading on meditation, Cayce lists a number of sounds that may be helpful in preparing for meditation: "... a drone of certain sounds [and] ... the tolling of certain tones, bells, cymbals, drums, or various kinds of skins" (281-13). In this context, a drone is a single, continuous tone, usually low in pitch. When you hear bagpipes played, you hear a drone underneath the melody.

Using special instrumental sounds in meditation makes sense. All such sounds have their unique pattern of vibrations, and the repetitions provide rhythms. We can experiment with these unusual sounds through audiotapes, selecting those we feel especially comfortable with, probably those that resonate with parts of us. Many "New Age" bookstores and health stores sell tapes of unusual sounds and instruments. Find your favorite drone, bell, or drumbeat! As you try each out, observe its impact on you. Remember that music does have a physical effect on you, and that effect may differ from one person to the next according to one's level of vibration. You may find some pieces very calming and uplifting; others — especially some drones or drum sounds — may be disturbing and even depressing. Be cautiously adventurous!

Of sea sounds. Another rhythmic, almost hypnotic sound is that of gentle ocean waves brushing on the shore. While I enjoy a variety of "environmental tapes" — sounds of rain forests, corn fields, canoeing across a lake, and thunderstorms — my favorite sound as a background for meditation is the rhythmic one of gentle waves lapping on the beach. Furthermore, because sea sounds do not have melodies or harmonies for me to get caught up in, I sometimes find it pleasant to leave a gentle wave tape playing throughout the meditation period. This taped sound is particularly helpful for masking other sounds in your environment during meditation.

Of chants. You may have heard of or even sung some of the unharmonized melodies in free rhythm called Gregorian chants or plainsong. While recordings of such music may be suitable as pre-meditation music, the chanting that Cayce suggests is quite different — usually the extended vocal sounding of a single tone. The primary value of the chant is in the internal vibrations it creates as you do it for yourself. Cayce speaks to the effects of such chants:

> ... the voice nerve center is the highest vibration in the whole nerve system ... (341-4)

> [Certain sounds, like ah-aum] respond to the [spiritual] centers of the body, in opening the centers ... (2072-10)

> Is it any wonder then that in all of thy meditation, Ohm — O-h-m-mmmmm ... is ever a portion of that which raises self to the highest influence and the highest vibrations through-out its whole being...? (1286-1)

During the chant, the mouth and tongue are used to modify the sound, as in pronouncing a succession of the vowels, A-E-I-O-U. Chanting is usually done by voicing the selected sounds aloud at a comfortable pitch, with enough volume to feel the vibration in the vocal organs in your throat. The vibrations may be felt throughout the head and, in some cases, throughout the body. The chant is usually done on a single breath ending with an "mmmm" sound that vibrates quietly until the end of the breath. On each repetition, the entire chant is repeated for a single long breath.

The Cayce readings suggest these sound combinations for chants, among others:

> OH-MMMMM or AH-OOH-MMMMM or
> OOH-AH-OOH-MMMMM
> AH-H-H-H-R-R-E-E-E-E-OH-H-H-H-M-M-M-M-M-M-M
> I-EE-OH-OOH-EE-I-OH-OOH-M-M-M-M

Experiment with these in different meditation sessions. Here are some general guidelines:
- For any chant, take a deep breath, sound the chant slowly, letting the MMM vibrate to the end of that breath. Then repeat the process at least twice more.
- Adjust your pitch if you feel you started too high or too low. The pitch should be comfortable for your voice range. Experiment with higher and lower pitches.
- During the MMM, try your tongue in different positions in your mouth

— resting at the bottom, against your upper front teeth, in the middle. You may feel some difference in vibration according to tongue position.
- The chant is often used just before focusing on the spiritual ideal or other affirmation. Experiment with it in various places in your preparation sequence.

Many people feel really weird chanting aloud by themselves. Another alternative is what psychic and spiritual teacher Jack Schwarz, in his book *Voluntary Controls*, refers to as "silent chanting" — an apparent contradiction in words. In brief, silent chanting is an unvoiced chant. The sound is prepared for and placed as if for chanting aloud, but the final voicing doesn't take place. Try an OH-MMM chant with your voice at a comfortable pitch and volume, and then simply withdraw your sound, but continue the air flow and vibration. The vibration will not feel the same, but some vibration does continue.

A chant is an opportunity to use your unique voice vibrations to help raise the level of vibrations throughout your body. Consider chanting at least as an occasional step of preparation. However and whenever you do it, try to relax your throat muscles and focus on feeling the vibration.

Other Vibration Raisers

Incense and odors. As the olfactory nerves are stimulated by smells, the vibrations in the olfactory system are raised accordingly, contributing to the raising of vibrations in the body as a whole in the attunement process. The specific odor — for example, lavender, sandalwood, cedar, and orris root are mentioned in the Cayce readings — may, for some people, also trigger helpful connections with the distant past. If your olfactory system reacts favorably to incense and other appropriate odors —flowers, sachets, wood — consider experimenting with odors of various kinds.

Stones. Stones, crystals, and metals also have their own vibrations. Holding and carrying certain stones on your person can, according to Cayce, help in your attunement. A stone specifically mentioned several times in the readings is the blue lapis lazuli:

> As to stones — have near to self, wear preferably upon the body, about the neck, the lapis lazuli; this preferably encased in crystal. It will be not merely as an ornament but as

116

strength from the emanation which will be gained by the
body always from same. For the stone is itself an emanation
of vibrations of the elements that give vitality, virility,
strength, and that of assurance in self. (1981-1)

I have a piece of lapis lazuli sitting on my computer as I write!

"Opening" the Spiritual Centers

Associated with seven ductless glands of the body's endocrine system
are seven spiritual centers, often referred to as "chakras." According to the
Cayce readings and many traditional Eastern writings, a source of energy
(often referred to as kundalini) normally rests at one of the lower of these
centers in the male testes and female ovaries. During meditation, this energy
is aroused so it will flow upward to a center at the top of the head, from which
it flows to another center in the head, and back down through the other
centers between the throat and the groin. Our interest in this chapter is not
on the individual centers, but on the total seven-center system through which
the energy flows during meditation. Attunement is not only facilitated by
this energy flow, but, according to Cayce, "spiritual contact is through the
glandular forces of creative energies..." (263-13). In other words, our
anticipated contact with God actually takes place through these centers when
the energy flows unimpeded during meditation.

In preparing for meditation, we can include steps to facilitate that flow.
For example, the head-and-neck exercise may help the flow of energy as well
as the circulation of blood to and from the head.

The energy flow is affected by the conditions at the seven centers. Each
of the centers may be fully ready for energy flow or may be in some degree
impaired, thus weakening the flow. They are often referred to as "open" or
"closed." However, some individuals such as Jack Schwarz say it is unlikely
that any of the centers is ever literally closed; if they were, energy flow would
cease completely and so would life, these people say. Consider instead that
the energy flow is greater or less according to the condition of the centers.
(The words "open" and "closed" may still be used, but with this understanding.)

The centers are all to be "opened" carefully and in an integrated manner,
not some to the exclusion of others. To help this take place in an appropriate way, the Cayce readings recommend using the Lord's Prayer (Matthew 6: 9-13). Key words within that prayer speak directly to the seven

117

centers; for example, "heaven" refers to the pituitary and "name" to the pineal — both in the head; "will" refers to the thyroid in the throat; "deliverance from evil" refers to the thymus near the heart; "forgiveness of debts" to the adrenals in the solar plexus; "freedom from temptation" to the cells of Leydig in the gonads; and "daily bread" to the gonads themselves (281-29).

When offering the Lord's Prayer in preparation for meditation, one may visualize the flow of energy from one center to the next as each key word or phrase is spoken. Visualization is not necessary, however, for the prayer to do its job of freeing up the centers *if*, when the prayer is offered either silently or aloud, the words are spoken mindfully — with meaning and sincerity, not just as rote.

One appropriate time for the prayer is during the period when you are relaxing the body; another is just before you begin focusing on your spiritual ideal. Experiment not only with the use of the Lord's Prayer, but also with where you insert it in your sequence of preparations.

Our attitudes and emotions directly affect the openness of the spiritual centers, especially the lower centers. Therefore, an important way of enhancing energy flow is keeping ourselves mentally and emotionally healthy. This is one reason for Cayce's continued emphasis on attitude adjustment, as I have called it.

Experiences in Meditation

Since most of the special experiences people have in meditation seem related to energy flow, this is an appropriate time to describe some of them. Remember, however, the cautions sounded when we talked about stillness: Experiences are not to be sought nor dwelt upon if they occur.

Movements and vibrations of the body. Edgar Cayce was questioned about several specific body sensations. The questions in the 281 series of readings listed below were asked by different members of the original prayer healing group called the Glad Helpers:

> Please explain the pumping sensation I experience in the lower part of my spine during meditation ... (281-12, Q-11)

> Please explain the unusual and vigorous movements in my body during meditation. (295-9, Q-11)

118

During a recent group meditation ... I felt a pulsation on the top of my head ... like a pulsation of the heart. Please explain. (281-27, Q-13)

Please explain the sensations during meditation of vibration running up through the body and ending in a sort of fullness in the head. (281-14, Q-7)

Please give me enlightenment concerning that which took place in my forehead while meditating ... like an opening and shutting of a valve, and was heard by another person in the room. (281-35, Q-6)

While each of Cayce's answers differed according to the needs of the person requesting, a single explanatory principle underlies his responses: Each of these experiences is of a physical sensation brought about by the movement of the energy along the path among the spiritual centers. In the case of the "unusual and vigorous" movement, Cayce suggested that if the individual's imagination or inner emotions were inducing the movement — trying to produce expected or desired movements — they should be controlled; otherwise, let them be. The sensations of fullness and pulsation in the head may indicate the need to send to others the healing energy built up during meditation or the "messages" received for others during meditation. The energy may be sent out toward others either through the laying on of hands or by thought containing the name of the intended receiver.

Cayce cautions about such body sensations and other phenomena — not to expect them, not to attempt to enhance them, and not to make them the focus of your attention. Many of these experiences are simply a sign that something is happening. If, however, one doesn't get the same signs someone else gets, or doesn't get any signs at all, things are still happening in the body. Cayce suggests that, when in doubt about sensations or images, the individual should simply refocus on the ideal or another spiritual idea.

My own experience may be illustrative. During most meditations, I feel a slight rhythmic pulsing through the upper part of my body. I have tried to ignore the movement and never focus attention on it, in line with Cayce's admonitions. This slight movement, visible only to someone near me, began suddenly after about ten years of meditating — after I started meditating weekly with the prayer healing group at A.R.E. called the Glad Helpers. I believe the energy flow within me was suddenly intensified by the vibrations raised in that group of long-time meditators during the two-hour meditation period each time we meet. And it was affected in such a way that the system seems to "remember" the flow, so it occurs in almost all meditations now, although it does become stronger in some group meditation periods than in others. My experience illustrates (a) that the number of years of meditation have nothing to do with the occurrence of meditation experiences, and (b) that meditation in a group of experienced meditators, as well as periodic long meditations, may alter your meditation experience.

Other sensations reported by meditators include feeling a pressure or fullness in the head, and feeling tingling at one or more of the spiritual center locations. Many experienced meditators, however, experience none of these sensations or movements.

Mental images and sensations of light, sound, and smell. In answer to the question about what happens in the body during meditation, Cayce replied that, in deep meditation, the channels are opened for the energy to flow (through focus on the spiritual ideal, for example, or by the words of the Lord's Prayer). The energy then flows to the spiritual centers, finding expression

> ... either through the movements of the body[,] in the hearing of sound, in the consciousness of odors, in the activity of the vision, or there is just the presence that may be read as the open book. (275-39)

A reading by Ray Stanford describes the rising of the kundalini from the cells of Leydig in the gonads to the pituitary and pineal centers in the head. As the energy fills and overflows the pituitary, Stanford says a reaction takes place between the pituitary and the pineal creating what is sometimes perceived as an explosion of white light. Stanford cautions that the white light is an *effect* of the process, not something to be sought as an end in itself (from *Speak, Shining Stranger*, pp. 19-20).

Some Cayce readings suggest that sounds and images may, in fact, be an inspirational effect of meditation:

> **Question**: Please explain the roaring sound in my right ear which I have heard in recent meditation.
> **Answer through Mr. Cayce**: Thou hast heard that the voice of Him cometh as the rushing of mighty waters; and that injunction which came with same, *"Peace — be still."* For it is not only in the storm, nor the rocks, but rather the still

120

small voice that comes after same.

Hence thou hast drawn, and do draw, nigh unto the brink of a greater understanding.

Hold fast to His hand, that leads the way! (540-3, Q-4)

Question: What was the form that seemed to be made up of light, that appeared in the room at the close of the meditation preceding this reading... ?
Answer through Mr. Cayce: The attuning of self to the high vibrations of love and life and joy — and is but that which heals and keeps peace among men. (5749-10, Q-3)

Question: Why do I see a cross so often in meditation?
Answer through Mr. Cayce: Has it not just been indicated? The Cross leads the way, *ever!* (307-15, Q-6)

As desirable as such sensations and impressions may seem, again the meditator is urged not to seek them actively or expect them to occur. The first priority in all meditation is attunement to God. All else follows as consequences of that at-onement, including most phenomena — physical, mental, and spiritual.

This may be Cayce's most articulate statement about expecting what will happen in meditation:

Question: Why don't I have more success with meditation?
Answer through Mr. Cayce: Oft we find ... that there is sought that this or that. . .reported to have happened to another, *must* be the manner of happening to self. And in this manner ... there is built the barrier which prevents the real inner self from *experiencing*. Let self *loose* ... Do not *try*, or crave, or desire a sign; for *thou* art in *thyself* a sign of that thou dost worship within thine inner self! For thou, as every soul, dost stand before the door of the temple where thy God hath promised to meet thee. Then, do not be impatient. For what thou asketh in secret shall be proclaimed from the housetop. (705-2, Q-6)

The most prudent way to approach meditation is to anticipate *nothing* unusual in the way of experiences: body sensations, movements, visualizations, or any other physical or mental sensations. Then if nothing occurs, disappointment has been avoided; and if anything does occur, it can be seen simply as an indicator of what goes on in the body of *all* meditators. As Cayce implies above — "for *thou* art in *thyself* a sign of that thou dost worship within thine inner self" (705-2) — the very fact that you exist, that you are a child of God, and that you are seeking to commune with God through meditation is in itself a sign of your success.

Still More Choices

It's a good thing that life is about choices! Just as at the end of the preceding chapter, I am presenting here a reminder list of activities and options that have been discussed in this chapter. You have probably noted those you want to experiment with, but just in case you missed some, here they are — all of them optional activities, most of them with many possible variations:

Optional activities
• Using various styles and lengths of music as preparation.
• Using quiet music during meditation.
• Using inner music.
• Using sounds of bells, drones, drums, etc.
• Using incense, odors, and stones.
• Listening to gentle ocean waves as preliminary to or even during meditation.
• Using Cayce's yogic breathing exercise.
• Using the breath observation as a preliminary focus.
• Combining your spiritual ideal focus with your breath focus.
• Chanting in one or more of the variations.
• Using the Lord's Prayer mindfully to facilitate the flow of energy through the spiritual centers.

"Try Me!" Here again is your opportunity to experiment. Strongly recommended for your consideration: the breathing exercise and the Lord's Prayer. To stretch yourself and get extra practice in concentration, try listening for your inner music. For variety, try chanting, stones, incense, sea sounds, and unusual music.

Continue planning and experimenting with variations on a weekly basis, and carrying out meditation periods on a daily basis. You now have seen most of the choices for preparation activities. Remember not to abandon an activity too quickly when it doesn't seem to have any effect, unless you find it very difficult or very distracting to your preparation and attunement.

The next chapter concludes this part of the book on creating your own meditation style. Reading it should give you a feeling of accomplishment as well as reassurance about your meditation process.

Chapter 9

Commitment, Creativity, and Inner Peace

"You stayed in your room when the tornado came through?"
"I was there the whole time."
"Didn't you hear the warnings to get into the basement or to evacuate to a shelter?"
"Sure, but it was time for meditation!"

Experimenting with your meditation process may result in both "good news" and "bad news": The good news is that you recognize the meditation process as a flexible, creative technique, readily adaptable to your needs, circumstances, and experiences. The bad news is that you may "wander around" in your meditation practice, so fascinated by its variations and by the possibilities of beneficial outcomes that you lose sight of its fundamental purpose — attunement to God, at-onement with life.

Furthermore, experimenting may seem to excuse you from making a commitment to meditation. However, even if you plan to continue experimenting, the time for excuses is over, and the time of commitment is at hand. I don't recommend you ignore tornados, hurricanes, and earthquakes to meditate, but short of that ...

Committing Yourself to Meditation

I recommend you commit yourself to three responsibilities: to meditate daily, to meditate mindfully, and to meditate creatively.

A commitment to meditate daily. If you buy the idea that your life can get recharged by universal Spirit and can also be guided by signs and messages from God, then it's not hard to understand why you should plan on a daily visit to God's message and recharging center:

> Take time daily, then, to commune with thy better self, thy God. (3488-1)

> Don't let a day go by without meditation and prayer ... (3624-1)

Even when you schedule a daily meditation period, it comes down to your choice of action at the scheduled time: Do you choose to meditate, or do you feel you'd rather not meditate, or do you allow something else to fill that time? This is where your priorities get tested. Let's consider two kinds of potential interference with meditation.

The first kind of interference I'll call reluctance: You find yourself thinking, "I'd rather not take the time to meditate today," or "I've got some problems today, so I better not meditate," or simply, "I'm not up to meditation today." Someone asked Ray Stanford during a reading, "Which is better ... to meditate regularly, even if improperly, and/or when otherwise upset and unable to concentrate; or not to meditate except when with a group so inclined, or when one rarely feels in the mood?" (from *Speak, Shining Stranger*, p. 25). Stanford's "Source" simply replied that the first alternative — less-than-perfect meditation — is better. Even one or two minutes of quiet time just sitting, focused on your ideal, is beneficial. It is also a meaningful expression of your commitment to the process.

A second kind of interference comes from competing commitments and responsibilities. Such interference is minimized if you set your meditation time for a period when there are usually no other potential demands on your time. No matter how hard you try, however, other responsibilities or unforeseen events (like a tornado?) may occasionally interfere with your scheduled meditation. Meditation is a high daily priority for me, and I schedule it to be first every morning before other activities and responsibilities make their demands. Almost nothing interferes with that time. But what

126

Discover the wealth of information in the Edgar Cayce readings

Dreams
Soul Mates
Karma
Earth Changes
Universal Laws
Meditation
Holistic Health
ESP
Astrology
Atlantis
Psychic Development
Numerology
Pyramids
Death and Dying
Auto-Suggestion
Reincarnation
Akashic Records
Planetary Sojourns
Mysticism
Spiritual Healing
And other topics

Membership Benefits You Receive Each Month

EDGAR CAYCE FOUNDATION and
A.R.E. LIBRARY/VISITORS CENTER
Virginia Beach, Va.
OVER 50 YEARS OF SERVICE

NO POSTAGE
NECESSARY
IF MAILED
IN THE
UNITED STATES

BUSINESS REPLY CARD
First Class Permit No. 2456, Virginia Beach, Va.

POSTAGE WILL BE PAID BY

A.R.E.®
P.O. Box 595
Virginia Beach, VA 23451

if I wake up on a cold day and discover no heat in the house, and an elderly family member needs immediate attention? Of course, I immediately get out the extra blankets and the space heaters, get the elderly person bundled up to get warm, check the furnace and the oil supply, and either restart the furnace or make an emergency phone call. When all that's done, I meditate if time is still available — even if I'm distracted or upset at the moment — or I reschedule it for evening — perhaps leaving a reminder on my pillow so I won't forget it at the unaccustomed time.

After you have been meditating regularly for several weeks or months, you will begin feeling more at one with life, and you will experience other benefits of meditation. Then, meditation becomes its own reward, and you may need less prompting at scheduled times. It also helps if you come to regard meditation as one of your fundamental responsibilities to your physical, mental, and spiritual health — at least as important as brushing your teeth!

So first and foremost, commit yourself to *meditate daily*. In addition to your gaining the benefits from regular meditation, the discipline of a daily commitment is in itself excellent training for your will. Rudolf Steiner recommends the building of rhythms into life as an exercise for the training of the will. In his book on will, *Paradox of Power*, Mark Thurston uses meditation as an example of this training:

> The will is awakened and trained through repetition in more than one way. First, there must be willed effort to maintain the pattern. Once the pattern is established, the will can, in turn, begin to draw sustenance from the rhythm itself.
>
> This process is illustrated in the discipline of keeping a regular meditation time each day. At first it takes effort. All kinds of excuses to procrastinate or avoid keeping the appointed time arise from the mind. By acts of will the regular pattern is established. However, with the creation of such a personal rhythm, a remarkable thing begins to happen. The rhythm has a life of its own. Keeping the meditation time becomes easier, no longer requiring a struggle of undue effort. The will itself begins to be fed and strengthened by the purposeful pattern. (p. 104)

I must admit to a day now and then when I do not meditate, and to other days when I meditate briefly or shallowly. Although I know I benefit from even those minimal efforts, I sometimes sense on those occasions that a

127

pattern has been disrupted, a vital life rhythm broken. Such occasions serve as a reminder of how much my life is lifted and sustained by regular meditation. In effect, meditation is addictive — in a positive sense. Not meditating means missing the spiritual recharging of my batteries and the spiritual recalibration of my directional systems.

A commitment to meditate mindfully. The second part of the commitment is to *meditate mindfully.* "Mindful" here has a twofold meaning: the first relates to seeking diligently the stage of mindfulness beyond the stage of concentration; the second relates to keeping activities in the meditation process from becoming rote, without conscious thought.

In her book *Mindfulness*, Ellen Langer refers to the use of preflight checks required on all commercial airlines. Such checks must be mindful, she points out, lest the pilot or other crew member look at a meter or a switch setting without really seeing it and call it OK when in fact it is not OK. Langer cites the tragic crash of a commercial airliner that apparently resulted from just such a mindless check of a critical setting. One of the key activities of meditation that can readily succumb to mindlessness is the repetition of the spiritual focus, up to now usually the spiritual ideal in one of its several forms. Although the words even without thought still have power, mindfulness will facilitate reaching the essence behind the words — the spiritual thread along which one moves toward God.

Most preparatory activities can be done mindlessly as well as mindfully, and the meditator should be alert to signs of mindlessness. Since variety helps keep one mindful, changing an activity or the sequence of activity in the preparation phase may encourage mindfulness. However, the primary route to mindfulness is the training of attention, learning to keep the mind focused and alert.

A commitment to meditate creatively. The third part of the commitment is to *meditate creatively.* This means keeping vitality and joy alive in your meditation through your creative use of the meditation process. Allow meditation not only to bring you the inner peace and feelings of well-being, but also to quicken your spiritual self and to tap into the well of joy that may be experienced through your visits with God. When these experiences are lacking, reawaken your experimental curiosity and inject new life into your process with different preparatory activities, new aids to attunement, or a change in your spiritual focus.

"Try Me!" Commitment time is here. I recommend that you now write a statement of commitment about your meditation practice as you will carry it out for the next several weeks or months. Your "contract" should state approximate daily time or times of meditation, normal location, alternate times or places when regular periods must be missed, and frequency of "self-observation" of your meditation practice and its effects. Attach to your contract an outline of your personal style of meditation, or a plan for your continued experimenting over the time period in your contract. For example:

> Beginning now and continuing for six months, I will meditate mindfully and creatively for at least 15 minutes every day at about 7 a.m. in my bedroom. On days when I must leave home before 7 or when I am away from home at that hour, I will meditate before I go to bed that same day wherever I happen to be. The first Saturday every month, I will make notes about my meditations — the process I am using and any observations I have about feelings or effects. I will follow the meditation procedure outlined on the attached page.

Date and sign your contract, and display it where it may give you an extra little nudge to keep the scheduled time in meditation. Even if no one sees the contract but you, there is something self-motivating about a written commitment.

At the end of the designated period, "renegotiate" or simply "renew" your contract for another period. Committing yourself for several successive short periods may be less overwhelming than committing yourself for one long period. Follow your intuition!

The Creative Meditation Experience

Since this chapter completes Part Two, *Creating Your Own Meditation Style*, a check on your meditation experience is timely, to see how it tallies with our aim — the inner peace that is "being at one with life."

Meditation can reward us with some of the most significant experiences we ever have. Its effects can reshape and sustain every facet of our lives from the spiritual to the physical. We have cited specific benefits experienced by people who meditated — physiological effects, mental effects, and behavioral effects. Perhaps as consequential for us, meditation may change our lives in ways we probably never expected.

Marilyn Helleberg describes beautifully how meditation may increase the subtle "coincidences" we experience:

> There is Something in the universe — call it what you will — (the Way, cosmic flow, divine plan, will of God) that, *totally beyond the laws of chance or coincidence*, directs the lives of those who are in tune with it. *If you can position yourself in the flow of that force*, you will find that, more and more, you just happen to be at the right place at the right time; you manage to find the right words to say what needs to be said; you find yourself doing the kind of work you enjoy and do best; and when you have a need, the right person or thing just happens (?) to come along to fill that need. Almost everyone has had an experience or two like this, and most often, such events are chalked up to coincidence. But when one is really "in the divine flow" they become the rule rather than the exception.
>
> ... Just the act of meditation itself will greatly increase your ability to tune in to the cosmic flow... (From *Beyond TM*, pp. 102-103)

For me, such experiences are some of the most helpful outcomes of my meditation. This ongoing form of guidance and assistance from "the universe" — God — allows you to cope productively with your challenges through the strategy of "Doing It!" more often than you ever could without meditation.

In *Centered Living: The Way of Centering Prayer*, M. Basil Pennington talks about another benefit of meditation (which he calls "Centering Prayer"):

> ... people who Center regularly seem to have such boundless energy. They are constantly refreshed even in the midst of their labors. This enables them to cut back on their sleep and other recreative activities, so they have more time for productive work. The investment of Centering Prayer is amply paid back. Anyone who says he or she has not the time to Center should perhaps take another look. If they are so hard-pressed they are perhaps the ones who most need Centering Prayer, not only to gain time and energy but to find leisure and worship and God in the midst of all their labors. (pp. 122-123)

This energy renewal makes meditation a strong candidate for the coping strategy I have labeled "Revitalize for It."

An Edgar Cayce reading describes a third general effect of meditation that, perhaps unexpectedly, extends beyond the meditator:

> As the [individual] may experience in some of its moments of meditation, the finding of peace in self enables the [individual] to give more assurance, more help to others; just by being patient and not attempting to control or to appear overanxious.
>
> ... Thus as harmony and beauty and grace reign within the consciousness of an [individual], it gives that to others — and others wonder what moved them to feel different, when no one spoke, no one even appeared to be anxious. This is the manner in which the spirit of truth operates ... (3098-2)

You are not the only "winner" through your meditation.

Now that you have been meditating regularly, take a look at your own experience:

"Search Me!" During and after your periods of meditation, what effects have you been experiencing? Don't be critical of your meditations — simply describe feelings and emotions or other effects you are aware of any time after meditating. Make notes of your observations.

Have you begun to experience any of the feelings and other qualities you described as "being at one with life"? Look back at the responses you made for Self-Inventory 3 in Chapter 2. Add to your written notes any similarities you find between the noticeable effects of your meditations and the desirable state of being at one with life.

> If you are new to meditation, don't be concerned if your experiences do not yet match the inner peace and feelings of well-being you anticipate. Be patient with yourself and your meditations. Whatever you do, *keep on keeping on* with daily meditation.

About once a week, observe your feelings, internal states, and other effects you attribute to your meditations. Make brief notes about them along with the date and the activities in your meditation.

131

The Effect of Meditation on Creativity

"Creativity" is the ability to go beyond known forms to develop new forms. The "forms" may be objects, patterns, knowledge, ideas, principles, or relationships. If we understand that everything — whether thought or substance — is of the one energy that is God, it follows that our ability to be creative can only be enhanced by our ability to connect with God, the original Creative Force. Through this God-connection we are also connected with a universal consciousness in which all thought, memory, and knowledge can be reached.

Psychological studies of creativity suggest that the creative person has some of the same characteristics as a person who meditates. According to psychologist Patricia Carrington in her book, *Freedom in Meditation*, the highly creative individual appears more able to direct awareness inwardly than the less creative person. That allows the individual to do more "primary process thinking" — thinking that uses highly symbolic and pictorial means of expression, often in bizarre or absurd ways, as in our dreams or hallucinations or any state where the mind is not confined by ordinary logic. The content may be drawn from the unconscious mind of the individual. (I suggest further that, through attunement in meditation, it may also be drawn from the universal source of creative energy — the "mind" of God.)

When primary process thinking is controlled and integrated by the conscious mind, highly creative ideas may result. Carrington reminds us about the dream origins of ideas such as Elias Howe's sewing machine needle, Friedrich Kekulé's structure for the benzine ring, Francis Crick's DNA molecule, and Robert Louis Stevenson's inspirations for books. Psychological research demonstrates a positive relationship between meditation and controlled primary process thinking, suggesting that meditators are probably more capable of primary process thinking than non-meditators — one step toward creativity.

Research also suggests that meditation may enhance three other traits typical of the creative person: openness to experiencing emotion, the assurance of allowing oneself to respond to problems on an intuitive level, and perceptual openness — a willingness to perceive things in new ways. From other research and experience, Carrington cites three specific characteristics of the creative process which apparently improve through meditative practice: increased productivity of ideas, improved quality of creative work, and strengthening of creative stamina — the ability to sustain long periods of creative work.

All of these results imply that meditators have the *disposition* for greater creativity — not necessarily that they will be creative. The qualities available to the meditator must be developed and applied before creativity is actually manifested. If you, for example, are motivated to enhance your creativity, I suggest that, in addition to incorporating *creative meditation* into your daily life, you become especially aware of the four mental processes referred to above. Your sensitivity should be especially keen immediately after attunement, but remain on the lookout for them at any time, if you are meditating daily. These are the mental processes to look for:

- Primary process thinking (symbolic and pictorial imagery often in unconventional or illogical contexts or relationships): Record them as you might your dreams, noting with them any concern or project to which you have been giving a lot of attention.
- Openness to experiencing emotion: Be aware of emotions emerging during meditation or soon after, and note any reactions you have on their appropriateness to what's going on in your life.
- Willingness to respond to problems on an intuitive level: Any time you are stuck for an answer or trying to solve a problem or make a decision, notice *first* whether or not you have an intuitive response as an alternative, and notice *second* whether you are inclined to use it or not. Keeping a simple log of your intuitive impulses, hunches, or unexpected information can help you realize how frequently intuition occurs. By paying attention to it, you will experience it all the more frequently.
- Perceptual openness: Notice times when you perceive things you never noticed before, or when you perceive objects or ideas or relationships in ways that are new to you, from new angles, or yielding information or impressions you never had before. When you are walking in your neighborhood or riding in the car in normally familiar territory, observe your environment as if seeing it for the first time. Notice when you see objects that you do not usually see. You can do the same in any familiar surroundings, such as your own home, your office, your library, or your place of worship. Prize those new little details and thus reward your alerted senses so they will continue their careful work.

To the degree that you notice more frequent occurrences of any of these traits, you are probably increasing even more your *capability* for being creative. Then all you need to do is find the medium to which you want to apply it — problems to solve, artistic endeavors to undertake, writing to do, and so on.

Let's try an application in creativity right now:

"Try Me!"

1. Select an idea, an activity, or a relationship in your life about which you would like to be more creative. Encapsulate that item in a few words, such as "the renovation of the kitchen," "next year's vacation," or "my relationship with Pat." Write those words of your "creativity project" at the top of a sheet of paper and set it within reach before starting your meditation. Now release the project from your mind, using inspirational reading or music to divert your attention.

2. Carry out your meditation without any reference to the project. If the thought of it comes to you, move it along as you do any other thought, without giving it any special attention. Use your spiritual focus for concentration. Spend a few minutes in mindfulness without the focus.

3. As you complete your meditation, without moving from your position, read several times the project words you have written on the sheet. With the sheet and a pen or pencil handy, close your eyes again, repeating mentally the project words as a focus in two ways:

   a. Use the project words as a focus for 20 to 30 seconds and then release them to a clear mind (30-40 seconds). Repeat this alternating pattern for three to five minutes. If new thoughts or ideas come to mind, write them down with as little disturbance of the process as possible.

   b. Now try the approach of starting with the project words, letting them lead you wherever they go. Let your mind free associate, even if it seems to wander far from the subject. If it doesn't return in a minute or so, bring it back to the project words. As you encounter new thoughts or ideas, write them down with as little disturbance of the process as possible. Continue this for three to five minutes.

4. When you leave your meditation location, take your paper with you and add ideas or thoughts as they come to you during the rest of the day (or the next day, if you are meditating just before bedtime). Sometimes the flow does not begin until after the meditative period and you are in the

midst of other activities. Try to remain sensitive to impressions relating to your creative project, and add them to your notes.

5. In a day or two, at a time other than meditation, look over your notes to see what might be of help on your creative project. Work with the same project for several days. You may also want to focus on it before bedtime to get information from your dreams.

To illustrate:

> I am starting to think about my next major writing project. Although I have considered several ideas for books on metaphysical topics, I would like to give my thinking a creative boost. On paper, I write "my next writing project." After meditating, I reread these words and then use them as a focus, alternating them with stillness and listening. Aside from some metaphysical topics I have already considered, the clear new thought that comes to me is "children," and I write the word down.
>
> Always underlying my writing projects is the philosophy of the Cayce readings. Writing for children on some aspect of the Cayce philosophy is not a new idea for me, but I haven't considered it for a long time. I add to my written note "on Cayce topic." No other clear thought comes to me, but "Cayce for children" keeps coming back.
>
> Now I let my mind free associate on "Cayce for children." Some of the thoughts that come along: my grandchildren, dinosaurs, castles, kings, beautiful princess, Atlantis, buried treasure, mysterious stranger, mystery. I write as many of these down as I can remember. After other meditations, some of the same thoughts come to mind, but mystery leads me to ESP, psi, and psychic. Outside of meditation, I begin to think about Atlantis as a possible topic. Then something about mystery and buried treasure triggers the idea of psychic archaeology, and later I am reminded specifically of Stephan Schwartz's fascinating psychic archaeology project in Alexandria, Egypt.

I am still developing this idea, in and out of meditation. I have gone so far as to talk with Stephan about it. At the moment, "my next writing project" may be a fiction or non-fiction book for young people on Schwartz's Alexandria Project. Watch for it!

According to past research, your meditation experience will help you be more and more creative as time goes on. You may see this manifested both in greater productivity of ideas and in better quality of ideas from such a process. Now that's truly *creative meditation*! May you find useful ideas for your own creative project!

Attunement First!

When you know about benefits that may be realized through meditation, such as increased creativity — and especially once you have experienced some of them — you may be tempted to begin your meditation process with a purpose in mind other than the fundamental goal of at-onement/attunement. In the procedures soon to be presented for seeking guidance and healing, for example, you may be inclined to let your mind and emotions be drawn toward the anticipated outcomes as you prepare for meditation and even as you direct your focus. Such results-directed expectations can interfere with the attunement process, during which you must stay focused spiritually; and that attunement — your connection with God — must occur before you have access to God's resources, such as guidance and healing. In every meditation, therefore, you must try to free your mind, body, and spirit from their "hidden agenda."

The tendency for us to think about anticipated benefits as we go into meditation seems to have a long history. Meister Eckhart uses an engaging analogy in discussing this inclination in our relationship with God:

> Some people, I swear, want to love God in the same way as they love a cow. They love it for its milk and cheese and the profit they will derive from it. Those who love God for the sake of outward riches or for the sake of inward consolation operate on the same principle. They are not loving God correctly; they are merely loving their own advantage. (From Matthew Fox's *Meditations with Meister Eckhart*, p. 61)

Joel Goldsmith goes directly and unsparingly to the point:

> Any meditation that has within itself a single trace of a desire

136

to get something from God or to acquire something through God is no longer meditation. Good is to be realized, yes, but not to be achieved: the infinity of good is already where I am; the kingdom of God is within me. (From *The Art of Meditation*, p. 21)

And that is the point: The outcome will occur as the result of the attunement, not as its objective.

With the same concern, Cayce's readings frequently refer to a familiar verse from the gospel of Matthew:

But seek ye first the kingdom of God, and his righteousness; and all these things shall be added unto you. (Matthew 6:33 KJV)

Mark Thurston shares this helpful idea about the attitude being held as one goes into meditation:

Meditation is like *loving* — as in loving God — and the language of love is *giving*. I should approach each meditation with the intention to give of myself — not to get. The only genuine criterion for a successful meditation is the feeling of authentic self-surrender to something bigger than self. (From personal correspondence with the author)

In summary, hold to the principle of "attunement first" in every meditation. On those occasions when you are puzzled or disappointed about what is *not* happening in your meditations, about the effects you are *not* experiencing, examine your motivation and intention during the attunement process. Are you allowing desires for outcomes or expectations of benefits to override your desire for attunement/at-onement? Putting your at-onement first is really putting God first. All else must follow.

A Peaceful Meditation

As a closing experience for Part Two, here's a special meditation suggested by Peace Pilgrim:

"Try Me!" Follow your current process of meditation, with one exception: Instead of using your spiritual ideal as the focus, use the words below, suggested by Peace Pilgrim. You may want to copy them onto a card to hold in meditation. Most of the words are from Psalm 46, Edgar Cayce's favorite psalm. You may want to say each word or short phrase on an inhalation or exhalation of breath. When you have finished, find the essence of peace within yourself and hold on to it for the mindfulness stage.

Peace . . . be still . . . and know . . . that I am God.
Peace . . . be still . . . and know . . . that I am.
Peace . . . be still . . . and know.
Peace . . . be still.
Peace . . . be.
Peace . . .
        Peace . . .
            Peace.

Part Three extends the process of meditation into every corner of your life. You may want to proceed to it right away, or you may prefer to wait until you have completed your experimenting and have developed your new personal baseline style of meditation.

When you're ready, I'll be waiting for you patiently in Part Three.

PART THREE

TAKING CHARGE OF YOUR LIFE

Chapter 10

Who's in Charge of Your Life?

"This business used to be run by someone who was lazy, ignorant, fearful, irresponsible, and always looking for a scapegoat. It was really in trouble. Fortunately, the new manager is intelligent, enthusiastic, courageous, energetic, and dependable. Now the business is really becoming successful."

"Who's the new manager?"

"Me."

"And who was in charge before?"

"Me."

As you are discovering, meditation is a remarkable means for creating your own inner peace even in the midst of outer chaos. But as the song says, "We've only just begun!" If you are new to meditation — or recommitting to meditation — you've only just begun to experience how that calm and at-oneness can help you cope with the "slings and arrows" syndrome. Part Three is dedicated to moving *creative meditation* from its sheltered existence in a daily corner of your life out into the full spectrum of your world.

Creative meditation is a strategy that can help you cope with the toughest of challenges. If circumstances are giving you more challenge than you need right now, you have two choices for dealing constructively with the

SELF-INVENTORY 4
"Would You Believe ... ?"

Consider each statement below as a possible expression of your sincere belief right now. At the left of each statement, write either "A" (meaning "I basically AGREE") or "D" (meaning "I basically DISAGREE"). Leave blank any about which you are undecided.

A = I tend to *AGREE* with this statement.
D = I tend to *DISAGREE* with this statement.

_____ 1. I frequently find myself in circumstances which I had no part in selecting or bringing about.

_____ 2. I may become ill because I have something to gain from the illness.

_____ 3. I am predisposed to act in certain ways because of the positions of the planets at the time I was born.

_____ 4. My life has a specific spiritual purpose for me to fulfill.

_____ 5. Whether I believe in a particular medical treatment or not has no effect on my being healed through it.

_____ 6. I have put myself into the conditions resulting in my present financial status.

_____ 7. I have lived previous lives on earth.

_____ 8. If I keep my thoughts to myself, they have no effect on anyone else.

_____ 9. I attract to myself the situations I need for my spiritual growth.

_____ 10. My attitudes and emotions have a significant effect on my susceptibility to catastrophic illness such as cancer and heart disease.

_____ 11. If I was involved in an accident but not at fault, I was not responsible for experiencing the accident.

_____ 12. I can find the answer to any question by looking within myself.

_____ 13. My future circumstances have already been determined for me.

_____ 14. I have the capability for being psychic.

_____ 15. What appears to be an unjust event in my life may be the result of an unjust action of mine in a previous life.

140

challenge: (1) you can incorporate *creative meditation* into coping strategies (such as the one labeled "Revitalize for It") to reduce the effects of the challenge; or (2) you can begin to reduce the challenge itself by changing the conditions that cause it. "What? You mean I can change the circumstances of my life without walking away from them?" The answer to that question must be preceded by another one: Do you believe you can?

What Do You Believe?

Your attitudes and your actions are powerfully influenced by your beliefs. For example, if you sincerely believe that men and women should be paid the same if they do the same work, your words and actions will tend to support this equality. The strength of your belief will help to determine if it prevails over other considerations or not. If your belief in the equality principle is very strong, you may, for example, even stick your neck out to get attention to the issue in a situation where it might otherwise be overlooked.

Your attitudes and actions regarding your circumstances are influenced by your beliefs about your circumstances and about life in general. Here's an opportunity for you to look at those beliefs.

"**Search Me!**" Complete Self-Inventory 4, responding honestly to each item according to your current beliefs. The instructions for scoring and interpretation are at the back of this book.

Your responses on this self-inventory are interpreted in terms of how close your beliefs are to the following idea: *You are responsible for your present circumstances.* If that seems like bad news to you, the good news is that *you can change your circumstances!*

How can you possibly be responsible for getting yourself into a difficult personal relationship, for having a car that doesn't work half the time, for getting colds so frequently, for being in an untenable work situation, and for not having enough money to pay your bills? If it was up to you, you would choose the opposite of those circumstances, right? Then what has stopped you from getting a better deal in life? Has Fate dealt with you unfairly? Have other people gotten all the breaks or put blocks in your way?

In his recent book on personal transformation, *You'll See It When You Believe It*, psychologist Wayne Dyer expresses his view on this:

141

I have lost my ability to blame others for the circumstances of my life. I no longer view the world in terms of unfortunate accidents or misfortunes. I know in my being that I influence it all, and now find myself considering why I created a situation, rather than saying, "Why me?" This heightened awareness directs me to look inside of myself for answers. I take responsibility for all of it, and the interesting puzzle becomes a fascinating challenge when I decide to influence areas of my life in which I previously believed I was not in control. I now feel that I control it. (p. 33)

This concept of our responsibility for putting ourselves where we are permeates the Cayce readings. This one idea has changed my life more than any other single concept. I have brought myself to where I am, including the circumstances that seem troublesome and unwanted. I have not reached this point because of "them" out there nor because of a mysterious roll of Fate's dice. As a Cayce reading succinctly puts it: "Nothing happens by chance..." (136-12).

I'll illustrate with two contrasting personal examples:

On the negative side, my body has two sites of chronic physical weakness, both caused by injuries many years ago. Periodically, I reinjure or aggravate those areas so that I have a frequent reminder of these weaknesses. I accept responsibility for the injuries as well as for the frequent discomfort. They serve a useful purpose in my life — keeping me a regular swimmer, to mention just one. I still work at changing these painful conditions, and I have been moderately successful with both of them.

On the positive side, the opportunities to write two books on the Cayce philosophy seemed to fall into my lap. I didn't have to go through most preliminary agonies of trying to find a publisher and selling an idea. But I accept responsibility for creating these opportunities also. I didn't know they would be these books, or when they would be written, but I created the circumstances which culminated in my writing them, as I will describe later in this chapter.

A view that holds you responsible for your circumstances is not usually an easy one to accept, especially if you experience a lot of the "sling-and-

142

arrow" syndrome. As tough as things may be for you, it may be tougher to accept the idea that you have chosen your condition. Tougher yet may be figuring out what needs to be done to bring change about, and the toughest of all may be exercising the will to carry it out.

The idea that I am responsible for my circumstances became much more believable to me once I understood this next point: "Creating circumstances" doesn't necessarily mean just bringing into existence a specific set of conditions your mind and body desire. Rather it means setting in motion the conditions that will produce a result that will satisfy your ideal and purpose. It may be what you desire, if that's consistent with your ideals and your spiritual purpose, or the result may be different from anything you might have considered in advance. That's why it's often a challenge to mentally track backward from a current circumstance to find the cause you set in motion.

We tend to resist change because, as challenging as our circumstances may be, we are somehow being "rewarded" for staying with the seemingly undesirable circumstances. This is as true of illness and disability as it is of a work or relationship problem. One of our first steps after identifying a challenging condition, especially one of long standing, is to search deeply inside ourselves to discover "What is reinforcing me to hang onto that situation? What's in it that gives me comfort or gratification? What benefit results from it?" I am periodically forced to reexamine my physical problems with such probing questions. It helps to be able to look at the situation with perceptual openness, the willingness to look at things in new ways. Meditation can facilitate such perception.

Once you accept the burden of responsibility for being where you are — and take the credit and comfort when they are due — you can select circumstances you desire to change and can plan strategies for bringing about this change. You will be better able to create strategies for change if you understand the operation of "spiritual laws," often referred to as "universal laws."

Understanding the Laws of the Spirit

Most everyone realizes that a multitude of *"physical laws"* appear to govern — that is, help us explain, predict, and manipulate — the behavior of matter and energy in the physical world. Obvious examples are the laws relating to gravity and to the reflection and refraction of light. Understanding the law of gravity, for example, helps us not only to explain why rivers flow downstream, but also to design waterwheels, canal locks, and hydro-electric power systems.

As research unfolds in today's science and technology, what scientists over the years accepted as immutable physical laws no longer appear absolute and unchangeable. For example, physical laws once assumed that objects like rocks and chairs were "solid" matter with readily specifiable, constant properties. Then along came Einstein and his relativity theory with its conclusions that an object's mass is *not* constant and that mass and energy are in fact the same thing. Fields like particle physics and high energy physics turn our ideas of physical properties inside out, to the point where we must now qualify our statements of physical laws with specifications of the conditions under which they operate. (As an aside, the principles of modern physics look more and more like the principles of *meta*physics.)

Just as physical scientists attempt to identify physical laws and the principles under which they operate, scientists of the mind in fields such as psychology, psychiatry, and neurology try to find "*mental laws*" and their qualifying conditions. Such laws and associated principles are intended to help explain and predict human behavior as controlled by mental functions. For example, the mental "law" of behavior reinforcement holds that an individual is likely to repeat an action for which he or she is positively reinforced. Because of the complexity of the human mind and the comparative youthfulness of the research on it, such mental laws require even more conditional qualifications than physical laws.

If people were asked about "*spiritual laws*," many would probably cite either prohibitions such as the Ten Commandments or the Golden Rule, "Do unto others ..." God's universe is governed by spiritual laws most people know nothing about, although their lives respond to these laws continuously. These spiritual laws are absolute and immutable. Just as with physical and mental laws, whether we know about them or not, they still operate fully in our lives. How much more harmoniously we can live in God's universe when we understand and work *with* spiritual laws! For example, when we sincerely want to bring changes about in our life circumstances, we can best do so by cooperating with the laws that govern those circumstances.

These words written by spiritual teacher and mystic Emmet Fox in the 1930s reiterate the idea of personal responsibility, relating it clearly to the action of spiritual law — or simply "Law," in Fox's terms:

> There is no such thing as luck. Nothing ever happens by chance. Everything, good or bad, that comes into your life is there as the result of unvarying, inescapable Law. And the

only operator of that law is none other than *yourself.* No one else has ever done you any harm of any kind, or ever could do so, however much it may seem that he [or she] did. Consciously or unconsciously you have yourself at some time or other produced every condition desirable or undesirable that you find in either your bodily health or your circumstances today. You, and you alone, ordered those goods; and now they are being delivered. (From *Power Through Constructive Thinking*, p. 265)

Spiritual laws do not lend themselves to neat, logical organization and identification. Perhaps instead of God's providing us with a concise list of readily defined, mutually exclusive laws — such as the Ten Commandments — God prefers for us to discover them, label them if we must, and define them for ourselves as part of our individual spiritual journeys.

I will describe and illustrate four spiritual laws: the law of manifestation, the law of cause and effect, the law of abundance, and the law of ideals. Although I will present them one by one, they all operate simultaneously and continuously. In fact, when you imagine that one of the laws may not be operating, it's probably only because the effects of another law are being felt more strongly.

The law of manifestation. This spiritual law is embodied in the principle quoted dozens of times in whole or in part throughout the Cayce readings: *"... the spirit is life; the mind is the builder; the physical is the result"* (349-4). What this says to me is this:

1. *The spirit is life:* Everything that exists is of the one energy (which we may call Creative Force, Spirit, or God), and conversely, Spirit is the origin of everything that exists. The implication for taking charge of my life is vital: To change or create a circumstance in my life, I must address it first through the spiritual. The creative life force that is within the difficulty I encounter is the same life force that I'll use to create a solution.

2. *The mind is the builder:* The mind draws upon that infinite energy resource and shapes it to some thought-form through the action of the mind at both the conscious and unconscious levels. The thought-form is strengthened through repetition, strong emotion, clear visualization, and other more subtle aspects of the mind. Cayce's concept of the mind extends beyond today's

145

typical psychological definitions to a more all-encompassing "bridge" between spirit and substance.

3. *The physical is the result:* The thought-form dwelt upon by the mind may eventually be perceived in the physical world as an actual physical form, as an attitude or conscious idea, or as an action, influence, or effect. The physical result may be manifested through the exercise of *ordinary* physical processes (such as growing, assembling, or raining), equipment (such as factories, surgical instruments, or computer chips), and agents (such as yourself or another person). It may also be manifested through *extraordinary* processes (such as extrasensory perception, spontaneous manifestation, or laying on of hands). The physical result may occur after a long period of time or it may be instantaneous — or anything in between.

This law of manifestation suggests that, whether you are talking about an issue in a relationship or an ignition problem with your car, your circumstances result from what your mind builds on the foundation of the spiritual.

As suggested earlier, you can examine a disturbing or challenging situation to see what is reinforcing it, what is making it comfortable for you. For example, why would your mind build an ignition problem? Possibilities include: to give you a reason to ask others for a ride; to allow you to stay home and rest; to give you an excuse to buy a new car; to prevent you from sticking to an overdemanding schedule; and on and on. Motives of self-protection or self-esteem may have moved you to create circumstances in which they would grow. Your desire was deep enough that the spiritual connection was made, energy was given to it, and your mind operated on that energy, producing the ignition problem as one result. Sometimes, even when the physical circumstance appears negative (erratic ignition), what you discover as the hidden desire of the mind is really positive (the need to slow down, to take a rest, to let others help you). Your understanding of the operation of this "spirit/mind/physical" law will help you to find reasons for undesirable circumstances, as well as to change them.

The law of cause and effect. In its simplest form, this law says that every cause (action) has an effect (reaction). Stated the other way, every effect is preceded by a cause. One of Cayce's readings puts it this way:

> For, nothing — as is known in a causation world — happens of itself or without a cause. (1998-1)

146

This law as applied to human activity has many familiar forms and counterparts. One of the quotes most cited by Cayce is from Paul's letter to the Galatians: "... for whatever a man sows, that he will also reap" (Galatians 6:7 RSV). Two corollaries of this law of cause and effect frequently appear in the Cayce readings as "like begets like" (349-17) and "what ye expect ye receive" (954-5) — sometimes called the law of expectancy. The statement cited earlier — Nothing happens by chance (136-12) — is also a principle within the law of cause and effect.

The effect may occur long after the cause. The time period is God's time, not ours. In fact, the cause and effect may be in different lifetimes, in which case it is the law of karma — what is caused in one life without effect in that life will have its effect in a subsequent life. The word "karma" is often used as if it were only a negative condition — the negative effect of a negative cause, if you will. Karma may just as easily be a positive effect of a positive cause. For example, Mozart's early musical genius may have been karma from preparatory musical disciplines in previous experiences.

The law of abundance. This law, sometimes called the law of supply, takes several forms, but underlying all of them is the principle that there is no limit on the resources available to you. However, obtaining those resources depends on how you use what you have already been given. For example, in the Gospel of Luke, Jesus says:

> ... give, and it will be given to you; good measure, pressed down, shaken together, running over, will be put into your lap. For the measure you give will be the measure you get back. (Luke 6:38 RSV)

Do you notice the thread of cause and effect there also? Variations of this also appear in the Cayce readings:

> As ye apply, as ye make use of that in hand, more is given thee. For, day unto day is sufficient, if use is made thereof... (1206-13)

> How ... will ye use that which has and that may come from the use of the material gains? How hast thou used them in the past? (657-3)

Still other conditions on experiencing abundance are suggested in the

147

Cayce readings: the sincere seeking and following of the spiritual ideal in one's life; the giving of needed service to others; and the absence of self-indulgence or self-aggrandizement. Furthermore, abundance and supply apply to more than material possessions and financial resources. They apply equally to new ideas, talents, health, physical energy, and of course love. The only limitations on abundance are those that we ourselves impose.

The law of ideals. You've been introduced to the spiritual ideal and its counterparts in mental and physical ideals. Although your primary work with the ideal has been as your spiritual focus in meditation, the ideal plays a much more significant role in your life, being a tool for assessing your progress in life, for evaluating alternative choices, and generally for guiding your day-to-day behavior. You will soon experience using the ideal in such ways.

To me, the influence of the ideals is so pivotal in our lives that I consider it the basis of a spiritual law. It might be stated: We progress spiritually in our lives to the degree that we guide our lives according to our spiritual ideals. One of many Cayce readings on this law states it this way:

> ... what the [individual] may do with its abilities in the present experience will depend upon what the [individual] does about that which it chooses as its ideal in this present experience, and what it does about such an ideal in dealing with the problems that concern things, conditions, and individuals. (4082-1)

Each of the other three laws I've presented depends on the action of this law of ideals: their effect in your life is always influenced by whether your actions are or are not in accord with your spiritual ideal.

Because of the critical role of the ideal, I have suggested reviewing your ideals periodically, confirming that you have identified your lifetime spiritual ideal and making sure your working level ideals — spiritual, mental, and physical — are stated in terms relevant to your life. The following exercise provides such a review.

"Search Me!" Find your "bull's eye" worksheet on ideals (from Chapter 4) or whatever other lists you have made of your ideals.

Before meditating, read all the ideals and affirmations you have written, noting any changes you may want to make in them. You may also want to review the notes you made in the exercise in Chapter 4 about your personal heroes and your own gifts. See if your answers at that time still ring true.

In this meditation, you will check to see if the ideal you've been using is *still* the best for you. So set your notes and worksheet aside, as well as the words and feelings of the ideal with which you have been working.

Prepare for meditation in the style you are currently using. Then, for the concentration stage, use the word "love" and its feelings as your spiritual focus.

After concentration and mindfulness, offer a simple prayer for guidance on your spiritual ideal. Remain in the stillness for two or three minutes, being alert to any words or feelings that come to mind. The ideal you have been working with may come to you. If so, express thanks, set it aside, and continue to listen and observe. This is an opportunity to receive other messages about your ideal. Write down any that appear.

After this meditation is over, continue to watch your ideas and what happens in your environment over the next day or so. A message might come in thoughts, events, or feelings experienced outside of meditation.

If you perceived a change in your ideal — one that rings true with you — plan to make a bull's-eye chart with that new ideal, and redevelop whatever affirmations you need. Use this revised ideal in your subsequent meditations.

In a few months, repeat this "ideals checkup." After that, I recommend an annual checkup — maybe at the beginning of the New Year as the basis for new resolutions.

Empowerment Through the Spiritual Laws

The more you understand, accept, and cooperate with the spiritual laws, the more you will realize the power you have to create your own circumstances. This is true *empowerment* — the ability to plan, direct, and control your life for your own fulfillment through progress in spiritual growth.

Paradoxically, your ability to *control* your life is counterbalanced with

149

the need for *surrender* to a higher power — to God and to your ultimate spiritual ideal of oneness with God. In a sense, the more we "let go and let God," the more we realize we are ultimately in charge of our lives. *Creative meditation* can first awaken in you the wisdom to know what kind of future is best for you — a process of "surrendering to your good." Then, *creative meditation* can make available to you the creative force of the universe; spiritual laws can guide you in understanding how the force operates; and your personal spiritual ideal can enable you to draw the force into your own life and create circumstances consistent with your ideal and God's purpose.

The spiritual laws do not need to be invoked or put into operation — they operate all the time. We may ignore them, we may try to "beat" them, or we may cooperate with them. Regardless, they will have their impact on us. Cooperating with the laws is simply planning and performing our actions according to our understanding of how the laws work. If we want to do something more, we can affirm the operation of the laws and our trust in the outcome.

A detailed personal example is presented to illustrate the process of empowerment through cooperation with spiritual laws. The example will show how the laws work together, not one at a time as presented earlier. The situation is adapted from circumstances in my own life, although I have simplified it for purposes of this presentation. I will narrate it in the present tense to keep time sequences and processes clear. I apologize for the long personal story, but I can best illustrate the cooperative process in a setting I know best — myself. The story begins about eight years ago:

> I am considering a change of occupation for my approaching later years. In a couple of years at age 55, I will be able to retire from over 30 years in "big business," with adequate benefits and a reduced pension — a continuing income that would need supplementing. Now that I know about spiritual ideals and life purposes, I would like to move toward an occupation that not only makes effective use of my capabilities — especially my writing — but also permits me to work more openly with the Cayce-type philosophy. The new situation must be consistent with my lifetime spiritual ideal of "loving service."
>
> The law of manifestation leads me to plant this idea in spirit and then build it with mind. "The spirit is life" phase starts by talking it over with God in prayer and at the end of meditation, using my spiritual ideal as the focus. I try to be

receptive at all times — listening, observing, being patient, continuing spiritual study. A lot of self-analysis goes on during this period: How big a risk can we take as a family (there are three of us at home)? Do I just want a change, or is the spiritual orientation really vital? How will others be affected? Journal writing is very helpful during this period, as is dream recording and interpretation. I also have my first psychic reading.

"Mind is the builder" does not mean putting a lot of limits or labels on the idea, but affirming that the right occupation for me and the right living situation for my family are available. I ask if we should move from New Jersey to Virginia Beach and if working for A.R.E. is a possibility. I also suggest other locations and possibilities for professional work — the "research triangle" in North Carolina, for example. I affirm the capabilities and talents I would like to share —especially organizing and writing. I don't prescribe the settings (other than mentioning the A.R.E. "if it is Your will"). Through all this, I continue to affirm (and confirm) my ideal. Meditation is my fundamental discipline throughout this process.

Considering the law of abundance, I know that there is no lack of financial supply to adequately supplement our retirement income. My wife and I agree on living within a moderate income — much lower than the current one — keeping in mind that we have a permanent dependent in our daughter Lyn, who is mentally retarded. We are not seeking any form of "self-aggrandizement." I examine whether I have been a good steward of my resources —my capabilities as well as my finances. Have I been using these resources in "loving service"? I have given many years of unstinting, loyal, and loving service to my employer. In my personal life, about two years ago, I made significant recommitments to my marriage and family, and initiated changes in attitudes and habits that refocused my attention on loving service at home.

As to the law of cause and effect, I focus a lot on "you get what you expect" and "you reap what you sow." I feel certain that the most suitable situation for me and my family will manifest. It's difficult to express how strongly I believe that. With that faith is also the paradoxical idea of surrender. I am so sure the right thing will come about, that I can "let go and let God," without putting any qualifications on my expectations.

An example of sowing in order to reap, as well as of abundance: On my job, I accept some responsibilities not normally mine — responsibilities to help my department out of a bind and, in fact, to help several individuals in major career decisions — like "Should I shape up, should I stay and get fired, or should I leave?" (I am not consciously seeking assignments to demonstrate loving service — they come to me, one after the other, during this period when I am especially focused on my ideal.)

Throughout this period of a year or more of "creating my future," I have many opportunities to contribute to this spiritual preparation, as well as to see signs of confirmation that I am on the right track. Many remarkable "coincidences" occur. During it all, I continue to affirm my faith in this process and my willingness to let God be my guide. Meditation is a primary means both for sustaining my inner calm and for being open to God's guidance.

Later, during the period in which my circumstances have begun to change, I take the opportunity to explore my soul's purpose through Mark Thurston's teaching and writing (see Thurston's *Soul-Purpose: Discovering and Fulfilling Your Destiny*). My mission in life appears to be "to communicate spiritual truths in ways that will further the cause of peace and justice." My lifetime ideal is frequently confirmed as loving service, with the reminder that loving service begins at home!

What were the results of this extended effort? I contributed significantly to my present circumstances with that effort begun eight years ago. Understand that some conditions were set in motion long before (e.g., my lifelong interest in writing, my prior employment resulting in generous retirement benefits, and an extraordinary marriage relationship that has accommodated several radical adjustments in our lives and circumstances).

The results included some circumstances more fulfilling and beneficial than I had imagined, as well as several others never anticipated, but replete with loving service opportunities. Here are just three examples:

- The opportunity to work at the A.R.E. in two very different capacities, one particularly oriented to service within the organization which also allowed me to move from full-time to part-time employment, as a transition to full-time work at home.
- The opportunity to take on a full partner share of home responsibilities, including not only the supervision of our daughter, but also the care of an elderly parent who now lives with us. ("You want opportunities for 'loving service in the family'? All right, you have your wish.")
- The opportunity to write two books, back to back, based on the Cayce philosophy, one of which emerged from a newly experienced area of loving service: aging, the elderly, and those who care for them.

This partial list of results illustrates the reason for the admonition: "Be careful what you wish for — you may get it!"

As you become aware of other spiritual laws, you will increase your own potential for empowerment — taking greater control of your life by cooperating with the laws through the help of *creative meditation*. Maybe we should label a new coping strategy "Empower Yourself!"

"Try Me!" You now have an opportunity to take the first step toward being in charge of your life.

1. Select a circumstance or condition in your life that you have tended to accept as out of your control. Self-Inventory 1 may remind you of several such circumstances. Don't choose the most severe condition, nor one that is trivial, but one over which you would like to have power.
2. Describe the circumstance or condition in detail. Who have you felt was responsible? When did it begin? How has it affected your life? What would happen if it changed or disappeared?
3. As the basis for your empowerment, consider all four of the spiritual laws discussed. You may choose to concentrate on only a couple of them, although all of them (and others) will be operating. The law of ideals will be essential to your success in bringing about change.
4. Develop a plan for changing your selected condition, meeting the requirements of each law. Use *creative meditation* to develop your ideas and strategy. Write out a brief plan of action.
5. Using *creative meditation*, put your plan into action — if you dare. And why shouldn't you? If you feel you have no control

right now, what can you lose? And you will not lose, although you may not be completely successful in your first experience. Remember the analogy about trying to play Bach or Beethoven after your first music lesson!

The next two chapters will present specific strategies for taking greater control of your life: the first for using inner guidance in solving problems and making decisions; the second for healing the hurts of your life, mental as well as physical.

You're on your way to becoming a new style of "take charge" individual. That term sometimes implies a presumptuous, impatient, authoritarian person with exalted ideas about leadership. That's not for you! Your style is that of an individual empowered to take responsibility for your own life, all of it, in a thoughtful, thankful, spiritual manner, ready to create the circumstances that will allow you to follow your ideals. Does that sound like anything you want to happen?

To replace all those scapegoats you used to have, I offer this piece I wrote for myself after my own "grand illumination" about responsibility:

WHERE HAVE ALL THE SCAPEGOATS GONE?

I wasn't satisfied with yesterday,
Although I played creator for it
Just the day before.

I used to think that others were the cause
Of many of my problem situations,
And often did I blame the circumstances
That were way beyond my personal control.
It often seemed I was the victim
Of "a cruel fate," "a heartless God," "the times"...
And though my talents cried for recognition,
How could I rise if others kept me down?

But now I've come to realize
That what I first create within my mind,
That what I think about and dwell upon,
Will someday be in my reality.

So when I see myself as helpless victim,
Being pushed around by circumstance,
I now remember who has set this up,
And that I have no one to thank but me!

I wasn't satisfied with yesterday.
I have a lot to do today
To set up my tomorrow.

Chapter 11

Being Psychic and Sensible, Too

"I was sorry to hear your mother died."
"Thanks. She was a wonderful person, but frankly, it's a relief not having her tell me how to run my business and my life."
"How *is* business?"
"So-so. But I just got some wonderful advice from a psychic. Can you imagine? She channeled a message especially for me."
"Did she tell you her source?"
"Sure. It was my mother!"

When we don't know much about psychic ability, we may assume that everything coming from psychic sources is accurate and worthwhile. That assumption may lead us to accept psychically received information uncritically — just as we probably accepted what mother told us when we were children.

Information professed to be for our guidance and well-being is readily available these days from an abundance of psychic sources — through individuals labeled "psychics," "psychic counselors," "readers," and "sensitives," and through esoteric systems and devices as diverse as astrology, numerology, palmistry, Tarot, regression, I Ching, and Viking runes. If we perceive such ready guidance as infallible, we may tend to relinquish responsibility for some of our decisions and actions by yielding to a wisdom "out there" that seems bigger than life. In fact, the source may be smaller than life, and the information may have deteriorated as it filtered through the interpreter, resulting in guidance less valid than what we can receive directly ourselves. The quality of the music you hear over the radio is no better than the quality of the original performance or the quality of the radio receiver system.

This does not mean we should abandon the idea of receiving information through outside psychic sources. It does mean that we should use caution and common sense in evaluating and using such information. We can, however, learn to be our own best psychic — and *creative meditation* can play a significant role in the process.

We will first explore what "psychic" really means, so you can see how it applies to you as well as to others. We will also profile several frequently used esoteric arts and sciences, such as astrology and numerology, I Ching and Tarot, defining terms like "oracle" and "synchronicity" along the way. Then we will weave these different threads into a special *creative meditation* process that encourages you to combine psychically received information with knowledge from your conscious mind and information from other outside sources, thus allowing you to be psychic and sensible, too, as you take charge of your life.

"What Do You Mean — Psychic?"

The word "psychic" is a direct descendent of the Greek word *psychikos*, meaning "of the soul," which is part of the first definition of "psychic" in the *Random House Dictionary* and is exactly the way Cayce defined the word (e.g., 513-1).

Defining *psychic* as "of the soul" is helpful only if you have some concept of what the soul is. For our discussion, your *soul* is an inner spiritual nucleus that holds the God-like qualities and capabilities you are learning and accumulating through your experiences on earth. A Cayce reading says that the soul is "the God-part in thee, the *living* God" (262-77). The definition of "psychic" suggests then that, since you have a soul, you are psychic. The more highly developed you become spiritually — that is, in soul development — the more your psychic abilities may manifest themselves.

As you develop qualities consistent with your spiritual ideal and demonstrate their action in your life, those qualities "reside" in your soul. The

158

unique pattern of soul qualities you have developed over the period of your soul's existence in the cosmos is called by Cayce your *individuality*. Other qualities that you develop — the traits you exhibit for others to see and recognize as you, the habits and attitudes you develop to meet the circumstances of this life — are all part of your *personality*.

How do "soul" and "psychic" relate to meditation? In preparing for meditation, you try to awaken and exercise those inner qualities of your soul that constitute your individuality. They will facilitate your attunement with God. Your attempts to clear petty and unspiritual thoughts from your mind and to focus on your spiritual ideal in *creative meditation* are efforts to raise your consciousness to your soul level. Then, at the soul level, your vibrations begin to approach the high vibrations of God. In my conception, when your vibrations reach a high enough level, entrainment occurs and you may sense oneness with God at that moment. When you are in contact with God — that is, with all universal energy and consciousness — you may obtain information from God and other higher sources according to your attunement. At such times, you are exercising one function of your psychic ability.

Contact may also be made with other sources in spirit, instead of directly with God. This includes, according to Cayce, guides, angels, other evolved spiritual entities, and also entities that are not highly evolved. Sometimes the sources may identify themselves, as the "Brothers" did for Ray Stanford, and as "Michael" did when he occasionally spoke through Edgar Cayce. We invoke a prayer of protection in meditation to protect ourselves from influences by spiritual beings who are not at higher vibrational levels "near the throne of God."

So where does that lead us? "Psychic" means "of the soul," which in turn means "pertaining to those God-like qualities in your inner spiritual nucleus." If you are seeking psychic guidance, you are looking for information and direction with the help of those inner qualities that bring you close to God. That suggests you can go directly to God for guidance — that you need not use a psychic agent who goes to God for you.

This also suggests that if a psychic does not make the connection through the psychic's own soul and its pattern of God-like qualities, the information the psychic receives and reports may be from sources other than God, and perhaps considerably lower in vibration than God. Even a person who has high spiritual ideals and a proven "track record" as a psychic sometimes experiences periods when the psychic ability is not operating. Also, psychics may be more gifted in obtaining information about some subjects than about others — for example, more skilled at obtaining physical health information than past-life information. In such situations, information given by the psychic may simply be stimulated by his or her imagination.

This leads to two important principles on obtaining psychic guidance through another person. First, the psychic's own personality and spiritual development influence the sources to be reached and the manner in which the information is communicated. Second, the range of sources for information is very wide — from the ultimate source in God to entities severely limited in their capacities and understanding. Every effort must be made to obtain guidance only from highly evolved sources, if not from God Himself. These principles can be expressed as questions about the psychic:

1. Do the thoughts and actions expressed by the psychic reflect the use of spiritual principles and "God-like qualities" in the psychic's own life? In other words, is this psychic likely to become attuned to our common Primary Source, or at least to a source of very high vibration? And will the psychic's "reading" be presented through attitudes uncontaminated by biases and stumbling blocks in the psychic's own personality?

2. What spiritual sources does the psychic reach? What kinds of spiritual entities channel through the psychic? Are they of high vibration?

These are not simple questions to answer about someone else, especially if you know nothing about the psychic and his or her life. Yet, without assurance about the source and about the influence of the psychic on the reported information, you must be especially cautious in making decisions or choices based on that information.

Instead of abdicating to outside sources of psychic guidance, why not become your own channel, using *creative meditation* as part of your preparation? When asked how best to develop psychic talents, Cayce's answer emphasized "keeping in close association and communication with those inner forces in self, as is found in entering into the silence at the periods as have been set" (5424-1) — in other words, through regular meditation.

The "Esoteric Arts and Sciences"

The word "esoteric" truly fits systems like astrology and numerology, and oracles like I Ching and Tarot: They are, as the word implies, understood only by the "select few" who have special knowledge about them. If you're not really "into" astrology, for example, listening to two astrologers talk can be like listening to a foreign language. Most of the esoteric systems are not for the casual or the dilettante. They require serious, patient study and application.

The Greek root *esoterikos*, meaning "inner," gives another connotation to the word: pertaining to information which is subjective (inner) rather than objective (outer). The validity of esoteric information cannot be proven in advance of the results any more readily than you can prove in advance the advice of a stockbroker, a psychologist, or a physician. In all cases, the professional collects available information and evidence about a personal problem or a situation and then applies principles and guidelines from the relevant "science" and from the professional's own knowledge and experience, tempered with intuition. The physician and psychologist may have more scientific, research-based data supporting their diagnosis and recommended treatment, but the advice to the individual is still subjective. Probably the most effective practitioners in all these professions are those with the most highly developed intuitive skills.

The Cayce readings address the question of how much credence to give esoteric information. Cayce was asked to what extent palmistry, for example, may be relied upon. His response applies, he says, more broadly than to palmistry:

> ... in regard to any and every omen [esoteric sign], it is an indication — yes. As to whether or not it will come to pass depends upon what the [individual] ... does *about* [what] it knows in relationship to itself. It may be depended upon, then, about twenty percent as being absolute — and about eighty percent "chance" or what a body does with its opportunities. (416-2)

The greater contribution to what happens comes from "what we do with our opportunities"— that is, from our free will, if we will only use it wisely.

The guidance process in *creative meditation* allows you to incorporate information from esoteric sources. We'll take a quick tour of several of these esoteric arts and sciences, noting what each may contribute to a guidance process.

Psychic readings. The previous discussion about psychics may discourage you from using another person as a channel for psychic information. My purpose was one of caution rather than prohibition. If you are considering obtaining a psychic reading, here are some suggestions:

- Find out in advance as much as you can about the psychic so you can address the two kinds of concerns expressed earlier — how the psychic's own life reflects higher principles and from what sources of information the psychic draws.

- Write your questions for the psychic clearly and without suggesting alternatives or answers, if you can. Appropriate for a psychic reading are questions about your soul's purpose in this lifetime, past lifetimes, health concerns, relationships, and even the future.

- If you are present at the reading, and if the psychic's information doesn't seem responsive to your question, ask for more information or ask the question in a different way.

- Record the questions and the psychic's responses on tape so you can listen to the information more carefully at your leisure. It may be helpful to transcribe the tape for ease of study and reference.

- Summarize the information, answers, and suggestions by the psychic in your own words. This will help you realize what is clear and what is not clear, and will facilitate using the information in a guidance process like the one to be described.

Astrology. Astrology is surely the most misused, misunderstood, and maligned esoteric system. Probably the most frequent misuse of astrology is the labeling of everyone exclusively by one of 12 sun signs — Aquarius, Pisces, Aries, and so on — followed by a detailed character analysis based on profiles of their signs.

The foundation of an individual's astrological identity is a lot more than the sun sign; that identity is based on the unique pattern of energy into which the individual was born. That pattern is determined by the positions of *all* the planets in the solar system, *plus* the moon and sun, at the exact time and place of birth. The primary aim of astrology is to identify an individual's predispositions and tendencies created at the moment of birth by the existing patterns of energy. A great many of the Edgar Cayce readings, primarily the "life readings," include astrological information on tendencies and predispositions.

Astrological readings may include three kinds of information: (a) the astrological data itself — the signs, the aspects (e.g., conjunctions, squares, and oppositions), the transits, and sometimes the progressions; (b) an interpretation of the patterns within that data; and (c) suggestions for the subject's subsequent planning and action. To the person untutored in astrology, the first type of information will be of little value, so the benefit rests entirely with the interpretation and recommendations, if given.

The first kind of information — the astrological data — can readily be generated by computer, as can a primitive kind of interpretation. As with psychic readings, the astrologer's own motivations and ideals can influence the interpretation of astrological data. The most helpful interpretations and suggestions require a talented and intuitive astrologer-counselor who selects the most helpful, relevant information and relates it to known facts about the counselee's life.

What are sometimes expressed as astrological predictions are not really predictions; they are the logical outcome of current trends, expressed as probable events if the trends continue without disruption. The object of astrological counseling is to provide insightful information concerning these trends and predispositions, so the counselee can choose actions that will either go along with or go counter to the apparent trend. The counselee always has control over future events through the activation of free will.

Remember that the information from even the most gifted astrologer is not a form of divine guidance to be followed blindly. You are never relieved of your responsibility for choosing your actions through your own free will, even if you have the best astrological reading (or psychic reading).

I find the book by Myrna Lofthus, *A Spiritual Approach to Astrology,* very helpful in interpreting my own astrological readings, because of its spiritual bias and its foundation in the astrological information from the Cayce readings.

Numerology. This esoteric system is less popular than astrology and also less ridiculed by the uninitiated. It is probably no less ancient than astrology, having a significant bond historically, for example, with the Jewish Kaballah. Many non-numerologists acknowledge the significance of certain numbers. For instance, in both the Old and New Testaments, the number seven — probably signifying completeness and perfection — appears many times as a significant number, as well as do multiples of seven —e.g., 49 and 70 and "70 times 7."

Because of its less complex structure than astrology, numerology is easier for the amateur to learn and use, given an excellent textbook or teacher. I find the two-volume series by Matthew Oliver Goodwin, *Numerology: The Complete Guide*, an excellent, easy-to-follow reference. The elements needed for personality profiling are the day, month, and year of birth, and the complete name, preferably as written on the birth certificate (with the exception of adopted children). The letters of the name are converted to single digits by a standard table, and then those digits and the digits of the birth date are used in various combinations to arrive at specified sums that represent, for example, the life path, the expression (the individual's potential natural abilities), the soul urge, the karmic debt, and the challenge (an obstacle encountered in the early years of life). More advanced numerology combines the above elements with other dates and data such as address and telephone numbers. For guidance purposes, these advanced calculations may be more helpful than the basic personality data.

Oracles. Did you know that the words "Know Thyself" were apparently engraved in ancient Greek over the door at the renowned Oracle of Apollo at Delphi? I take that as a reminder that, even with the most inspired type of guidance, we must still decide how it fits with what we know about ourselves.

An *oracle* is sometimes defined as a divine revelation or communication, often in obscure or ambiguous form. If we accept "divine" as meaning "operating through Spirit," I'll accept that definition. To explain how an oracle such as I Ching works, I also need to explain the concept of "*synchronicity*," a term created by physician-psychologist Carl Jung.

Start with the idea of a meaningful coincidence: I was considering using some Biblical-period Cayce readings as a basis for writing a fictional treatment of John, the disciple of Jesus. I had not discussed this with anyone other than my wife. In one week, three different people spontaneously mentioned something to me about the Gospel of John! Another example: My wife went to the library at a time when we were considering a move from New Jersey to Virginia as part of our change in circumstances. Having asked for guidance, she picked up a children's book at random and opened it to a paragraph that said, literally, "Go south and plant new crops"!

According to the Jung definition, another element must be identified before classifying either of these situations as synchronistic: a subjective, mental state relating to the objective event must be present in the observer. In the example on writing about John, my mind — at both conscious and subconscious levels — was developing and sorting out many different ideas about short stories or a full-length book on John. This inner focus was the subjective state to which Jung referred. In the library example, my wife's mental state included serious concern about the potential move. The connection between the inner state and the outer event is *not* one of cause and effect. The inner state did not cause the three people to tell me about John, or cause my wife to pick up and open the book. The principle is *a*causal — meaning without cause — but of equal importance to the principle of physical causality. Jung points out that Chinese thought gives the acausal principle the same importance we give the causal one.

Synchronicity is the principle underlying oracles such as the I Ching and Tarot. As you will see, synchronicity can play several significant roles in the psychic guidance process.

I Ching. This ancient Chinese "Book of Changes" may be the oldest written document on the planet. The earliest ideas in it may be even older, having come from elders of Siberian nomadic tribes that sired both the Oriental and the Native American cultures. The first set of 64 "hexagrams" — each a microcosmic view of life — were created about 4,800 years ago. These simple six-line symbols encapsulated the ideas from the oral tradition into archetypes of how things are in the world according to universal principles and laws. On one hand, the hexagrams and the several traditional "commentaries" that have become associated with them over the centuries comprise a book of universal wisdom and metaphysics that can be studied in its own right. On the other hand, if the book is consulted as an oracle, it is a remarkable system for getting guidance on any subject.

The traditional method for consulting the I Ching was a complex manipulation of 50 yarrow sticks. The ritual of sorting, laying them out, and counting them provided an interval of time for the seeker to fix the concern or issue clearly in mind, almost in a meditative way. The most frequent modern method for consulting the I Ching requires only three coins of the same denomination and a set of rules for throwing and reading the coins, which lead the seeker to either one or two hexagrams for study and interpretation.

Carl Jung was particularly impressed with the I Ching as an oracular system, relating its functioning to his principle of synchronicity. The concern you hold in mind as you throw the coins and draw the hexagrams is the necessary inner state; the results of the coin tosses (and thus the selected hexagrams) are the outer events. I find the I Ching to be a useful trigger for ideas and often surprising considerations in my own psychic guidance experiences.

Many readily available books teach interested individuals how to consult the I Ching. A number of novices have found, as I have, *The I Ching*

Workbook, by R. L. Wing an effective way of learning and practicing the system. Several traditional translations are available — for example, that of Richard Wilhelm and Cary F. Baynes with a foreword by C.G. Jung — as well as some recent new translations. Attempts have been made to relate the original ideas and symbols to today's circumstances and challenges. A book by Guy Damian-Knight, for example, adopts a form and language applicable to today's business organization, with advice on investment, marketing, advertising, sense of timing, and risks, among other considerations (see *The I Ching on Business and Decision Making: Successful Management Strategy Based on the Ancient Oracle of China*).

Tarot. This ancient system may have its origins in oral tradition 35,000 years ago! It is oracular in nature, but is more often referred to as a form of "divination" — a means for obtaining knowledge about the unknown or the future.

Tarot employs a series of 78 different cards, each of which can be interpreted in two ways: normal and reversed. The full meaning of the symbolism on each card is reputedly known only to highly developed souls, but texts are available for explaining the meaning and use of each of the cards in divination and guidance (for example, Eileen Connolly's *Tarot: A New Handbook for the Apprentice*). After the deck is prepared by shuffling and cutting and the seeker's questions have been written down, cards are drawn from the deck and laid out in a "spread" according to one of several traditional arrangements. The reading consists of interpreting the individual cards as well as some of the interrelationships among the cards. For this to be more than a superficial recitation of symbols and their meanings requires an interpreter familiar with some other esoteric systems, such as astrology, numerology, and parts of the Kabbalah, and with substantial experience in interpretation under a knowledgeable Tarot practitioner.

Viking runes. This form of oracle is of ancient origin but of recent accessibility. Without detracting from the system in any way, I see it as a "poor man's" substitute for the I Ching and Tarot: The 25 small "stones" with runic characters can be consulted like an oracle, but the interpretation is much more simple than the I Ching: One stone is drawn from a bag of stones; or several stones are drawn and laid out in a spread not unlike Tarot.

We are indebted to anthropology scholar-writer-publisher Ralph Blum for his effort in reviving the runes as an oracular system (see *The Book of Runes: A Handbook for the Use of an Ancient Oracle, The Viking Runes*). His interpretations of each character — and its reversal where it applies —

are both inspired and inspiring. Many individuals who find other esoteric systems too complex or time-consuming have found the runes a helpful, meaningful, synchronistic form of guidance. Other texts and workbooks have appeared in the wake of the recent new interest in these stones.

The Creative Meditation Approach to Self-Guidance

The guidance process I am about to describe is an extension of suggestions in the Edgar Cayce readings about solving problems and making decisions. To cover the wide range of situations to which the process applies, we will use the word "question" to mean the problem, the decision, the concern, or the issue on which you are seeking guidance. The word "answer" will refer to whatever guidance information emerges from the process. You are already familiar with all the principal elements of this approach:

- your spiritual ideal;
- a statement of the question(s) on which you seek guidance;
- information on the topic available to you from both inner and outer sources: experience, facts, opinions, psychic sources, esoteric arts and sciences, dreams, intuition, and synchronicity;
- a meditation process for attunement.

The recommended process has five phases, all essential to productive and valid self-guidance:

Phase 1: Preparation
Phase 2: Data Collection
Phase 3: Formulation of Answer
Phase 4: Evaluation of Answer
Phase 5: Follow-Through

As an overview of the process, each phase is first defined briefly, with references to the Cayce readings on guidance. Following the overview, a detailed example will be presented. Then you can work on a question of your own.

Phase 1: Preparation. The two principal activities in this phase are expressing the question clearly and completely, and reviewing your spiritual ideal, restating it if necessary to make it directly relevant to the question. The question should be stated in an open-ended manner that doesn't limit the possible answers. On the other hand, the question should not ask for everything on the issue to be resolved in one answer.

Your ideals will be used as a yardstick to measure your answer in the guidance process. Asked if the judgments made from information received in an introspective (meditative) process were valid, Cayce responded that they were when they were consistent with the ideals (1466-1).

Phase 2: Data Collection. This phase is pivotal to the rest of the process because, if you don't have the necessary information, you won't be able to formulate the best answer. The primary activity is gathering information from a variety of sources — both inner and outer. The amount of information should be appropriate to the importance of the question. The Cayce readings repeatedly emphasize first trying to get an answer "through [your] own mental reasoning" (1246-4), thoroughly analyzing the whole situation on the basis of all the information you can collect.

Phase 3: Formulation of Answer. This phase begins with summarizing and organizing the information collected. It is probably the most difficult because it is often a process of sorting through and analyzing a wide variety of different information, seeking common themes and the structure of an answer that may be buried in the data. The data may be weighed and prioritized as to credibility and relevance, sorted, and combined in several logical ways to develop the single best answer to your question.

Phase 4: Evaluation of Answer. Your "best answer" is measured against your ideal. If it is consistent with the ideal, the answer is then confirmed with God through meditation. For this purpose, the question is put into a yes/no form — for example, repeat your answer and add, "Is this correct?" or "Shall I do this?"

> Ask self in [your] own conscious self, "Shall I do this or not?" The voice will answer within. Then meditate, ask the same, Yes or No. You may be very sure if thine own conscious self and the divine self is in accord, you are truly in that activity indicated, "My spirit beareth witness with thy spirit." (2072-14)

If you cannot arrive at a single answer, you may develop alternative answers. Measure each answer separately against the ideal. Any answer not consistent with the ideal is dropped. Meditation is used to confirm or reject each of the remaining answers.

If you are left with several confirmed but seemingly contradictory answers, you may need to return to the initial question or to the data and make sure that the question is stated in the clearest possible way and that all summaries are valid based on the data you collected. By repeated recycling through the phases and steps, you should eventually be able to arrive at a single confirmed answer or a series of consistent, related answers.

Phase 5: Follow-Through. The guidance process is not complete until steps have been taken to put the answer into action. "Do not become one that asks and does not abide by the answers!" Cayce warned (1246-4). A final critical activity is observing the results of your guided actions for signs that either confirm or reject the results. Good solutions ought to bear good fruits for you and for everyone else involved in the situation. Synchronicities can provide clear signals of confirmation or rejection.

For those who find diagrams helpful, Figure 2 depicts the main steps just described.

My extended example of the guidance process is related to a challenging relationship with a work colleague whom I will call Charles. The example is based on past experience, but the details have been modified to simplify the example and to preserve anonymity. I will narrate it in present tense, identifying the phases as I go. You may find it helpful to keep track of my activities on the flow diagram in Figure 2. This example of the self-guidance process extends over about two weeks. The sentences and phrases in italics represent some of the notes I would write in my guidance process notes as I go along.

Phase 1: Preparation. I write my question as *"What can I do to overcome my feelings of resentment and anger toward Charles?"* This concentrates my efforts on the areas about which I have greatest concern — more so than "How can I improve my relationship with Charles?"

My lifetime ideal is *loving service*, and for guidance I adjust it only slightly to *loving service in my work relationships* for my working level ideal.

Phase 2: Data Collection. As part of the data collection, I search my own memory and feelings for relevant information. For example, how long have I been resentful or angry toward Charles? What circumstances trigger these feelings? What other circumstances or people in my life trigger similar feelings? What have I tried to do about them so far? What are the probable consequences of doing nothing about them? I write down the key facts and

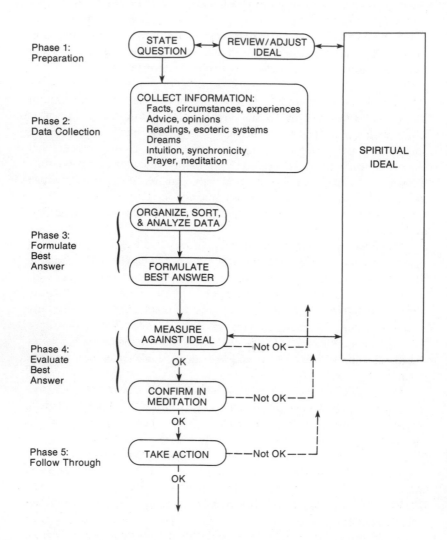

Phase 1:
Preparation

Phase 2:
Data Collection

Phase 3:
Formulate
Best
Answer

Phase 4:
Evaluate
Best
Answer

Phase 5:
Follow Through

STATE QUESTION

REVIEW/ADJUST IDEAL

COLLECT INFORMATION:
Facts, circumstances, experiences
Advice, opinions
Readings, esoteric systems
Dreams
Intuition, synchronicity
Prayer, meditation

SPIRITUAL IDEAL

ORGANIZE, SORT, & ANALYZE DATA

FORMULATE BEST ANSWER

MEASURE AGAINST IDEAL
Not OK
OK

CONFIRM IN MEDITATION
Not OK
OK

TAKE ACTION
Not OK
OK

Figure 2. Flow Diagram of Creative Meditation Self-Guidance Process

170

any insights I get by going through this process. For example, I write: *triggered when my boss or other supervisors commend his work and when he talks about himself; don't feel the same when others get praised; cannot work well together as long as I have these feelings; tried to bury my feelings and pretend everything is OK.*

I also gather both factual and opinion-based information from some mutual acquaintances who know that Charles and I have a difficult relationship. I ask if they sense my anger and resentment — they do. Do they have any opinions on what it comes from? One friend feels that Charles has some obnoxious traits, not directed exclusively toward me — for example, he's *got "a big mouth"* when it comes to his own accomplishments and activities. Also Charles *tends to "butter up" higher management.* Another friend says my feelings may come from the fact that *Charles is seen as high potential by upper management and I am seen as a strong team member and good contributor* — not singled out as high potential. Another friend says he thinks *I may not be getting along with Charles because I stay in the background too much. I need to challenge him sometimes, and I should let him know how I feel.*

I talk the situation over with my wife, who knows Charles and has heard my complaints. She reminds me of her occasional advice about Charles: *consider Charles as equal colleague, not as competitor.* My own opinion of what's happening includes these points: *Charles gets all the showy assignments* and *goes out of his way to be unpleasant and uncooperative with me.*

I have several astrology readings in file, and I also like to work with the I Ching and runes. In my astrology transcripts, for example, I find several helpful statements about interpersonal relationships; for example, *I tend to take interpersonal relationships for granted* and *I tend to back away from unpleasantness in relationships.* I add these statements and others from my readings to my guidance process notes.

I "throw an I Ching" related to my relationship with Charles. One of the hexagram themes jumps out at me and I write down: *only friends and immediate followers waste thoughts on one who dithers irresolutely to and fro.* This might refer to my "dithering" about working things out with Charles, or it may reflect Charles's opinion of me — I don't think Charles is "dithering irresolutely."

To get dream information on my question, I "program" a dream before sleeping. After the third night, I recall a dream as I wake up, and I write down as much of it as I can. In one scene, for example, Charles and I are sitting on a long staircase, Charles several steps higher than me. I am writing down

171

what Charles is saying, which seems to be in a foreign language. Is this a confirmation of his higher potential, or just a reflection of the remark my friend made. Is he talking above my head? Or is he talking gibberish? I probably need more dream information and other facts to interpret that appropriately. In my guidance notes for now, I just write *dream scene on stairs with Charles.*

One day driving to work, I suddenly remember an incident in which Charles made a technical comment that I thought was quite innovative. I also remember that I assumed he had picked up the idea from someone else. Later, I write that memory down as *innovative idea: was it his?* At another time, I go into a work project file for something and find instead a copy of a letter Charles had written in which he commended several people on the staff for their efforts on a particularly sticky problem. (I was not involved.) I add *Charles' commendation letter* to my list.

At the end of a regular meditation, I had a cartoon-like image of a man who might have been Charles, who had an enormous mouth and tiny eyes. This may have been a psychic impression, in symbolic form, of how my higher self perceives certain of Charles' characteristics. I note down *cartoon with big mouth, little eyes: Charles?*

I now have quite an assemblage of information — the preceding paragraphs illustrating only a sample of the notes and statements I collected. After about two weeks of data gathering, on and off, I decide I should sort out what I have and try to find an answer. I can always get more information later if I need it.

Phase 3: Formulation of Answer. One way I sort my data is according to whether it relates primarily to Charles, to me, to both of us, or to our relationship. (This way of sorting occurred to me after a meditation.) As a result of this sorting, I find I have two types of information about Charles: (1) a lot of unfavorable traits and opinions, my own included but not exclusively; and (2) some highly favorable traits and talents, unaffected by Charles' own opinions. I also get a good picture of my own weaknesses in this situation: backing away, taking relationships for granted, no indication of "high potential."

Another analysis pulled out everything that stimulates my anger or resentment. Still another pulled out everything that consists of advice or guidance of a positive nature, such as being more assertive with Charles, taking the initiative to build a better relationship, looking for his real talents and accomplishments.

I also sorted the information into outer sources and inner sources, to see if there was any difference in the message. In fact, much of the outer source data had a strong theme of rebuilding my relationship with Charles; the inner source theme had more to do with Charles' personality and talents. I may have been less open to hearing my friends talk about his talents, so that came more from inner sources — although not exclusively.

When formulating my best answer, I keep in mind what comes from factual data and what comes from opinions. I also give added weight to my inner sources. There was some information I couldn't fit anywhere, but I felt comfortable using what I did.

My best answer seems to be for me to *take the lead in building a new relationship with Charles, emphasizing openness between us and an honest recognition of Charles' talents.* I don't qualify the answer with any negative behaviors or traits of either of us, nor with a concern about the eventual result of such a relationship. Could I have reached this answer by simply thinking about it logically? Perhaps, but I had struggled with the relationship for many months and had some blind spots until I undertook this guidance process.

Phase 4: Evaluation of Answer. The first step in evaluating the answer is comparison with my working level ideal, *loving service in my work relationships.* Without having thought much about that ideal during the analysis and formulation of an answer, my answer seems especially consistent with the ideal. So that's a good sign.

The second step of evaluation is the critical one of getting confirmation of the answer after attunement to God. To get a confirmation, I need to express the answer as a yes/no question. I have my notes handy when I go into meditation. After attunement and a period of mindfulness, I read my answer and add: "Is this what I should do?" I wait for a confirming response of any kind. I sometimes get a clear rejection if I've missed the answer, but seldom do I get a clear confirmation at the end of meditation, even after asking in several meditation periods. I have learned to assume that, after about three tries, "no news is good news."

Phase 5: Follow-Through. So I proceed to the follow-through/action stage where I get confirmatory responses through synchronicity. For example, I go for my regular swim at the YMCA and encounter Charles, never having seen him there before. We exchange pleasantries. To me, a positive sign!

One of my first steps in carrying out my answer might be to become more familiar with what Charles has accomplished. Another would be to initiate some social time with him — over lunch, for example. When we are at lunch for the first time, Charles expresses concern over a major computer problem he has just experienced; I solved that same problem for myself before

173

breaking for this lunch — synchronicity rides again!

That completes my personal example. Now it's your turn!

"Try Me!" For the first time through the self-guidance process, select an issue that is significant to you, but not life-affecting — more significant than what you should have for dinner and less significant than making a career change. You may want to choose a relationship issue, paralleling my example above. Later, as you become more experienced and confident, you will be ready to tackle highly significant questions you face.

You may find it helpful to prepare worksheets for your activities, especially for summarizing the data you collect. You can use the headings on the flow chart as headings on your worksheets.

Enjoy the process. Feel free to adapt it to your own inclinations and needs. You'll use it only if you find it practical for you, as well as helpful in its results.

Below are several pointers you may find instructive as you work through your first guidance example. Or they may be relevant only on later experiences. Or you may never need them. Use them accordingly.

Preparation ideas:
- As you develop your question, a series of related questions may come to mind. Start with "first things first" — the question that must be answered first. Work through other questions later — if they still exist. Or you may choose to work with several related questions at once, evaluating each of them separately in the fourth phase.

- The main concern about the ideal here is whether or not in its present form it can be used as a yardstick for the answer you get to your question. That is, will you be able to say that an answer is consistent with your ideal? If not, adjust the words or add specificity so you can.

Data collection ideas:
- As you make notes of information gathered, don't be concerned about style and form. Get the points down in whatever words and phrases come to you. Include any insights you get as you collect your data.

- Readings by others — for example, psychic, astrological, or Tarot readings — may be simply another form of outer source information, unless you feel assured about its spiritual grounding. On the other hand, readings you give yourself — such as I Ching, runes, or your own numerology reading — may be considered inner sources if you feel strongly influenced by your intuition.

- Your dreams may give you some of the most valuable guidance from your inner source, because they often reveal information you get no other way — options you would not think of, alternatives you prefer not to consider, surprises, and cautions, for example. For instruction and guidance on recording and interpreting dreams, I recommend *Dreams: Tonight's Answers for Tomorrow's Questions* by Mark Thurston and *Getting Help from Your Dreams* by Henry Reed. Also Reed's videotape, *Dream Interpretation Workout* is a very useful, step-by-step guide to help the viewer interpret one of the viewer's own dreams from several perspectives.

- Discerning between intuition and wishful thinking is a challenge. If you can avoid giving form to any predetermined alternatives, you are less likely to experience the effects of wishful thinking.

- In the later evaluation step, prayer and meditation will be used to confirm or reject the final solution. In data collection, however, information may emerge spontaneously in the silences of regular prayers or meditation periods, perhaps indistinguishable from intuitive information.

Answer formulation ideas:
- There is no best way to organize, sort, or analyze the data collected. The form, diversity, and amount of data will all vary widely according to the issue and how much effort you give to it. Consider the following ideas: (a) Your question may provide clear categories or dimensions for your organizing of data, such as it did in my example. (b) If the issue has two or more clear alternatives, try sorting the information according to which alternative it supports. (c) Assign weights to various kinds of information, according to its credibility for you. For example, mark with a plus sign (+) anything with high value for you, with two pluses (++) anything of really high value. Use minus signs (– –) on anything you feel should not weigh heavily in the answer. (d) Consider summa-

rizing separately the data from outer sources and that from inner sources and compare them. They may provide different, but compatible answers, as in my example.

• Watch for guidance on the process itself — that is, how to analyze your information — at the end of meditation periods, through intuition, or through synchronicity. In other words, you may be guided in how to find an answer, as well as in the answer itself.

• If no answer is clear to you, you must either collect more information — especially from inner sources — or go back to the beginning and revise your question. On the other hand, if several possible answers emerge, you may collect more information or change the question or proceed to the evaluation of answers, checking each of the acceptable alternatives in turn.

Answer evaluation ideas:
• When you prepare to seek confirmation of the answer in meditation, it should be framed in a form requiring only "yes" or "no" as an answer. It will be easier for you to detect a simple confirmation or a rejection, than to receive a detailed reply of substance.

• Designate one or more meditations for this confirmation process — I suggest three times. These can be regular meditation periods, extended by a few minutes at the end. Set aside the question and the entire guidance issue during attunement (remember, attunement first!). After the concentration stage with the spiritual ideal as the focus and a minute or two in mindfulness, state your tentative answer along with a yes/no question, such as "Is this correct?" or "Shall I do this?"

• Be sensitive for any symbol, word, or feeling that indicates either "yes" or "no" to you: It could be the actual word "yes" or "no" visualized or heard inwardly, an image of approval or disapproval (e.g., someone smiling or frowning; someone nodding the head "yes" or shaking the head "no"; flowers springing up or flowers dying; etc.), or a feeling that "things are OK" or that "things are not quite right."

• When you first try this guidance process, you may not receive a clear answer in the first few meditations. Be persistent and keep trying in your meditations. Since you haven't had a negative response, you may want to assume the "no news/good news" position like I do, and go on to take initial actions — something not too momentous. The answer may appear through intuition or synchronicity later in the day.

• If the answer is rejected, you must return to previous steps — perhaps all the way back to rethinking the question.

• If you see that your answer has several steps or facets to it, you may want to formulate a sequence of questions to be evaluated. I would probably divide my final question and answer into two parts — the first on my taking the lead, the second on openness and recognition.

Follow-through ideas:
• The industrious Shaker communities deserve the credit for the saying: "First you move the Spirit, and then you move your feet." That principle applies perfectly in the guidance process. Action then may be accompanied by indicators of either confirmation or nonconfirmation: In my case, either the way seems to unfold before me, clearing anticipated obstacles, or the way is cluttered with hindrances of all sizes and difficulties.

• When you make plans to take action based on your answer, don't begin with the biggest, most irreversible step. For example, don't quit your job or sell your house immediately. Start with smaller but still definite steps. That allows time for signs of confirmation or nonconfirmation to take place before you pass the point of no return in your actions.

That completes the five-phase process of guidance using both psychic and sensible sources and methods. Just ahead lies another way *creative meditation* can help you take charge of your life — self-healing.

Chapter 12

"Meditator, Heal Thyself!"

"You should be feeling great, getting rid of your asthma all on your own."

"Physically I feel fantastic! But sometimes I think I'm missing something."

"You probably miss how everyone used to fuss over you when you got an attack."

"No, but I miss complaining about how big my medical bills were and how little the doctor was doing for me. Now the only one I can complain about is me."

The ability to take charge of your own circumstances is another "good news/bad news" paradox: The good news is that you can always take some action to have greater control — to reduce your challenges, to accept more peace and contentment in your life. The bad news is that you have no one to blame if circumstances don't improve. This is as true for your physical and mental health as it is for your relationships, your debts, and your work situation.

The guidance process in the preceding chapter can help you diagnose and receive helpful information on your health problems, especially those founded in your attitudes and emotions. As medical science recognized the relationship between mind (psyche) and body (soma), the field of psycho-somatic medicine evolved. And now we have the field called "psychoneuroimmunology" — a wonderful, rhythmic word, one that eclipses even "epidemiology." This new field combines three disciplines: psychology, neurology, and immunology. The research in these fields suggests that virtually every physical ailment may be rooted in psychological causes. If you add spiritual and karmic causes to emotional-psychological causes, you probably account for 100 percent of all disease and injury as well.

This chapter will add to your *creative meditation* repertoire the ability to facilitate your own mental and physical healing. After some fundamental guidelines for staying healthy, we will consider how healing relates to beliefs. Then I will present a unique approach for healing yourself and keeping yourself in good health — an approach that involves the seven spiritual centers.

Staying Healthy and Whole

Wellness in a healthy body is our natural state. This condition depends on our observance of some fundamentals that I will list here without discussion:

- A nutritious, well-balanced diet suited to your age, activity level, and lifestyle, emphasizing uncontaminated fresh fruits and vegetables, grains and legumes, fish and poultry, and plenty of good water.
- Regular, moderate exercise, also suited to your age, normal activity level, and lifestyle.
- Sufficient sound sleep, probably seven to eight hours daily.
- Regular, healthy eliminations.
- Good personal hygiene and grooming, especially skin, teeth, and hair.
- Management of attitudes and emotions, using effective techniques to release and transform feelings that are potentially illness-producing — feelings such as anger, guilt, fear, and hopelessness.
- Proper balance throughout your life — between work and relaxation/ recreation; among the physical, mental, and spiritual aspects of your life; between left-brain activities (language-related, logic, linear, organized) and right-brain activities (spatial, visual, intuitive, non-linear); among social activities, family/close relationship activities, and time alone.
- Clothing conducive not only to comfort and pleasant appearance, but also to proper circulation, energy flow, and mood control.

- Living accommodations that provide healthful light, good temperature and humidity control, air circulation, and privacy space.
- Personal growth and creativity opportunities.

Incorporating these fundamentals into your life will significantly increase the likelihood of your being healthy. Following through with *creative meditation* and the self-healing process to be described will not only increase that likelihood, but will help you overcome health concerns of every kind.

"As You Believe ..."

You now realize how much your beliefs can influence your control over your life. In Self-Inventory 4 (Chapter 10), three of the statements were directly related to your belief about your health — items 2, 5, and 10. How did you score on those items?

Because health is completely self-contained in us — that is, it is delimited by our own individual physical and mental states — it is a factor over which we can have greatest control. Furthermore, we can effect change more quickly and easily in our health than for issues involving other people and for activities such as relationships, finances, and employment. Although our health may be affected by some outside circumstances and people, we can take charge of our health unilaterally — that is, without the involvement of others. In a Cayce reading, a woman asked, "Is there [the] likelihood of bad health in March" (two months away)? Cayce's reply is a classic:

> If you are looking for it, you can have it in February! If you want to skip March, skip it — you'll have it in June! If you want to skip June, don't have it at all this year! (3564-1)

The fact that all disease comes from within and can be healed from within should not surprise us when we consider the law of manifestation: "the spirit is life; the mind is the builder; the physical is the result." In a reading addressing many basic concepts of healing, including the role of the spiritual ideal, Cayce says:

> Healing for the physical body, then, must be first the correct choice of the spiritual import held as the ideal of the individual. For it is returning, of course, to the First Cause, First Principles...

Do the first things first. Lay the stress on those things that are necessary. Remember ... all healing comes from within. Yet there is the healing of the physical, there is the healing of the mental, there is the correct direction from the spirit. Coordinate these and you'll be whole! (2528-2)

Even when we can accept our responsibility for our illnesses, it takes a little more faith and trust for us to accept the idea that the same law with its same responsibilities governs our accidents and injuries. Yet they may be even more critical for us to understand. A personal example will illustrate:

Recently, I was on the next-to-top step of an aluminum stepladder, trying to reinstall two pieces of wood paneling high on an interior wall of our screened-in porch. After several unsuccessful attempts, a strong intuitive message said, "Get down off the ladder." Ignoring that, I decided to give it one more try. The accident that followed was a remarkable experience: The aluminum ladder bent and collapsed under me. Time slowed to a crawl as I felt myself falling toward the cement floor below. I saw my glasses leave my face, I saw the hammer hit the floor, and I saw the box of nails scatter its contents on the way down. I think I shouted, "Oh, God, no!" and my thought was, "I don't want to get hurt!" My rear end took the first shock of the landing, and my back and head quickly followed. As I lay there, time resumed its normal pace.

My first thought before moving was, "Help me, God, not to be hurt." (You need to know that I have had more broken and cracked bones from falls in my lifetime than a team of competitive skiers.) My next thought was, "Why did I do this?" Several answers appeared. I considered them and responded, "I understand, but I don't need this!"

As I began mentally searching my body for injury, I knew I should immediately call the Glad Helpers' prayer chain and my chiropractor. Everything seemed to move without the pain I associate with broken bones. (My past experiences have *some* value.) I cautiously dragged my aching body across the floor through the door into the house where I managed to get up on my knees to reach the telephone. I made my calls, telling the chiropractor I'd get there somehow in the next hour. My wife arrived home just as I was trying to get into my van to drive myself.

To conclude this story: I did not break any bones, I was walking — slowly! — within 15 minutes, and I later had some lower body muscle and bone discomfort that limited some activities, but I was whole and able to function almost normally within days. I attribute my lack of serious consequences and my rapid recovery to my immediate, spontaneous prayers, the prayers of the Glad Helpers, the chiropractic treatment that I knew would help, the application of a castor oil pack (a frequent Cayce remedy) to my lower back all that night, plus — perhaps most significant — my immediate reflection on why I had taken the fall.

That analysis of cause was like a brief meditation as I lay on the porch floor, before I had the courage to move. I immediately accepted responsibility for the fall ("Why did I do this?") and searched for reasons relating to me and to anyone else who would be affected by my incapacitation. Several possible reasons occurred to me and, without selecting just one of them, I admitted how petty they were, asking that they not get in the way of my mobility and health. I urgently asked God to keep me from creating work or stress for my wife. I think my "responsibility analysis" indicated I truly did not need any injuries and that I had learned a lesson from the experience even without broken bones this time. That "owning up" is as important to recovery — and to prevention in other situations — as the healing prayer.

Healing takes place in accordance with our beliefs. This goes beyond the fact that I can bring about healing if I sincerely believe I can. If I believe surgery is necessary for certain conditions, then surgery will help in my healing; if I believe medication prescribed by a physician is needed, then it will help heal; and if I decide the chiropractor's skills are needed, I am healed accordingly. However, these beliefs are not acting in a setting where nothing else is going on.

As you now understand, the spiritual laws interact with one another; they do not operate singly or just during the time when you remember them. The spiritual laws are being expressed in you in several different conditions simultaneously. Bringing about a change through the action of one spiritual law may have no effect on the continuing actions of other laws. For example, suppose the cause/effect law has created a catastrophic illness, such as cancer, in response to a situation of hopelessness and repression. The illness may not respond to attempts for healing, in spite of intense beliefs in the self-healing process, even through the use of treatments believed in — if the healing process is not also directed at the underlying causes. After my fall, for example, I attended to the causes for the fall, as well as to the treatment of the body.

Our beliefs are based on our past experiences in large part, and since we differ from each other in those experiences, we differ in our beliefs about what will and won't work in healing. Of course, we can alter our beliefs given time and a justification for doing so. I certainly have altered many of mine over the past ten years, because I see the results of changed beliefs in others as well as in myself.

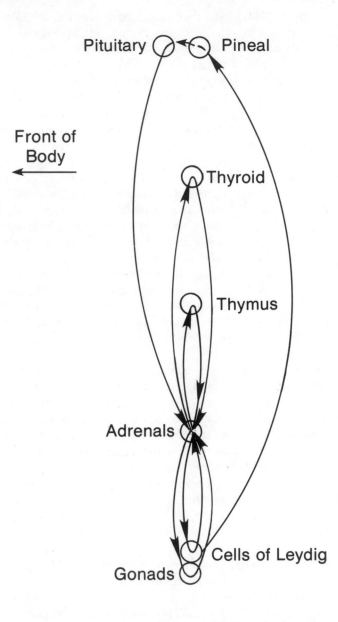

Pituitary ⭕ ◄ ⭕ Pineal

Front of
Body
←——

⭕ Thyroid

⭕ Thymus

Adrenals ⭕

⭕ Cells of Leydig
Gonads ⭕

Figure 3. Diagram of Energy Flow Through Spiritual Centers
During Meditation

As you read about and try the healing process I will present, you may find an immediate affinity to some of its ideas and activities, and want to experiment with them. Other ideas may not seem as credible when you read about them, but when you try them you feel a sense of possibility about them. I hope you will try them all with an open mind.

As you work with self-healing, keep in mind the interactive effects of all the spiritual laws. Although the healing process will focus your attention on the present conditions of body and mind, remember that those conditions are results of other causes, some of which are probably hidden deep within your consciousness. Begin the process by seeking guidance to understand and release yourself from those causes.

Self-Healing Through the Spiritual Centers

Several references have been made earlier in this book to the spiritual centers in the body (often called "chakras") and the flow of energy that connects them during meditation. Figure 3 depicts the relative positions of the spiritual centers in the human body (facing left in the figure), as well as the complex pattern of energy flow described in the Cayce readings.

Some inconsistencies. Although most knowledgeable individuals and many spiritual traditions identify seven spiritual centers/chakras, the sources differ in their association of glands with the centers, in their description of functions and ideas associated with each of them, and even in the pattern of energy flow. The model I describe is based primarily on the information in the readings by Edgar Cayce and the series of readings by Ray Stanford collected in *The Spirit unto the Churches: An Understanding of Man's Existence in the Body Through Knowledge of the Seven Glandular Centers*. Stanford's readings closely paralleled and expanded upon those of Edgar Cayce's.

I will often refer to a center by the name of an endocrine gland associated with it — the pituitary center, for example, or simply the pituitary. The centers are not just small points interior to the body. Every spiritual center is also associated with at least one major funnel-like vortex of energy, with its base at or near the gland and extending outward from the body into the etheric field.

Because the reader is likely to encounter other models of the centers/ chakras, I will address two areas of seeming discrepancy between the Cayce/ Stanford material and other sources, especially those drawing from Eastern traditions. These differences relate to the names and locations of the two lowest and the two highest centers/chakras:

1. The Cayce source refers to the second lowest center as the Leydig gland — actually the cells of Leydig — indicating that it is physically located in and above the gonads (the testes in the male, the ovaries in the female) and that the Leydig's activity (energy) passes through the gonads (281-53). Medical research has shown that the cells of Leydig are also found in the adrenals. I have heard it said that they may also be found in the spleen, which would be an interesting point because, in other chakra systems, the spleen is the gland often labeled as the site of the second chakra. Everyone seems to agree that there is a second center/chakra in the area of the lower abdomen, and this can be verified with the pendulum technique described by Barbara Ann Brennan (in *Hands of Light*, p. 81ff.). Which gland it is associated with seems less critical than the function it serves and how it operates in the center/chakra system, and that is more similar among systems than the labels.

2. All models identify two centers/chakras in the head, and most models associate them with the pineal and pituitary glands. Most systems other than the Cayce/Stanford model imply that the energy flows from the four lower centers through the thyroid and pituitary centers on the way to the pineal. The Cayce/ Stanford material, on the other hand, gives the pineal a special function as the "Appian Way" with a "long thread activity" that carries the energy directly from the Leydig/gonad centers to the pineal at the center of the brain (281-13 and -53). This direct connection is analogous to an express train originating at the cells of Leydig with its first stop at the pineal, skipping the intermediate stations of adrenals, thymus, and thyroid. That direct rise of energy to the pineal is essential: A kind of spiritualization of energy takes place at the pineal; if the energy were to rise sequentially through the other three centers, it might be transformed in undesirable ways or even blocked before reaching the pineal. From the pineal the energy flows forward to the pituitary — the master gland — located only a couple of inches in front of it, and then back down to the solar plexus/ adrenals. From there it is dispersed to all the other centers (281-

53). Figure 3 attempts to illustrate this complex energy flow. The sequence of the two highest centers is usually reversed in other models, the pineal being listed as the "highest" — the seventh counted from the gonads. Cayce acknowledged a possible reversal in his labels on these two centers (281-54), suggesting — as with the lower two centers — that it is less important what they are called or the sequence in which they are listed than how well we understand their function.

Regardless of what picture and set of labels you see for the centers/ chakras, keep in mind that the energy is not simply flowing in a simple loop up and down the centers. After attunement takes place, the energy flows in a series of loops — somewhat like "figure 8's" with the adrenals as a kind of distribution center at the center of the 8. Also, visualize that the energy flow is not only within the physical body, but flows in the aura, the etheric body, especially at the centers. The cells of Leydig, adrenals, thymus, thyroid, and pituitary centers all have major energy vortices extending both to the front and to the back of the body into the aura. The single gonad vortex opens downward near the base of the spine, and the single pineal vortex opens upward above the crown of the head.

A caution. In one of his readings, Cayce cautioned against working with the spiritual centers or other "structural portions" individually without fully understanding the "anatomical structure of the body":

> For, applying such would then become dangerous, unless there is the full comprehension, physically, mentally, spiritually of such structure, such functioning, such activities of a body.
> If the body finds in these, that which answers from within self, use it. If the body chooses to do otherwise, it is privileged to do so and pay the penalty. (3368-1)

It is beyond the scope of this book to provide you a "full comprehension" of such structures and functions, so you should approach this healing activity with caution and sensitivity. I believe, however, that the positive orientation of the healing technique presented here allows you to try the suggested activities and find out if they "answer from within self." I further believe that this approach is consistent with another Cayce principle: Mental suggestions (including affirmations) held in the mind with sincere intent (as in meditation) can stimulate healing, resuscitative forces. Here's how Cayce put it:

> ... the *mind* acts upon the resuscitating forces of the physical being, by and through suggestion... Thus a meditation, a centralizing, a localizing of the mind upon those portions of the system affected, or upon the activities needed for the physical being, *influences*, directs the principal forces of the system. And it does resuscitate, if kept in sincerity; not merely said as rote ... (1992-3)

The self-healing approach presented here also follows another Cayce injunction — to "open" the centers in an integrated fashion (as through the Lord's Prayer, for example), rather than concentrating on some centers to the exclusion of others.

Overview of the healing process. According to many traditions, each center is associated with certain physical, mental, and spiritual functions and ideas. For example, the thyroid center near the throat is associated with the voice, speech, and expression, and also with the human will; the adrenals are associated with strong emotions and their control, with persistence and strength of purpose as well as with anger, hostility, and pride. The *creative meditation* healing approach concentrates on the strengthening of the positive attributes at each of the centers, without giving any energy to the negative ones.

This approach to self-healing is presented for the first time in these pages. It has been stimulated by the Cayce and Stanford readings, together with some ideas by Brennan, McClellan, and Schwarz. The technique is also influenced by my experience with meditation in weekly healing sessions with the Glad Helpers. The formulation further benefited from several creativity meditations.

The creative healing process is designed to be performed after a meditation that is followed by prayers for others. After a period of mindfulness, the meditator offers a prayer, asking that each named individual be surrounded with golden light of love and protection. These may be individuals about whom you have concern, whether they have asked for prayer or not. You may also wish to surround difficult situations from your life or from the daily news, affirming that the light will shield the situation or person from outside negative influences. After completing those prayers for others, the self-healing process may begin.

The first step in self-healing is to ask God for information and guidance on the cause of any unhealthy condition in your body; for example, "Father-Mother God, I am truly thankful for my whole being — physical, mental, and spiritual. Please help me to know and understand the cause of any unhealthy condition within me. Guide me in releasing that cause from my being. I thank you as that is being done." (You may include specific conditions if you wish.) Attend to the stillness for a minute or two, observing any response to your prayer.

The next step is a simple diagnostic scan, described below, to determine where healing is especially desirable. Then the remainder of the self-healing procedure is one of focusing on and communicating with each of the centers, the purpose of which is to infuse the energy passing through that center with the positive attributes of the center. If there is sluggishness or blockage at the center, the healing is intended to relieve those conditions in a positive, controlled manner. After considering each center in turn, all centers are acknowledged, and the healing process is completed. The meditator may continue in meditation or may end the meditation session at that time.

The process always includes all seven centers. However, more time and healing activity may be concentrated on one or a few of the centers, according to your intuition, the diagnostic scan, or a known need. The attention may be focused with the mind only, or the hands may be used to provide a strong physical association with the healing activity, somewhat in the manner of the laying-on-of-hands technique as suggested by Cayce (281-5).

A diagnostic scanning technique. After the prayer for self-healing guidance, take a minute or two with eyes closed to focus yourself mentally at each of the centers in turn, starting with the pituitary and ending with the gonads. For each one, visualize being at that spiritual center near the associated gland.

You may find it helpful to use your hands in the following way:

Place your left hand gently across your solar plexus, fingers spread; place your right hand over the center being considered — first the forehead, then the crown, the throat, the chest at heart level, the solar plexus (on top of the left hand), the lower abdomen, and the area of the genitals.

Experiment with the right hand touching the body at each center and also with the right hand hovering an inch or so away from the body directly over the center.

As you concentrate on each of the centers in turn, be alert for indicators and impressions of possible healing needs:

- If you know what color of the spectrum is usually associated with each center (specified in the tables of spiritual center healing information at the back of this book), be sensitive to any grayness or muddiness in color, indicating a possible need for healing.
- Be sensitive to any negative impressions you receive in words or images, or to any sense of poor energy movement.
- If you are using your hands for the scan, be alert for any temperature variation felt on the hands and any other changes in tactile sensations, such as a tingling against the skin or an external pressure.

Any contrary indicators may signal the need for concentrating some healing activity at that center. A response to your prayer for guidance about cause may also occur during this diagnostic survey.

Spiritual center healing activity options. By now in this book, you should be used to options and alternatives. (Did I hear you say, "Here we go again!") In this healing approach, as in meditation, there is no single best action for each center. You must experiment to find out what rings true to you and what appears to work most effectively at the time.

I have prepared seven "Tables of Information for Healing Through the Spiritual Centers," located at the back of this book, so you can readily find them in future self-healing meditations. Each of the tables lists information relating to one of the seven centers. The major source of the details in these tables is Stanford's *The Spirit unto the Churches*, supplemented by the Cayce readings and the work of Barbara Ann Brennan, Randall McClellan, and Jack Schwarz (all referenced at the back of this book). Turn now to one of the tables at the back of the book and follow this roadmap of what's included and how it may be used in healing:

Location and energy vortices: To help in your visualization of the center and of the movement of energy near it.
Position of hands: Alternative ways to use your hands in self-healing, if you so desire.
Associated physical, mental, and spiritual functions and ideas: You

may choose one or more of these to emphasize in a healing session, according to intuition or scanning; the word or phrase or a related feeling or image may become a brief focus or used in an affirmation or prayer.

Symbolic color of center: What to be sensitive to in scanning; not for healing.

Positive external color influence: For visualizing during the healing process, instead of using the symbolic color.

Sounds or chants: Specified syllable to be sounded aloud to increase the vibrations at that center; other sounds or chants that have a positive influence on the center.

Meditative attitude and affirmation phrases: Specific ideas from the Cayce or Stanford readings for your mental set or visualization during healing activity at the center; phrases may be spoken aloud, used as brief spiritual focuses, or simply repeated silently several times.

Illustration of healing through the spiritual centers. Let's say I have completed my regular meditation and have sent light for the surrounding of others. Then I offered a prayer for insight into my healing, like the one cited earlier.

Now I begin my diagnostic scan of the centers, using visualization without hands. I visualize the pituitary center (no negative indicators), then the pineal (no negative indicators). At the thyroid, I get a feeling of heaviness. Nothing unusual at the thymus, but I perceive a lot of churning energy at the adrenals. The cells of Leydig and gonads appear satisfactory. So I have healing work to do at the thyroid and adrenals centers (big surprise!). I have my book beside me, open to the tables in the back, so I can refer to the information on healing through the centers.

I start with the pituitary center, using my hands this time — left hand at the solar plexus, the right on my forehead. I visualize brilliant white light behind my forehead, concentrate on my ideal for a few moments, and say, "Let me be a channel of blessings."

Moving to the pineal, I leave my left hand in place and move my right hand to the crown of my head. Again I visualize brilliant white light below my right hand, and I release myself to God and to oneness. I say, "I am one with God and the universe." (Notice I'm not trying to use the exact words of suggested phrases, since they are meant only as general guidelines.)

Moving to the thyroid, I leave my left hand in place and move my right hand to partly encircle my throat. Since chanting is especially important for the thyroid center, I chant aloud, using the HAAAH-MMMMMM sound, repeating it for a total of three times. I picture my throat filled with beautiful blue-green light, while I repeat aloud "Not my will, but Thine, O Lord" several times. Then in silence, I hold an image of my will bowing down before the will of God, and I try to feel an essence of that surrender. I hold that for a couple of minutes.

Then I proceed to the thymus, and so on through the other centers, taking more time at the adrenals — the other center that I felt needed healing. At the end, I acknowledge each center in turn, proceeding up the body — gonads, cells of Leydig, adrenals, and so on — saying, for example, "Thank you, gonads center, for doing your job well."

If you have a specific physical ailment you would like to heal, determine from the tables at the back whether the organ or function involved is associated with a specific center. If so, do extra healing work at that center for several days. If there is no specific association listed, then concentrate on the thymus center (related to the immune, lymphatic, and circulatory systems) and on the adrenals center (related to the general health of the body because it is so closely linked with the emotions and the distribution of energy to other centers).

Some final suggestions about adapting the healing information and activities to your own meditation session:

- Always give attention to every center on the way down, and then, at the end, acknowledge every center on the way up.
- Feel free to find other positions for the hands relative to the centers. For example, the vortices at the back may be given more attention, or you may find more comfortable positions for your hands. One of the purposes for using the hands is to help you keep your attention and visualization focused in that area and to help you feel a tangible connection with the center. Your hands may also feel sensations during healing, and they are a means for stimulating energy flow through the minor chakras in the hands.
- If you frequently encounter negative indicators in the same centers, vary your healing work with them, experimenting with different ideas, affirmations, and visualizations.
- After you become familiar with the functions and ideas for each center, create your own affirmations and meditative attitudes.

Now it's your turn.

"Try Me!" In your next meditation, or at a separate time, include a healing session with the spiritual centers. Do not be concerned if your diagnostic scan does not give you any indicators at all, especially if you have not done that kind of visualization before. Unless you have other intuitive feelings about where to concentrate attention, you may give equal time to all centers, or you may choose to focus on one idea, such as strengthening your determination and your control of emotions (adrenals), or overcoming sexual desire (cells of Leydig), or controlling your eating (thyroid — for will, for assimilations, and for proper thyroid gland functioning).

You are now in possession of two valuable tools for personal empowerment in taking charge of your life: an approach for receiving guidance on decisions, choices, and problems, and an approach for healing yourself physically, mentally, and spiritually.

The next phase of *creative meditation* is aimed at spreading its benefits throughout your life by carrying the meditative process with you wherever you go and in whatever you do. "What? Meditate while I'm in line at the supermarket?" Maybe, and while you're eating and walking and sitting in a committee meeting. "Impractical!" you say? Let's find out.

Chapter 13

Extending Inner Peace

"All this shopping and waiting in lines and making decisions is beginning to get to me. If only I could meditate. . ."

"Don't be silly. You won't find a quiet spot any place around here. And you can't just sit down on one of those benches over there and do your thing. Everyone would think you'd gone bonkers... You'll be home in an hour or two. You'll have to wait until then... Too bad you can't meditate here while you're standing in line, waiting to check out."

"I just did."

Meditation is your opportunity to visit God's recharging and message center — now also a guidance and healing center. Is one daily visit enough to get through the day in peace and at one? Joel Goldsmith says that a meditation in which "the Christ in us is awakened" lets us go on for a while,

... but not for too long, because the mesmerism of the world forces itself upon us, and six hours later, sensational newspaper headlines and radio news impinge on our consciousness, and the Christ begins to slip into the background. (From *Practicing the Presence*, p. 98)

195

To counteract this, he says, we must find additional times to meditate, even if only briefly:

> Gradually, these periods of meditation become a regular part of our existence, and we are meditating at any or every hour of the day or night, sometimes for only half a second or for several minutes at a time; sometimes while driving a car or doing housework. We learn to open consciousness, if it is but for a second, and find ourselves in a state of receptivity. (From *The Art of Meditation*, p. 30)

What's a reasonable response to the continuous wear and tear on our well-being and self-control? To extend the inner peace and at-oneness from our daily meditations into every corner of our lives. We will explore some of the techniques used by mystics and other meditators — even meditating while driving!

Practicing the Presence of God

The Cayce readings frequently direct our attention to the Gospel of John, especially Chapters 14 through 17. One of the predominant themes of that discourse by Jesus at the Last Supper is the special relationship the disciples (and we) have with God. Cayce used the term "Christ Consciousness" to refer to our awareness that we are part of the oneness of God. In this reading, Cayce paraphrases John's gospel in his reminder about the need to increase that awareness:

> Keep, in thine meditations, that of the *Christ* Consciousness being magnified *in* thee day by day ... for we — humanlike — so easily *forget* the promise, that "If ye abide in me, *I* will *abide* in thee," and "What ye ask in *my* name, *believing*, ye shall have ..." (1742-4)

Cayce gave a series of readings that resulted in the spiritual study texts called *A Search for God*. One of the lessons in Book I is titled "In His Presence." Repeated throughout the three readings related to that lesson (262-32, -33, -34) is the theme that we must strive to be conscious of being in His presence — not just in meditation as "a thing apart," but in our everyday experience. The lesson material that resulted from those readings elaborates:

When we separate ourselves or think ourselves apart from our Maker, we are like ships without rudders.

The oneness is ever existent, but it is only through our realization and our acknowledgment of its existence that the change is worked in us, and life takes on a new aspect. We are free-will agents. God is not a person in the sense that we think of persons; yet, to those of us who seek His presence, He is very personal. (From *A Search for God*, Book I, pp. 101-102)

In one of the readings for that material, Cayce points out: "... we are all *in* His presence whether we acknowledge it in the present or not; for ... in Him we live and move and have our being ... " (262-32).

Our personal spiritual practices — prayer, meditation, and spiritual study — are essential to sustaining that awareness of oneness. But only when we carry our spirituality into our day-to-day, hour-by-hour experiences can we truly express oneness and grow in Christ Consciousness:

> ... the abilities to combine the daily activities with the spiritual development. *This* is a virtue so few have attained, to make their religious experiences, their spirituality, *practical* in their daily lives! (1204-3)

> For only that character of spiritual thought that is a practical thing, that may be lived and experienced day by day, is worthy of thy acceptance. (1723-1)

> Know that there are those strengths, those assurances that may be found in the closer walk with the Christ Consciousness. Ye can make this very real, very personal in thy experience. This doesn't imply that you are to become a recluse, or that you are to become long-faced. It's the opposite. You must become cheerful! (3578-1)

Our interpersonal relationships and our opportunities for service to others provide fertile settings for our efforts to take our spirituality into daily life. But to keep us mindful of God's presence and connected to God's resources, we can take our meditative state of at-oneness with us into the world. The traditional term for this extension of at-oneness is "practicing the presence of God."

To make that transition from a once-a-day experience with God to the experience of God's presence throughout the day requires continuous exercising of the will through the choices made and through disciplining of the attention. This extension of at-oneness can, however, be experienced through many simple and diverse forms of meditative activity, some of which seem a long way from the meditations you have been practicing.

Four types of activity are presented for your consideration and experimentation: spontaneous meditations; "mindful doings"; mini-meditations; and momentary meditations.

Spontaneous Meditations

Let's say you meditate regularly every morning. One evening after supper, before you go out for the evening, the thought of meditation flits across your mind like a butterfly and is gone. Or in the middle of a busy day at home, you suddenly think about a friend or a family member. Or you have just checked into a hotel on a trip, and you feel moved to sit down and "get connected" before you proceed to your next activity. Or you wake up during the night and find yourself thinking about an unsettling situation. As a regular meditator, you may occasionally experience subtle invitations to meditate, to seek inner calm, to reach out to someone, to visit with God, to release a troubling circumstance. These are opportunities for "spontaneous meditation" — an unscheduled period when you respond to an inner call:

> **Question**: What is the best time for meditation for this [person]?
> **Answer through Mr. Cayce**: Whenever there is the call, as it were, to prayer, to service, to aid another. (275-39, Q-2)

> **Question**: Please give time for me to meditate other than the 6:30 period.
> **Answer through Mr. Cayce**: Well that [you] gain that consciousness [to] be instant in prayer; speak oft with thy God. (307-4, Q-8)

Your form of meditation at such times must obviously be suited to the time, place, and inspiration of the moment. The key: Don't hesitate or debate about meditating at such a time; just do it. And if you have only five minutes, that's all right, too. When you are meditating regularly at a scheduled time and place, these spontaneous meditations require less preparation than if they were the only times you meditated. My spontaneous meditations usually consist simply of relaxing my body while observing my breath to focus and relax my mind, and then I concentrate on my ideal or a simple affirmation. If a thought about a specific person or situation stimulated the meditation, then after attunement, I spend a few moments directing energy to surround the individual or circumstance.

Nothing says you need to wait for inner signals before you take a few extra minutes to meditate during the day or evening. Sometimes the opportunity comes as you change from one activity to another with several minutes to shift gears. A short spontaneous meditation will help you make those shifts smoothly and with renewed energy and clarity of purpose.

If you are in circumstances where you cannot meditate in your usual style — for example, in a public place, at a place of employment, in a committee meeting — alternative ways to get in touch with God and to center yourself in inner peace will be presented as this chapter continues.

"Try Me!" Over the next few days, take at least one opportunity for spontaneous meditation in response to an inner urge or to the thought of a friend or loved one.

"Mindful Doings"

Early in the book, I introduced you to Brother Lawrence, best known for his "practice of the presence of God." To many, he personifies the integration of attunement with mundane activities:

> The time of business does not differ with me from the time of prayer; and in the noise and clatter of my kitchen, while several persons are at the same time calling for different things, I possess God in as great a tranquillity as if I were upon my knees at the blessed sacrament. (From Laubach and Lawrence's *Practicing His Presence*, p. 105)

Rabbi Aryeh Kaplan points out that "one of the key teachings of Judaism is that one can experience a closeness to God in anything one does... Even the most mundane act can serve as a link to the Divine" (from *Jewish Meditation*, p. 141). He goes on to describe elevating the task of washing dishes to an act of worship!

199

Virtually any activity we perform can become a vehicle for "mindful doing." The exercises presented in Chapter 5 for the training of attention include a few such activities. Here are some others:

Mindful eating. Daniel Goleman's description of a meditative approach to eating makes us aware of the many sensations to be appreciated in this ordinary activity:

> It helps to eat very slowly, breaking down each movement so that you can attend to each nuance of sensation, sound, taste and movement...
>
> Explore the visual and tactile nature of the food you're eating. If it's a food you can eat with your fingers, feel its texture against your fingertips, note its shape and color and outline. Is it hard or soft? Rough or smooth?
>
> Slowly raise the food to your mouth. Notice the moment you can first smell it. If you've been attentive, you may notice you've started salivating before it even reaches your mouth. Be aware of the first brush of the food on your lips.
>
> Next, chew the food, slowly and deliberately. Notice the feel of your teeth biting through it. Note the taste, the sounds, the myriad sensations created by every bite. Be sure to chew the food completely and swallow it before you take another bite. Continue eating with the same careful deliberateness. Stay calm and focused throughout. (From *The Meditative Mind*, pp. 188-89)

Aryeh Kaplan presents ideas from Jewish teachings that enhance the spiritual dimension of mindful eating:

> [The person] should have in mind that the taste of the food is also an expression of the Divine in the food, and by eating it, he is incorporating this spark of the Divine into his body. A person can also have in mind that he will dedicate the energy that he will obtain from this food to God's service ... Therefore, eating itself can be a form of meditation as well as a means through which one can draw closer to God. (From *Jewish Meditation*, pp. 143-144)

Walking meditation. Any time you are walking — whether on your way to work or out enjoying nature — you have another opportunity to meditate. In *Beyond TM*, Marilyn Helleberg describes one form of walking meditation as a good way to defeat worry: Select a scriptural quotation or a one-sentence prayer (or, I would add, an affirmation) that really speaks to your situation. Then go out and take a walk with God, she says, repeating the passage or prayer over and over as you walk, letting the words flow naturally, perhaps in rhythm with your footsteps.

Another form of walking meditation is to keep yourself focused on the beauty and wonder of nature and God's creations, as so often suggested in the Cayce readings. Hildegard of Bingen was a 12th-century mystic, referred to by Matthew Fox as the "grandmother" of the Rhineland mystic movement of creation-centered spirituality. From her writings comes this meditative idea:

> Glance at the sun. See the moon and the stars. Gaze at the beauty of earth's greenings.
> Now think. What delight God gives to humankind with all these things. Who gives all these shining, wonderful gifts if not God? (From Uhlein's *Meditations with Hildegard of Bingen*, p. 45)

You can develop a habit of becoming meditative whenever you walk certain frequent routes — either outdoors or indoors — so that your surroundings trigger the process. As an indoor example, if you work in a large building or a complex of buildings in which you must regularly walk between certain work areas, you can use those occasions for walking meditations.

Mindful housework. Washing dishes was suggested earlier as an exercise for sensory focus. Just think of all the other household tasks that can be performed mindfully and meditatively: vacuuming carpets, washing windows, scrubbing floors, painting, folding laundry, washing cars, stacking wood, cleaning woodwork ... and on and on.

As a variation, consider using a spiritual idea as your focus, borrowing an idea from Joel Goldsmith: Consider your meditation task as washing windows, for example. Before you begin your task (your meditation),

> ... open the Bible or a book of spiritual wisdom and read for a short time. You may read only one paragraph, or you may need to read ten pages before some particular thought

attracts your attention. When this occurs, close your book and take that thought into your meditation. Think about it; hold it right in front of you; repeat it to yourself. Ask yourself: Why did this particular quotation come to me? Does it have an inner meaning? What is its significance to me at this time?

As you continue meditating another statement may come to your attention. Consider both of these thoughts: Is there any relationship between them? Is there any coherence? Why did this quotation follow the first one? By this time probably a third idea and then a fourth will have come, and all these thoughts will have come out of your awareness, out of your consciousness. In this short period of meditation which may have been of only a minute's duration, you have experienced God revealing Itself; you have opened yourself to divine Intelligence and Love. This is the Word of God which is quick and sharp and powerful. (From *The Art of Meditation*, p. 26)

Washing windows will take longer than "only a minute's duration," so you have plenty of time to explore a spiritual thought. An intriguing idea? I hope you'll try it. It does make work time fly, if that's of any interest to you, partly because you are integrating into your daily activity the condition of at-oneness experienced in a regular meditation period.

Carrying your peace. Marilyn Helleberg suggests another way of integrating your peace from meditation into the rest of your life. At the end of morning meditation, for example, sit quietly and try to store away in your memory the peaceful feelings you have:

> ... the heaviness in your legs, the soft, rhythmic nature of your breathing, the glow that seems to surround you, the emotional equilibrium you feel ... [perhaps] a profound sense of freedom, or an inner playfulness, or a floating sensation. *Notice* these mental states and any images that may accompany them (such as dancing on the clouds, drifting on water, or riding on a ray of light) and try to memorize them. (From *Beyond TM,* p. 95)

Then as you go about daily activities, stop occasionally and remember those sensations in detail.

Here's another suggestion adapted from Helleberg for getting through a day you anticipate to be hectic: When you wake up and remember you face such a day, mentally review what you plan to get done that day. Then meditate. After your prayers for others at the end, visualize yourself starting each task for that day in slow motion, not going through the whole task, but enough to get that graceful, slow-and-easy feeling planted in your mind — which is the builder, remember. Then as you start each of your activities that day, recapture that slow motion feeling linked to the peace and at-oneness of your meditation.

Mindful driving. Because driving a vehicle takes so much skill and attention, any meditative activity associated with it must be carried out without interfering with those critical faculties. On the other hand, since driving is such a frequent occurrence for many of us, it is worth considering as a period for extending our at-oneness — especially since some of our greatest aggravations and frustrations may be experienced while driving!

Here are several ideas for mindful driving:

- Be aware of how much you use your eyes in driving, not just to watch the road ahead, but to scan the environment for approaching vehicles, people, animals, and objects; to look at other drivers to assess their intentions or to exchange signals about turning, cutting in, going first at a four-way stop, and so on; watching for stoplights and signs. Express thanks to God for your sight and your alertness. Pray for His direction of your vision wherever it is needed.
- Be similarly aware of your use of your ears and hearing while driving, expressing thanks and praying for His direction as needed.
- When you are stuck in traffic, make a conscious effort to feel peaceful and calm. Remember that your anxiety about time or your annoyance about inconvenience will not change the situation one iota. Think peace and patience — try to recapture some of the feeling from your last meditation. See yourself and your car enveloped in a bubble of white light. When you feel at peace yourself, focus your attention on the people in the other vehicles around you. Visualize sending them the light of peace and surrounding each of them in their own bubble of light. Picture the road filled not with cars, but with great bubbles of light. That may even bring a smile to your face!
- As you drive along, pick out an object or cluster of objects at some

distance in front of you — a group of trees by the road, a barn, a tall building, the superstructure of a bridge. Consider the wonders of the process that put the object there: For a natural object, think about the miracles of earth formation, of planting and growing, of the seasonal changes, of the effects of rain and sun; for constructed objects, consider the bringing together of design and construction, the talents of the builders and makers, the effects of the weather and aging, the number and varieties of users. Express your thankfulness for all these miracles and demonstrations of the gifts from God. When you finally pass the object, celebrate it with a smile and a greeting. Then choose another distant object for your appreciation.

These suggestions will probably stimulate other kinds of meditative activities for driving. The state you are trying to re-create is one of peace and at-oneness, acknowledged with thanksgiving and praise. Any way you can do that while driving — with safety a top priority — will be appropriate for mindful driving.

"Try Me!" Within the next week, try at least one form of mindful doing as described or one from your own creative experience.

Consider one regular activity of your life which you can do mindfully/meditatively, and begin doing it that way whenever you can.

Mini-Meditations

Imagine that you are about to make an important presentation to a group. You are sitting in a waiting room and have about five minutes before you will be called. Or, in five minutes, the children will come bounding in from school, looking for food, asking for help, and complaining about a friend. Two perfect times for a mini-meditation!

In five minutes or less, you can carry out a segment of your usual meditation process, or you can use other techniques to help you find that calm inner core of peace. In answer to a question about how to overcome "the nerve strain I'm under at times," Cayce replied, "Quiet, meditation, for a half to a minute, will bring strength ..." (311-4).

Several forms of mini-meditation are described briefly, with the idea that they will stimulate your own ideas, suited to the occasion and circumstances.

Abbreviated meditation. This is a much-shortened version of your regular meditation, tailored to a three-to-five-minute period. For example, you sit straight, close your eyes, relax your shoulders and neck, and observe your breath, all in about one minute. Then you concentrate on your spiritual ideal for a minute or two and feel its essence in mindfulness for another minute or two. You can shift the amounts of time on each activity to suit your own needs.

Another variation is to spend the entire time observing your breath or focusing on the ideal. Still another variation — one especially suited for meditating in public — is to sit with your eyes open, focused on an object while you meditate for three minutes or so.

Create for yourself a preferred abbreviation of your usual meditation process — not as a substitute for regular meditation, but as a supplement at other times of the day.

As one of its Home Research Projects, the A.R.E. offered an opportunity for its members to participate in an experiment called "The One-Minute Meditator." The process actually required three minutes of activity: one minute of the Cayce breathing exercise described earlier; one minute of silent meditation focusing on an affirmation related to the spiritual ideal; and one minute in prayer for others. The participant was to follow this process once a day for seven days, in addition to whatever other daily meditation time was being observed. Participants then submitted a data form reporting on their experiences with the activity.

A total of 602 people participated, of whom about half were regular meditators and another fifth were formerly regular meditators. Some results:

- Those who were already meditating before the project experienced greater feelings of centeredness and attunement than those who were not.
- Those who had another longer meditation on the same day as a short one had better results than those who did not.
- The amount of stress people were experiencing seemed to have no effect on the "quality" of the meditations.
- Three relevant comments: "[It] seemed to help me cope better with the daily stress on my job ... There's always time for three minutes"; "A short meditation can be just as deep, peaceful, and centering as a long one"; "... it is not the amount of time spent but rather the quality that is most important."

One of the conclusions of this project was that the short meditation works best in the context of a fuller meditation life, and that's consistent with the recommendations here. These several approaches to "practicing the presence" are intended as extensions of the basic daily meditation period, not as substitutes.

Walking mini-meditation. You get a call from a frantic neighbor, asking you to come quickly and help with a crisis. On your way, you can focus on your ideal or on an affirmation such as, "Let me be a channel of blessing," linking the words with the rhythm of your steps. For example, this sentence falls into four parts to correspond with four steps: *Let*-me *be*-a *chan*nel-of *bless*ing.

If you tend to be a pacer — someone who walks back and forth, or around in circles — during a stressful period or while waiting for something, linking an affirmation to your pacing can reduce your tension, whereas pacing itself may increase it.

Chanting mini-meditation. Considering the value of chanting in the attunement process, you may well spend two or three minutes repeating one of the recommended chants. Vary the pitch and the loudness, remembering that the higher pitches and softer tones affect the upper spiritual centers and the lower pitches and louder tones affect the lower centers.

In place of the suggested chants, you can chant Gregorian-style on the Lord's Prayer or on one of the longer affirmations. Don't be concerned about melody line or rhythm; just start singing the words on a comfortable tone, and move your voice up or down in pitch as the words seem to suggest to you. Whether you consider yourself a singer or not, this form of singing chant is quite enjoyable as well as helpful when you take just a few minutes for it. This is a perfect extension of singing in the shower!

Mini-meditation for pain. Physical pain is as available to us as the next jogging session, or the next time we rearrange the garage, or the next time we catch a heel on the steps. Many people live with chronic pain or discomfort from an old injury, from a longstanding condition like migraine headaches or arthritis, or from a temporary condition like flu or muscle strain. You may never appreciate meditation more than when it can help either to reduce pain or to allow you to tolerate pain.

Biofeedback techniques are almost routinely available now to help a pain sufferer modify, for example, the blood flow in the hands and thus reduce the pain of migraine headaches. Such specific procedures should be learned and practiced under the supervision of a qualified biofeedback specialist and are not the subject of this discussion. However, as a person with several chronically painful joints, I have found several types of mini-meditation helpful in reducing the pain and its impact.

One technique might be called "becoming your pain." Tendonitis frequently flairs up in my right wrist. The pain usually tells me that I have put extra stress on my wrist, weakened by an injury long ago. (I'm the one with all the broken bones, remember?) When I can't ignore it any longer, I may take a few minutes to sit down and close my eyes, observe my breath briefly, and then try to send my consciousness into my wrist. It's hard to explain, but I try to let that pain fill my consciousness for a minute or two, so I can almost feel it all over my body — a kind of extraordinary sensory focus. Then I release it to God, bring my attention back to my breath and repeat an affirmation, such as "You have done your job, pain. I will remember your message as you leave me now."

If I don't take time for "becoming the pain," I may simply concentrate on the affirmation for a minute or two. I have also visualized the pain flowing out of the sore area, like a vapor leaving the body. At other times, simply carrying out the normal activities of meditation takes my mind off the pain, and by the end of the meditation the pain seems to be less or even to have disappeared.

Relationship mini-meditation. You are about to meet with someone who frequently upsets you or antagonizes you. Or maybe you have just had that encounter. How to restore sweet peace and reason to your consciousness? It's not your job to change the other person; and after all, he or she is also a child of God. You are connected through God. Joel Goldsmith uses a beautiful analogy that may inspire some affirmative thoughts:

> The wave is one with the ocean, indivisible and inseparable from the whole ocean. All that the ocean is, the wave is; and all the power, all the energy, all the strength, all the life, and all the substance of the ocean are expressed in every wave. The wave has access to all that lies beneath it, for the wave really is the ocean, just as the ocean is the wave, inseparable, indivisible, one ... There is no place where one wave comes to an end and the next wave begins ...
>
> As a wave is one with the ocean, so you are one with God. Your oneness with the universal Life constitutes your oneness with every individual expression of that Life... As

207

the infinity of God surges through you to bless all with whom you come in contact, remember that the infinity of God is also surging through every other individual on earth to you.

This is a tremendous idea if you can grasp it. It means that your interest is the interest of every individual in the world; it means that his interest is your interest; it means that we have no interest apart from each other even as we have no interest apart from God. (*The Infinite Way*, pp. 98-99)

In recognition of that inseparability one from another and from God, a mini-meditation consists of these activities:
- Center yourself with your spiritual ideal as your focus.
- Picture the other person as he or she is likely to be right now, and put a bubble of light around the individual. Hold that image for a few moments. Affirm by saying, "Lord, he (or she) is Yours."
- Visualize a bubble of light around yourself; hold that image for a few moments; affirm by saying, "Lord, I am Yours also."
- Now visualize the two bubbles meeting, and affirm by saying, "Lord, do with us as *You* will. Help us remember we are both Your children and one with each other."

When your time does not permit this visualization, you may find it helpful to spend the available time affirming, "Lord, she (or he) is Yours, and I am Yours. Do with us as *You* will. Help us remember we are Your children and one with each other."

"Try Me!" During the next week or two, try two or more of these mini-meditations, or those of your own creation. Find times that help you stretch your at-oneness from regular meditation into a variety of other activities in your life.

Momentary Meditations

These are the opportunities for truly practicing the presence of God in your life. Your pleasant task is to find as many opportunities as you can for "God thoughts" — feelings of God's nearness, praise and thanksgiving to God, a sense of being "in the flow."

One form of momentary meditation is the use of an affirmation outside of any formal meditation: "Where peace goes, I will follow" or "My healing is taking place just now." Use them as momentary prayers, especially in situations where your ideal needs to be called forth. For example, your spouse, your customer, or your boss is taking forever to make a decision for which you are waiting. Silent repetitions of "Patience is my way of life" will affirm that you do indeed feel that way — or are trying to.

You can go a step further and develop affirmations for mental or physical ideals relating to specific situations or people. Call these to mind (or to emotions) when you find yourself in challenging circumstances. For example, "Remember, Charlie is my test on patience" or "This committee always moves at just the right pace."

Another form of momentary meditation is the short spontaneous prayer you may utter at a moment of need: "God help me in this" or "God be with me." Another is asking for instant guidance: "God, please show me the way," or "What would You have me do just now?" And still another is being thankful for everything that happens: "Thank You, God!" To me, continual thankfulness is one way to insure staying "in the flow."

Frank Laubach, a missionary to the Philippines, a mystic, and a prolific writer, suggests a commitment:

> Try to call Christ to mind at least one second of each minute. You do not need to forget other things nor stop your work, but invite Him to share everything you do or say or think. There are those who have experimented until they have found ways to let Him share every minute that they are awake. In fact, it is no harder to learn this new habit than to learn the touch system in typing, and in time a large part of the day's minutes are given over to the Lord with as little effort as an expert needs to type a letter. This practicing the presence of Christ takes all our time, yet does not take from our work. It takes Christ into our enterprises and makes them more successful. (From *Games with Minutes*, p. 42)

I suggest a variation on this to be carried out occasionally: Think of God for a few seconds every waking hour during one whole day. If you have a watch with an hourly time signal on it, develop the habit of thinking of God every time the signal beeps on the hour. I have done this with no more than "Thank You, God," or "Not my will, God, but Yours." On those days when I was relatively faithful to this hourly commitment, I felt more of an ongoing connectedness with God. (I'm reminded here of the apostle Paul's advice: "Rejoice always, pray constantly, give thanks in all circumstances," 1 Thessalonians 5:16-18.)

Joel Goldsmith suggests another helpful use for momentary meditation:

> Whenever you leave one place to go to another place, such as leaving your home for business or leaving your business for church or going back to your home, pause for a second to realize that the Presence has gone before you to prepare the way, and that that same divine Presence remains behind you as a benediction to all who pass that way. At first you may forget to do this many times during the day, but by jogging your memory you will eventually find that this will become an established activity of your consciousness and you will never make a move without realizing the divine Presence ahead of you and behind you, and in this way you will find yourself to be the light of the world. (From *The Infinite Way*, p. 101)

I'm sure you get the idea of the momentary meditation, just as I'm sure you have to find the approach most appropriate for your lifestyle and concerns. Even if you are not interested in going very far to extend your at-oneness, you will find many opportunities to use momentary meditations for other reasons.

"Try Me!" Over the next few days, find several opportunities for momentary meditations to meet your own personal needs and experiences. If you have a watch with an hourly timer signal, consider linking an affirmation to the signal for a day.

You now have the complete picture of what *creative meditation* can be — from the basic meditation period with its infinite variations, to the possibilities for personal empowerment, for guidance, for self-healing, and now for spreading its at-oneness across your life.

The final chapter steps back to regain perspective of where we were heading in this book and how far we have come. Then, as an incentive to keep on keeping on with *creative meditation*, always looking for new opportunities to create at-oneness, I will present the ultimate extension of our inner peace — through our service to peace for the world.

Chapter 14

Creative Meditation
in the Service of Peace

"I keep having this vision of a council of world leaders — maybe the United Nations — starting its meeting with meditation."

"Do they discuss the peace affirmation for the month and the proposals for retraining military units in peace tactics?"

"That's it! How did you know about this vision?"

"I'm the person creating it! I'm working with every spiritual law I know to bring it about. But I've probably overdone it."

"Why?"

"I may have included the impossible. I even created a thought-form that the Berlin Wall would come down!"

Before I point you forward in the direction of world peace through *creative meditation* — is that ambitious or what? — I want to take a brief look backward with you. I owe you an opportunity to evaluate how well we did — the book and I — in doing what I said we would do to meet your needs for inner peace, at-oneness, and strategies for coping with day-to-day challenges. No long summaries ahead — just a few loose ends to tuck in and then we'll tie it all together with a ribbon of peace.

211

How Did We Do?

In Self-Inventory 3 (Chapter 2), you described what it would be like to be at one with life. Look at your responses to Part A of that inventory.

Do you feel you are moving toward at-oneness in meditation? Maybe you've had some meditations in which you experienced the kind of at-oneness you imagined. At the very least, I hope you feel you are moving in that direction, experiencing inner calm and relaxation, perhaps a sense of your spiritual nature, the wonder of being a child of God.

Neither you nor I expect you to become an overnight mystic — or any kind of mystic! But just because the word "mystic" smacks of "holier-than-thou," don't shrug off too quickly the concept it represents — putting yourself into contact with God and staying there much of the time, ready to be thankful, ready for guidance, ready just to feel close to God.

One of the wonderful characteristics of *creative meditation* is that you never have to stop growing in your experience of at-oneness, your closeness to God, feeling truly at one with the world. And just when you realize your meditation is so very satisfying, close to the best you anticipated, it goes beyond that — if you allow it to do so.

Over the months and years ahead, I hope you will continue to commit yourself to meditate daily, mindfully, and creatively. Empower yourself to create the kind of life you want in the future. Take charge of your life through God's guidance and healing power. And spread your peace and at-oneness throughout your life with your own versions of "practicing the presence of God."

Early in this book, I made a lot of promises about what *creative meditation* could do in bringing at-oneness into your life. Right in the Introduction, I made this promise:

• If you will meditate regularly with a clear spiritual focus,
and
• if you will creatively extend the resulting attunement throughout your life,
then
• you can experience ...
   • inner calm regardless of outer circumstances,
   • the realization of being at one with the universe, and
   • the assurance of making choices that lead to greater control over the circumstances of your life.

If you would like to assess how well the book and I have lived up to those promises, I suggest two activities:

- In Chapter 2, look up the nine criteria I proposed for the state of being at one with life. I summarized them as follows:

> *At-oneness with life* will eliminate the negative effects of our slings and arrows of all kinds and degrees, will be easily invoked and long-lasting, will help us think and act appropriately while feeling in control of our lives, will permeate our being, will stimulate personal traits consistent with its tone, will foster creativity and productivity, and will be consistent with our inner values and ideals.

How well did I do in giving you information and techniques for realizing these ambitious goals? Have you begun to experience the fruits of your meditation practice as defined by these nine criteria?

- In Chapter 3, look up the seven principles underlying *creative meditation*. Step by step I have presented ideas and techniques of *creative meditation* that were built on this foundation. They are probably more meaningful to you now than they were then. Have the book and I stayed within these principles? Is it clear how the principles have shaped the ideas and techniques?

You are in the best position to decide whether I fulfilled my promises to you or not. And regardless of how that rating turns out, you are the only person who can decide whether meditation — *creative meditation* — will continue as an integral part of your life.

One other loose end: How does *creative meditation* fit into the eight strategies for coping with the slings and arrows of life? In Self-Inventory 2 (Chapter 1), you looked at your own coping strategy profile. Would *creative meditation* be a ninth strategy?

I see *creative meditation* as an enhancer of your coping style, rather than as a new strategy in itself. Specifically, it will enhance your ability to *Do It!* — the most productive strategy. Through the use of the guidance and healing processes, as well as through some of the activities for extending at-oneness, you will be able to find solutions and take actions in situations that earlier may have led you to less productive strategies — like *Ignore It!*, *Escape It!*, or *Internalize It!* You will also find *creative meditation* an effective way to *Revitalize for It!* when you have done all you can do.

The strategy of *Displace It!* includes the positive option of transforming frustration, resentment, anger, or other negative emotions — often from not being able to *Do It!* — into more acceptable channels of service. Perhaps one of the most appropriate avenues of service for a meditator is the service of peace — peace in our immediate circle of contacts, in our communities, in our nation, and throughout the world. The remainder of this chapter suggests how the inner peace and at-oneness of *creative meditation* — sometimes fed by the transformed energy of day-to-day challenges — can reach far beyond your own well-being.

In the Service of Peace

Our first commitment and responsibility in the study of *creative meditation* has been for our own inner peace and at-oneness with life. Although such study may seem selfish, it's quite appropriate for meditation to be undertaken for its self-serving values. When we *live* that peace and at-oneness, however, extending it throughout our own lives, we also alter the experience of others around us — by our example, by our direct interactions with them, and by the raising of the vibrations of group consciousness.

If you gauge the existence of peace and noncontroversy in our world by news headlines, you must often conclude that there is little peace on any front — local, regional, national, or international. Yet the spirit within us longs for peace. When we are crushed by events such as those in Beijing, China, in June 1989, our hopes soar all the more during events in Berlin a few months later. When we are dismayed over the venom and violence with which two factions demonstrate over the issue of abortion, we are all the more ready to celebrate the peaceful negotiations of a strike or the resolution of differences between two friends. Must we then sit back to await the next event — will it be peaceful or violent? — as if there is no way we can actively contribute to peace? With the *creative meditation* process as an enabling strategy, I suggest instead a five-step personal program for peace:

> *Love peace*
> *Be peace*
> *Seek peace*
> *Live peace*
> *Counsel peace*

Love peace. Peace begins as an attitude, a motive, an emotion within. How deeply do you feel about the importance of peace in the world? Most of us have been raised in a society that gives high value to individual freedom, competition, contention, and results, rather than to cooperation, compromise, accord, and process. To create peace, we must first *love peace*, wanting to see it manifested so much that we can taste it!

We begin our path toward peace by examining our own values, our attitudes, and our ways of reacting. In a series of readings on world affairs, Cayce says:

> Let thy daily life be free from criticism, from condemnation, from hate, from jealousy. And as ye give power to the Spirit of Peace, so may the *Prince of Peace*, the love of God, manifest. (3976-23)

You influence as well as reflect your attitudes about peace in your choice of books and articles to read and programs to listen to, view, or attend. Can a fan of violence be an advocate of peace?

After we gain control over such deterrents to our love of peace, we can build a foundation for peaceful service from the same "fruits of the spirit" that we seek to create in ourselves through meditation:

> Patience, love, kindness, gentleness, long-suffering, brotherly love. There is no law against any of these ... they are the law of consistency in the search for peace ... they of themselves bring peace ... (3175-1)

They keep us connected with spirit to help us manifest peace through the law, "the spirit is life ..."

Be peace. You take a major step toward peace in the world when you create the state of peace within yourself:

> ... peace must begin within self before there may be the activity or the application of self in such a manner as to bring peace in thine own household, in thine own heart, in thine own vicinity, in thine own state or nation. (3976-28)

The frequent, consistent, and creative use of meditation is probably the most effective and long-lasting approach for establishing inner peace — the main theme of this book. Your efforts will be enhanced if you relate your spiritual ideal to the goal of peace — perhaps as one of the focuses in your bull's-eye summary of spiritual, mental, and physical ideals.

Seek peace. A woman asked Edgar Cayce if it was right for her to want only harmony and peace, to which he answered: "The whole of God's creation seeks harmony and peace!" (1742-4, Q-5) If that is true, the lack of peace and harmony may simply suggest that everyone seeks it on his or her own terms, which ironically often leads to conflict.

Peace must be actively sought, not just awaited. How do we earnestly seek peace? One meaningful approach as an individual is through prayer, meditation, and affirmation. We can use the idea and feeling of peace in our spiritual focus; at the end of meditation, we can ask for guidance on peaceful resolutions to controversies; we can request prayer to surround key individuals or situations with a light that acts "as [the] defense against influences that would hinder" (281-9, A-4); we can regularly affirm manifestations of peaceful activities and outcomes. In his readings on world affairs, Cayce says:

> For as the people of each nation pray, *and* then live that prayer, so must the Spirit work. (3976-23)

Every year since 1986, on December 31 between noon and 1 p.m. Greenwich Time, millions of people all over the world have been praying for "Peace on Earth." Isn't it reasonable to celebrate some of the "surprising" world events since 1986 — from the warming of relations with the Soviet Union to the fall of the Berlin Wall and other continuing struggles for individual and national freedoms? May we not assume that concerted worldwide prayer has in fact had a positive effect?

Live peace. This state of being, sustained through *creative meditation*, has two levels of effect: (1) peace is reflected in your visible demeanor and your actions, as well as in your less visible aura and energy field; and (2) others are influenced by your demeanor, your actions, and your higher vibrational energy.

> ... the finding of peace in self enables the entity to give more assurance, more help to others; just by being patient and not attempting to control or to appear overanxious.
> ... like begets like. Thus as harmony and beauty and

216

grace reign within the consciousness of an entity, it gives that to others — and others wonder what moved them to feel different, when no one spoke, no one even appeared to be anxious. This is the manner in which the spirit of truth operates among the children of men. (3098-2)

Demonstrating peace in your life means modeling such behaviors as resolving differences, avoiding the creation of conflict, creating "win/win" outcomes, and supporting peaceful endeavors by others.

Counsel peace. Beyond what you do in your own inner and outer life, you can actively find ways to bring ideas and ways of peace into the lives of others:

Remember, ye pursue peace, ye embrace peace, ye hold to peace. It is not something that descends upon thee, save as ye *have* created and do create it in the hearts, in the minds, in the experiences of others. (3051-2)

Activities for counseling peace might include the formation of small groups that would study peace from many points of view or that would use an existing, difficult situation as a case study for creating peaceful solutions. Also, consider joining or starting a group that meditates together regularly in the service of peace. Groups of meditators can have a remarkable influence on the surrounding area, according to the studies by Elaine and Arthur Aron. After demonstrating that a group using TM (Transcendental Meditation) could reduce the crime rate in a large city, for example, the Arons took the opportunity during the 1978 Iranian revolution to demonstrate the effect of group meditation on violence. For three months, groups of meditators visited Iran, staying in Tehran hotels. They meditated whenever shooting erupted near them — and the shooting stopped. They sometimes went to smaller cities where violence flared up, they meditated — and the violence immediately stopped — every time. Their theory was:

If a large enough group of people ... were all drawing on the calm, coherence, and wisdom deep within the silent human mind, then those qualities would prevail in the environment, and the right changes, whatever they were, would come about. (From the Arons' "Waging (Inner and Outer) Peace" in *Venture Inward*, p. 13)

217

Many such groups around the world, regularly meditating together, could have effects beyond what most people consider possible —like *glasnost* and free elections behind a falling Iron Curtain. But "group meditation doesn't seem like much of an activist role," you say. Consider this opinion by singer and sometime-political-activist Judy Collins in her autobiography, *Trust Your Heart*:

> The Buddhists and Thomas Merton say that when you are meditating, you bring the forces of evil and good into balance in your own life, and doing this for yourself is to do it for the planet, for the universe. In that sense I suppose that prayer and meditation are political actions as much as any march or demonstration may be. (p. 241)

If you become active in the service of peace, other roles for you will come clamoring to your door.

The five steps again: Love peace — be peace — seek peace — live peace — and counsel peace! I offer this summary, another of my few expressions through poetry:

IF YOU WOULD HAVE PEACE

Within yourself sign treaties
To come to terms with motives and desires
That keep you in a state of conflict and unease.
No need to look "out there" for peace
Until you find a pattern in yourself.

Once your inner battles are contained,
Become the mediator
In your strained relationships with others.
Cease fire unilaterally!
A peace talk hardly seems sincere
If you come armed with anger and resentment.

Beyond immediate concerns,
Consider this your guide:
Do all that's possible by you
To live in peace with everyone.

218

You say you need some help
In all these peace deliberations —
Wording treaties, mediating, talking peace?
Count on God and His resources
To support the makers of peace
"Who shall be called the children of God."
You need but seek His help
And know with faith that He provides.

So, if you would have peace, be peaceful.
From this beginning, you can heal the world!

My parting charge to you: Never let a day go by without practicing a form of *creative meditation*. As a consequence, not only will you experience your own wellness and at-oneness with life, but also the joy and serenity of helping to heal the world!

REFERENCES

Aron, Elaine, and Arthur Aron. "Waging (Inner and Outer) Peace," in *Venture Inward*, July/August 1986 (2:4), 12-16, 40-43, 45.

Association for Research and Enlightenment, Inc. *A Search for God*, Books I & II. Virginia Beach, Va.: A.R.E. Press, 1942, 1950, 1970, and 1978.

Association for Research and Enlightenment, Inc. *The Edgar Cayce Readings* (Library Series). Virginia Beach, Va.: A.R.E. Press, 1973-1987.

Benson, Herbert. *The Relaxation Response*. New York: William Morrow, 1975.

Blum, Ralph. *The Book of Runes*. New York: St. Martin's Press, 1982.

Bonhoeffer, Dietrich. *Letters and Papers from Prison*. New York: Macmillan, 1953.

Bonhoeffer, Dietrich. *Meditating on the Word*. Cambridge, Mass.: Cowley Publications, 1986.

Brennan, Barbara Ann. *Hands of Light: A Guide to Healing Through the Human Energy Field*. New York: Bantam Books/Bantam Doubleday Dell, 1988.

Carrington, Patricia. *Freedom in Meditation*. Garden City, N.Y.: Anchor Press/Doubleday, 1977.

Collins, Judy. *Trust Your Heart: An Autobiography*. Boston: Houghton Mifflin, 1987.

The Cloud of Unknowing and the Book of Privy Counseling (edited and with Introduction by William Johnston). Garden City, N.Y.: Image Books/Doubleday, 1973.

Connolly, Eileen. *Tarot: A New Handbook for the Apprentice*. North Hollywood, Calif.: Newcastle Publishing, 1979.

A Course in Miracles. Tiburon, Calif.: Foundation for Inner Peace, 1975.

Damian-Knight, Guy. *The I Ching on Business and Decision Making: Successful Management Strategy Based on the Ancient Oracle of China*. Rochester, Vt.: Destiny Books, 1986.

Dyer, Wayne W. *You'll See It When You Believe It: The Way to Your Personal Transformation*. New York: William Morrow, 1989.

Falk, William. "Meditation Merges with the Mainstream" in *Esquire*, March 1983, p. 249.

Fox, Emmet. *Power Through Constructive Thinking*. San Francisco: Harper & Row, 1979.

Fox, Matthew. *Meditations with Meister Eckhart* (Introduction, translation, and arrangement by Fox). Santa Fe: Bear & Company, 1982.

Fuller, John G. *Edgar Cayce Answers Life's 10 Most Important Questions*. New York: Warner Books, 1989.

Goldsmith, Joel S. *The Art of Meditation*. New York: Harper & Row, 1956.

Goldsmith, Joel S. *The Infinite Way*. San Gabriel, Calif: Willing Publishing Co., 1947 (20th ed., 1976).

Goldsmith, Joel S. *Practicing the Presence*. New York: Harper & Row, 1958.

Goleman, Daniel. *The Meditative Mind: The Varieties of Meditative Experience*. Los Angeles: Jeremy P. Tarcher, 1988.

Goodwin, Matthew Oliver. *Numerology: The Complete Guide*, Vols. I and II. North Hollywood, Calif.: Newcastle Publishing, 1981.

Govinda, Lama Anagarika. *Creative Meditation and Multi-Dimensional Consciousness*. Wheaton, Ill.: Quest Book/Theosophical Publishing House, 1976.

Harvey, John, editor. *The Quiet Mind: Techniques for Transforming Stress*. Honesdale, Pa.: The Himalayan International Institute of Yoga Science and Philosophy of the U.S.A., 1988.

Helleberg, Marilyn Morgan. *Beyond TM: A Practical Guide to the Lost Traditions of Christian Meditation*. New York: Paulist Press, 1980.

Herman, Nicholas (Brother Lawrence). *The Practice of the Presence of God*. In Laubach and Lawrence's *The Practice of His Presence*. Goleta, Calif.: Christian Books, 1973.

Horak, Michael. "Pressures at Home and School Are Turning Kids into Bundles of Nerves," in *The Virginian-Pilot* (Virginia Beach, Va.), pp. E1-E2.

Kaplan, Aryeh. *Jewish Meditation: A Practical Guide*. New York: Schocken Books, 1985.

Kepler, Thomas A., compiler. *The Evelyn Underhill Reader*. New York: Abingdon Press, 1962.

Langer, Ellen J. *Mindfulness*. Reading, Mass.: Addison-Wesley Publishing, 1989.

Laubach, Frank. *Games with Minutes* and *Letters by a Modern Mystic*. In Laubach and Lawrence's *The Practice of His Presence*. Goleta, Calif.: Christian Books, 1973 (originally published by New Readers Press, Syracuse, N.Y.).

Leonard, George. *The Silent Pulse: A Search for the Perfect Rhythm That*

Exists in Each of Us. New York: Dutton, 1978.

LeShan, Lawrence. *How to Meditate: A Guide to Self-Discovery.* New York: Bantam Books, 1974.

Loftus, Myrna. *A Spiritual Approach to Astrology.* Reno, Nev.: CRCS Publications, 1983.

McClellan, Randall. *The Healing Forces of Music: History, Theory, and Practice.* Amity, N.Y.: Amity House, 1988.

Murphy, Michael, and Steven Donovan. *The Physical and Physiological Effects of Meditation: A Review and Comprehensive Bibliography, 1931-1988.* Big Sur, Calif.: Esalen Institute, 1989.

Peace Pilgrim. *Peace Pilgrim: Her Life and Work in Her Own Words.* Santa Fe, N.M.: Ocean Tree Book, 1983.

Pennington, M. Basil. *Centered Living: The Way of Centering Prayer.* New York: Doubleday, Image Book, 1986.

Peterson, Richard. *Miles to Go: The Spiritual Quest of Aging.* San Francisco, Calif.: Harper & Row, 1989.

Puryear, Meredith Ann. *Healing Through Meditation and Prayer.* Virginia Beach, Va.: A.R.E. Press, 1978.

Ram Dass (Richard Alpert). *Journey of Awakening: A Meditator's Guidebook.* New York: Bantam Books, 1978.

Ram Dass and Paul Gorman. *How Can I Help? Stories and Reflections on Service.* New York: Alfred A. Knopf, 1985.

Reed, Henry. *Dream Interpretation Workout* (videotape). Los Angeles: Video Home Companion, 1989.

Reed, Henry. *Getting Help from Your Dreams.* Virginia Beach, Va.: InnerVision Publishing, 1985.

Roth, June. "The No-Sweat Diet: Meditate and Lose Weight" in *Harper's Bazaar*, May 1980, p. 128.

Rubin, Theodore Isaac, M.D. *Reconciliations: Inner Peace in an Age of Anxiety.* New York: Viking Press, 1980.

Schwartz, Stephan A. *The Alexandria Project.* New York: Dell Publishing, 1983.

Schwarz, Jack. *Voluntary Controls: Exercises for Creative Meditation and for Activating the Potential of the Chakras.* New York: E.P. Dutton, 1978.

Sherwood, John. "Psychographics" in *Port Folio Magazine* (Virginia Beach, Va.), August 29, 1989, pp. 8-10.

Sinkler, Lorraine. *The Spiritual Journey of Joel S. Goldsmith, Modern Mystic.* New York: Harper & Row, 1973.

Smith, Charles Merrill. *How to Talk to God When You Aren't Feeling Re-*

ligious. New York: Bantam Books, 1973.

Stanford, Ray. *Speak, Shining Stranger*. Austin, Tex.: Association for the Understanding of Man, 1971, 1973, 1974, 1975.

Stanford, Ray. *The Spirit unto the Churches: An Understanding of Man's Existence in the Body Through Knowledge of the Seven Glandular Centers*. 4th ed. Virginia Beach, Va.: InnerVision Publishing, 1987.

Swami Rama et al. *Meditation in Christianity*. Honesdale, Pa.: Himalayan International Institute of Yoga Science and Philosophy, 1983.

Thurston, Mark. *Paradox of Power: Balancing Personal and Higher Will*. Virginia Beach, Va.: A.R.E. Press, 1987.

Thurston, Mark. *Soul-Purpose: Discovering and Fulfilling Your Destiny*. San Francisco, Calif.: Harper & Row, 1989.

Thurston, Mark. *Dreams: Tonight's Answers for Tomorrow's Questions*. San Francisco: Harper & Row, 1988.

Thurston, Mark. *The Inner Power of Silence: A Universal Way of Meditation*. Virginia Beach, Va.: InnerVision Publishing, 1986.

Trent, Sydney. "Accidental Author" in *The Virginian-Pilot* (Virginia Beach, Va.), June 2, 1989, pp. B1 and B3.

Trost, Cathy. "What's Your Mantra?" in *The Wall Street Journal*, March 18, 1986, p. 1.

Uhlein, Gabrielle. *Meditations with Hildegard of Bingen* (Introduction, translation, and arrangement by Uhlein; Preface by Matthew Fox; Foreword by Thomas Berry.). Santa Fe: Bear & Company, 1983.

Underhill, Evelyn. *Practical Mysticism*. New York: E. P. Dutton, 1943.

Wilhelm, Richard (English translation by Cary F. Baynes; Foreword by C. G. Jung). *The I Ching or Book of Changes*. Princeton, N.J.: Princeton University Press, 1983.

Wing, R. L. *The I Ching Workbook*. Garden City, N.Y.: Doubleday & Co., 1979.

Instructions for Scoring and Interpreting Self-Inventories

These instructions are based partly on the design and intent of the individual self-inventories and partly on the results of trying them out on a preliminary sample of people while the book was being written. The sample of 23 included both meditators and non-meditators, men and women, A.R.E. members and non-members, ranging in age from the thirties to the eighties!

The instructions for interpretation are intended only to suggest ways of looking at your responses. They should not be considered rigid rules for interpreting your opinions and experiences.

SELF-INVENTORY I
Scoring

1. For each individual challenge area you rated, multiply the number in Col. A times the number in Col. B. Write the answer at the right of B. (For example, if Col. A was 2, and Col. B was 3, you would write 6 at the right of Col. B.) Label this new column of numbers Column C.

2. Obtain three separate totals: Add Column A and write the total at the bottom of the column on page 2. Do the same for Column B, and for Column C.

3. Your "challenge position" is the total of Column C. Locate your score in the ranges defined on the next page under *Interpreting* in Step I.

4. The total of Column A is your "frequency score," and the total of Column B is your "intensity score." Which is higher? Read the suggestions under Step II of *Interpreting* for whichever condition applies.

5. Circle all individual area scores in Col. C that have a value of either 6 or 9. Read the *Interpreting* information in Step III.

Interpreting
Step I: Your Challenge Position

0-15:   You experience a *low* level of stress from your challenges. This is probably a comfortable and desirable level for most people — enough to keep life interesting and keep the "juices flowing," but not so much as to tax your physical and mental well-being.

16-30:   You experience a *low to moderate* level of stress from your challenges, with occasional higher stress in one or two areas. This is probably an acceptable level of stress, if other physical and mental circumstances are satisfactory. Try to keep the level of challenge from increasing either by more challenges or by greater intensity of present challenges, or both. You may be more comfortable if you decrease the frequency or intensity of challenge in one or two specific areas.

31-45:   You probably experience a *moderate* level of stress from your challenges, with occasional periods of considerable stress in three or four areas. This is a borderline zone for unhealthy stress. It is probably desirable to reduce your challenge position, by reducing the number of different areas affected, by reducing the frequency with which any of them give you a challenge, or by reducing their intensity when they occur, or a combination of these. You may make reductions more quickly by concentrating on one or two areas of greatest challenge.

46-60:   You probably experience a *moderate to high* level of stress from your challenges, with periods of considerable stress in several areas. This is probably an unhealthy level of stress, especially if maintained over a long period of time. It is desirable to reduce your challenge position significantly, by reducing the number of different challenges, by reducing the frequency with which any of them give you a challenge, or by reducing their intensity when they occur, or a combination of these. You may make reductions more quickly by concentrating on your greater challenges one or two at a time.

Over 60: You almost certainly experience a *high*, almost continuous level of stress from your challenges. This is almost certainly an unhealthy level of stress, especially if maintained over a long period of time. It is highly desirable to reduce your challenge position significantly, by reducing the number of different challenges, by reducing the frequency with which any of them give you a challenge, or by reducing their intensity when they occur, or a combination of these. You may make reductions more quickly by concentrating on one or two of your greater challenges at a time.

Step II: Frequency/Intensity Balance

Your Frequency Score is higher than your Intensity Score: If the difference is greater than a few points, your level of challenge seems to result more from the number of occasions on which you experience challenge than from the intensity of the challenges. You may make the greatest progress in reducing stress by trying to reduce frequency of challenge — more difficult to control than the intensity. Watch yourself next time you are offered a new opportunity for challenge. Do you ever say "no"?

Your Intensity Score is higher than your Frequency Score: If the difference is greater than a few points, your degree of challenge probably results more from the intensity of the challenges than from the number of occasions on which you experience challenge. You may make the greatest progress in reducing stress by trying to reduce intensity of challenge — easier to control than the frequency. The regular use of meditation will be one way to decrease this intensity.

Step III: Handling the 6's and 9's

1. A "6" challenge area must be either frequent with severe intensity or continual with moderate intensity.

   A "9" challenge area must be a continual, severe challenge.

   Both of these situations are candidates for control and reduction of stress.

2. Frequency of occurrence may be difficult to control where the challenge is an ongoing circumstance of your life. The best of all possible

227

resolutions would be to take appropriate physical and mental steps to eliminate the challenge from your life, or the mental steps to change your perception of it as a challenge of this magnitude. When that's not possible, the primary way of controlling frequency may be simply not to accept responsibility for new challenges — where you have that option. (Re-read the first two quotations by Rubin in Chapter 1.) An alternative for some challenges is to divide the responsibility with, or transfer it to, someone else.

3. Intensity of occurrence may be significantly controlled through the ongoing use of *creative meditation*, which prevents the buildup of intensity or allows it to dissipate before the next challenging opportunity occurs. (Read the quotation by Daniel Goleman in Chapter 3.)

SELF-INVENTORY 2
Scoring

1. Your present coping profile consists of your dominant strategies — those you rated 3 in *frequency*, with the 2-rated strategies as backups. See Step I under *Interpreting* for more information.

2. The eight coping strategies may be assigned values as follows:
Do It! is 5.
Exercise It and *Revitalize for It* are both 1.
Ignore It and *Internalize It* are both -1 (minus 1).
The other three are zero, since potential negative effects in those strategies cancel out potential positive effects.
This scoring system gives by far the greatest weight to "doing it" — our primary constructive strategy.

3. To obtain a score for your coping profile, multiply the *frequency* rating you gave each strategy times the value assigned to it above. For example:

Do It!	rated 2	x	5	=	10
Ignore It	rated 1	x	-1	=	-1
Exercise It	rated 1	x	1	=	1
Internalize It	rated 1	x	-1	=	-1
Revitalize for It	rated 2	x	1	=	2
			Total	=	11

228

Locate the total in one of the ranges in Step II of *Interpreting* below.

4. In Column B, circle any ratings of 0 or 1. You experience little or no benefit from these "low benefit" strategies. See Step III of *Interpreting*.

5. Two combinations of responses are of special interest. To examine them, proceed as follows: Write "L/H" (low/high) at the left of any strategies in which you rated the frequency as 1, but the benefit as 3. Write "H/L" (high/low) at the left of any strategies in which the frequency was rated 3, and the benefit was rated 1. See Step IV of *Interpreting* on the next page.

Interpreting
Step I: Coping Profile

Almost everyone in the preliminary sample used at least four different strategies, of which *Do It!* was one. In fact, everyone in the sample uses *Do It!*

About half of those in the sample used seven or all eight strategies. In those cases, three to five of them were dominant (rated 3 in frequency). *Do It!* was usually — and should be — one of the dominant strategies.

The most effective coping profile theoretically would have *Do It!*, *Exercise It*, and *Revitalize for It* as dominant strategies. However, you may find significant benefit in other strategies as well — for example, effective use of *Displace It* through volunteer work or other service; healthful and relaxing forms of *Escape It*.

Step II: Coping Profile Score

The most effective "copers" score at least 15 — high frequency for *Do It!* with no negative strategies to detract from it. A score from 18 to 21 is probably best, allowing for at least one positive alternative strategy, such as *Exercise It* or *Revitalize for It*. A score below 10 suggests a weak coping profile.

Step III: Low Benefit Strategies

If these include *Do It!* or *Exercise It* or *Revitalize for It*, you are missing something in how you are using them, because they should be among your most beneficial strategies. Think about recent occasions when you used one of these. Could you have gotten more out of it? Where did it miss the boat? Try some other activities within those strategies in an effort to increase their benefit for you.

If these include *Escape It* or *Displace It*, you may be able to get more from them with a positive redirection of your use. Otherwise, let them go.

As for the others, don't worry about them.

Step IV: "Low/High's" and "High/Low's"

Low/high strategies: Low use, high benefit. These are strategies you apparently find of significant benefit, and yet you've only used them a few times this past year. If they were so successful for you and were positive strategies, perhaps you need to develop more of a habit of using them.

High/low strategies: High use, low benefit. If these were strategies that are usually of positive benefit according to the assigned values above, you will want to continue to use them, but find ways of making them more successful. If these are strategies of mixed or negative value, either shape them up to be more positive and beneficial, or drop them altogether. Change your habits of what strategies you call upon. Why waste your time on strategies of continuing low benefit?

SELF-INVENTORY 3

Part A: Here are examples of words and phrases suggested by a sample of respondents to this inventory:

I know all is well.
My life has a constructive purpose.
At one with nature.
Feeling in the flow of life.
I am never alone.
Totally at peace within and without.
My life adds light to the world.
Joyful to the point of ecstasy.
Total contentment.

Thankful for all things.
Uplifting and release.
Lightness of body and spirit.
No problem too big for God.
Simultaneous detachment and involvement.
Constantly experiencing and expressing unconditional love.
Self-actualization.
Knowing all things are possible.
Being aware that the heart is singing.
Melted into the Light.
Floating weightless in a sea of love and gratitude.
Unhurried, yet full of vitality.
Wisdom and clarity.
Feeling like invisible, loving forces are actively helping me.
Living in the now.

Part B: The ratings of "being at one" (0-10) ranged widely in the preliminary sample, but tended to be high on the six-month average — possibly a reflection of the fact that a majority of the sample are meditators.

The range for the six-month *high point* was typically from 6 to 10, with a median of 8.

The range for the six-month *low point* was typically from 0 to 4, with a median of 2.

The range for the six-month *average* was typically from 4 to 9, with a median of 7.

SELF-INVENTORY 4
Scoring

1.   Circle your answers for items 1, 5, 8, 11, and 13.
2.   Checkmark all the D's you have circled.
3.   Checkmark all the A's *not* circled.
4.   Count your checkmarks. The total is your "responsibility belief score." Locate your score in the ranges defined below under *Interpreting*.

Interpreting
The Responsibility Belief Score

The higher your score, the stronger is your belief that you are responsible for your own circumstances, that you have put yourself where you are, that you have created or set in motion all the conditions in which you find yourself.

10-15: You have a strong belief that you are responsible for your own circumstances. The ideas and exercises in Chapter 10 will be quite consistent with your existing views.

6-10: Your beliefs about your responsibility for your own circumstances are mixed — you feel responsible for some situations and not for others. You may find some of the ideas in Chapter 10 difficult to accept. It may be helpful for you to review the statements on the inventory that are not checkmarked. Those are statements of a possible difference between your beliefs and the beliefs represented in this chapter. You may also find it helpful to suspend your disbelief on those items while you read the ideas and try out the exercises.

0-5: You do not believe that you are responsible for most of your own circumstances. The ideas and exercises in Chapter 10 will be quite inconsistent with your existing views. You may find it helpful to suspend your disbelief temporarily and to read the ideas and try out the exercises without making up your mind about them beforehand.

Affirmations for
Selected Spiritual Ideals

(Adapted from the Edgar Cayce Readings)

THE CHRIST   May the desire of my heart be such that I become more and more aware of the spirit of the Father, through the Christ, manifesting in me.

THE CHRIST   Let the light of the love of the Christ be my guide.

CONFIDENCE   Help me to blot out all fear and doubt from my consciousness, and fill my life with love and peace.

COOPERATION   Not my will, but Yours, Lord, be done in and through me.

HAPPINESS   Let me find happiness in my love for You, Lord, and in the love I bear toward others.

JUSTICE   Help me to know that the spirit of truth and justice is at work in the earth.

LOVE   Through the love You have shown us through Your Son, the Christ, make us more aware of "God is Love."

LOVE   Let the light be within me so that I, as a child of God, may realize Your love for us.

ONENESS   As my body, mind, and soul are one, You, Lord, are one in the earth, in power and in glory.

PATIENCE   Be the guide that we, with patience, may run the race that is set before us.

PEACE   Bring peace first in self, that we may love the Christ spirit and have peace in our hearts day by day.

PEACE	As I come seeking peace and harmony, help me to know I will find them only as I manifest peace in my own heart and mind and body.
PEACE	Help me to know that only as peace comes to my soul and mind may I find relief from the turmoils of material life.
PURPOSE	Create in me a new purpose and a righteous spirit, that I may be a living example of what I believe.
RELATIONSHIPS	My brother, my sister, my friend, my neighbor, even my enemy are children of God, my loved ones. Let me not cause any of them to err or to stumble.
RELATIONSHIPS	Let the knowledge of God so fill my being that there is less and less of self and more and more of God in my dealings with my fellow human beings.
RELATIONSHIPS	May I so conduct my own life that others may know Your presence abides in me.
SERVICE	Let me ever be a channel of blessings to those I contact.
SERVICE	Let me do what You would have me do.
SERVICE	Here am I. Send me. Use me.
SERVICE	May the light of Your word shine for those I meet day by day.
SERVICE	Let my hands, my mind, my body do what You would have me do as Your work on the earth.
SERVICE	Use me in whatever way that I may be as a living example of Thy love.

Tables of Information
for Healing
Through Spiritual Centers

THE PITUITARY CENTER

Location: Behind forehead, slightly above eyes, toward the center of your head.

Energy vortices: One extends forward from forehead into aura, second extends outward from back of head near base of skull.

Position of hands: Left hand on solar plexus and right hand on forehead in vortex; or both hands cupping the front vortex.

Associated physical functions: All other glands; cell growth and change, especially from emotional and psychological influences.

Associated mental and emotional functions: Higher psychic functioning and ESP; selflessness; enthusiasm; capacity to visualize and understand mental concepts; ability to carry out ideas in a practical way; (also see cell influence in "Associated physical functions" above).

Associated spiritual functions and ideas: Spiritual ideals; soul's purpose; true identity of self; service and dedication; faith and inner knowing; spiritual ecstasy and peace; perfect, impersonal love.

Symbolic color of center: Violet.

Positive external color influence: White, true green, a limited amount of violet; the metal gold.

Sound to resonate area of center: EE.

Sound or chant to influence center positively: Silence; AH-OMMMMMMM; sound of brass or metal trumpet; chanting

OMMMMMM softly at fairly high pitch three times activates pituitary, pineal, thyroid, and thymus.

Meditative attitude: Service to others and to God; faith in one's spiritual nature and in the goodness of all peoples; communion with the spiritual ideal; consideration of the soul's purpose.

Phrases for affirmations:
(Your own spiritual ideal)
"Service to the glory of God."
"A channel of blessing to others, and thus to God."
"Here am I, send me."
"Open my heart to the faith You have implanted in all who seek to know You."
"Make me more aware of 'God is Love.'"

THE PINEAL CENTER

Location: Below crown at top of head, behind pituitary.

Energy vortex: One extends upward from crown of head.

Position of hands: Left hand on solar plexus and right hand on head at crown in vortex; or both hands encircling the crown vortex.

Associated physical functions: Strong relationship to cells of Leydig center; has the specific impulse that gives light inwardly; gastrointestinal system; stomach; ovulation cycle in females.

Associated mental and emotional functions: Quick, useful intelligence; discernment; mind as a tool of Spirit, as in "the spirit is life, the mind is the builder ... "; memory; control of bodily appetites.

Associated spiritual functions and ideas: Attunement to selfless purpose; connection with spirituality; intuition and higher psychic abilities; memory of oneness; the faculty by which the Akasha is contacted.

Symbolic color of center: Indigo.

Positive external color influence: White, yellow; sunlight.

Sound to resonate area of center: MM (sung in upper register or falsetto)

Sound or chant to influence center positively: OH-MMMMMMM; gentle sounds; tinkling bells; piccolo; flute; harp; (see OM chant under "Pituitary").

Meditative attitude: Devotion to set the body at peace and the mind at service; understanding that the mind (not merely the intellect) and spirit are holy; being conscious of God; receptivity to psychic information; visualizing transformation of energy from cells of Leydig; silence.

Phrases for affirmations:
"One with God and with the universe."
"The Spirit is life; the mind is the builder; the physical is the result."
"As the Father knows me, so may I know the Father, through the Christ Spirit."
"Show me the way."

THE THYROID CENTER

Location: Throat.

Energy vortices: One extends forward from throat, second extends backward.

Position of hands: Left hand on solar plexus and right hand encircling front of throat with thumb and forefinger; or both hands encircling the front thyroid vortex, thumbs against the body.

Associated physical functions: Constructive use of voice; hearing; sympathetic nervous system; body weight; physical energy level; bronchial and vocal apparatus, lungs, alimentary canal.

Associated mental and emotional functions: The will; listening; awareness of time; use of words and forms of verbal or vocal expression; psychological energy level.

Associated spiritual functions and ideas: Surrender of will to God; awareness of our threefold nature (spirit, mind, and body); inspiration.

Symbolic color of center: Blue.

Positive external color influence: Blue-green, green; sunlight.

Sound to resonate area of center: AYE.

Sound or chant to influence center positively: Chanting especially important for this center — HAAAAH-MMMMMM; gentle sounds; tinkling bells; piccolo; flute; harp; sitar; music of composers dedicated to God's service; words of love and understanding; (see OM chant under "Pituitary").

Meditative attitude: Expectancy of knowing God's will; awareness of body, mind, and spirit.

Phrases for affirmations:

"I have heard Thee, O God. Use me!"

"Not my will, but Thine, O Lord, be done in me and through me."

"Thy will be done in earth as it is in heaven."

"May the words of my mouth and the meditations of my heart be acceptable to You, O Lord."

THE THYMUS CENTER

Location: Center of upper chest at heart level.

Energy vortices: One extends forward from chest, second extends backward.

Position of hands: Left hand on solar plexus and right hand spread on the chest at the heart level; or both hands encircling the front thymus vortex, thumbs against the body.

Associated physical functions: Sense of touch; immune system; heart; blood; circulatory system; lymphatic system.

238

Associated mental and emotional functions: Devotion; compassion; empathy; unconditional, unselfish, nonjudgmental love; "fruits of the spirit," such as gentleness of character, forbearance, and willingness to abide long-suffering; fearlessness.

Associated spiritual functions and ideas: Psychic contact with loved ones; arbitrator between spiritual and physical; the "fruits of the spirit" (see "Associated mental and emotional functions" above); spiritual love; oneness with others; openness to life.

Symbolic color of center: Green.

Positive external color influence: Green, mother-of-pearl, radiant pinkish red.

Sound to resonate area of center: AH.

Sound or chant to influence center positively: YAAAAH-MMMMMM; (see OM chant under "Pituitary").

Meditative attitude: Compassion and selfless love; qualities of the fruits of the spirit; visualization of a rose at the heart center; odor of the rose.

Phrases for affirmations:
"O God, enter my heart this day that I in every way might know Your hand, Your word, Your thought, Your love, Your truth, Your light."
"Deliver me from evil."
"In earth as it is in heaven."
"Let there be less and less of self, more and more of God, in my dealings with others."
"Make me more aware that 'God is Love.'"
"Create in me a pure heart, O God."

THE ADRENALS CENTER

Location: At the solar plexus.

Energy vortices:
One extends forward from solar plexus, second extends backward.

239

Position of hands: Left hand on solar plexus and right hand open on the back, opposite the solar plexus, palm outward; or both hands encircling the front adrenals vortex, right hand above (thumb against the body), left hand below (little finger against body).

Associated physical functions: Sense of sight; physical protection; health of entire body; body temperature control; circulation.

Associated mental and emotional functions: Persistence; determination; drive; strength of positive purpose; control of emotions; ability to laugh; pleasure; expansiveness.

Associated spiritual functions and ideas: Patience; faith in the spiritual teachings, in the spiritual nature of every human being, creature, and thing.

Symbolic color of center: Yellow.

Positive external color influence: Green, white.

Sound to resonate area of center: OH (in medium to low pitch).

Sound or chant to influence center positively: RAAAAH-MMMMMM; also AAAH-OMMMM; words addressing God; chant OM three times at moderate pitch, moderate loudness.

Meditative attitude: Visualize the energy flowing freely to all other centers from the adrenals; feelings of joyfulness; desire for a higher direction in your life; admission of weakness of self and the strength of God; transformation of negative emotions into positive uses of the energy.

Phrases for affirmations:

"God grant me the determination to control and transform my emotions just now."

"Forgive me my debts as I forgive my debtors."

"Give me the patience, Lord, to run the race which is set before me."

"Let me find happiness in my love for You and for my fellow human beings."

THE CELLS OF LEYDIG CENTER

Location: Lower abdomen, at or above testes or ovaries.

Energy vortices: One extends forward from lower abdomen, near genitals, second extends backward.

Position of hands: Left hand on solar plexus and right hand open on lower abdomen; or both hands encircling the front Leydig vortex, little fingers against the body.

Associated physical functions: Physical sense of taste; physical vitality; positive sensuality.

Associated mental and emotional functions: Moderation and transformation of sexual forces; control of sexual desire; freedom from temptation; constructive, controlled, creative imagination.

Associated spiritual functions and ideas: Service to God within your body that its forces are not wasted; upward surging of energy, especially in meditation.

Symbolic color of center: Orange.

Positive external color influence: Green, white.

Sound to resonate area of center: OOOOH.

Sound or chant to influence center positively: VAAAAH-MMMMMM; also AAAH-OMMMM; words addressing God; (see OM chant under "Adrenals").

Meditative attitude: Spiritual ideals and purposes; upliftment of consciousness through the upsurging of energy in meditation; awareness of God, peace, love, and grace; visualization of light and Christ forces at this center.

Phrases for affirmations:
"Lead me not into temptation."

"Father, let Your desires be my desires."

"Create in me, O God, a righteous spirit."

"Let virtue and understanding be in me, for my defense is in You, O Lord."

THE GONADS CENTER

Location: Lower abdomen, at or above testes or ovaries.

Energy vortices: One extends downward from genital area.

Position of hands: Left hand on solar plexus and right hand lightly resting over genital area; or hands linked at thumbs, resting in lap or hanging between the legs, partly encircling the gonads vortex.

Associated physical functions: Physical sense of smell; reproductive system; generation of life.

Associated mental and emotional functions: Positive purposefulness and passion; industriousness; persistence; clarity of thought; discernment.

Associated spiritual functions and ideas: Creative power; transformation of energy through conscious purposefulness; service at the highest level, devotion to God in action.

Symbolic color of center: Red.

Positive external color influence: Green, white.

Sound to resonate area of center: UH.

Sound or chant to influence center positively: LAAAH-MMMMMM; also AAAH-UMMMMM; (see OM chant under "Adrenals").

Meditative attitude: Realization of your spiritual nature, of being a child of God; turning the mind toward God; peace, stillness, and love; wonder of the creation of new life.

Phrases for affirmations:

"Give me this day my daily bread."

"Let me be more aware of the divine spirit within."

"Let the desire of my heart be such that I may be more and more aware of the spirit of the Father manifesting in me."

"May the peace and the light and the love of the Christ be my guide."

"Help me to know the peace that passes understanding."

INDEX

affirmations, from ideals, 68-71, 103, 205; from Cayce readings, 69, 94, 233-234; other, 69-71, 150, 208; in self-healing process, 191-192, 236-243; with breathing, 112. *See also* ideals; as spiritual focus in meditation
Aron, Elaine and Arthur, 217
Arpita, 35
Association for Research and Enlightenment (A.R.E.), xi, xii, 58, 205
astrology, 162-163, 171, 175
at-oneness with life, criteria for, 22-24, 213; defined, 17-18; indicators of, 17-19, 20-22, 86, 129-136, 212-214, 230-231
attention in meditation, 78-84; distractions to, 53, 70, 73, 82-85, 87, 96, 103; retraining of, 68-69, 78-82, 128
attitudes, before meditation, 84, 94-95, 100, 103-104, 118
aura, 108-109, 187

beliefs, as conditions for self-empowerment, 140-143, 181, 183
bells (and other instruments), use of, before meditation, 100, 114, 122
benefits of meditation, xi-xii, 35, 39-43, 127, 129-131, 136. *See also* at-oneness with life
Benson, Herbert, xi
Bible, references to, 4-5, 13, 24, 43, 70, 95, 101, 117, 137, 138, 144, 147, 163, 196, 209
Blake, William, 36
Boehme, Jacob, x, 36
Bonhoeffer, Dietrich, closeup, 41-42; on meditation, 42, 82-83
breath, 109-112, 113; exercises, 100, 110, 122, 205; focus, 53, 111-112, 122
Brennan, Barbara Ann, 108, 109, 186, 188, 190

Carrington, Patricia, 132
cautions, about meditation, 87, 114, 118-119; about spiritual centers, 187
Cayce, Edgar, closeup, xv-xvi
Cayce, Hugh Lynn, 38
chakras, 109, 117, 185. *See also* spiritual centers
chanting, as meditation, 206; before meditation, 100, 114-116, 122; in self-healing process, 191-192, 235-243
cleansing before meditation, 100, 104
Collins, Judy, 218
colors in self-healing, 190-192, 235-243
concentration, defined, 74-75. *See also* attention in meditation